CELTIC

CELTIC

A Biography in Nine Lives

KEVIN MCCARRA

faber and faber

First published in 2012
by Faber and Faber Ltd
Bloomsbury House
74–77 Great Russell Street
London WC1B 3DA

Typeset by Ian Bahrami
Printed and bound by CPI Group (UK) Ltd, Croydon, CR0 4YY

A CIP record for this book
is available from the British Library

ISBN 978–0–571–23435–6

FSC
www.fsc.org
MIX
Paper from
responsible sources
FSC® C101712

2 4 6 8 10 9 7 5 3 1

For Susan Stewart
North Stand Upper
Section 408

CONTENTS

LIST OF ILLUSTRATIONS

INTRODUCTION

There is no other football club like Celtic. The point was proved when an estimated 80,000 supporters were so besotted that they made their way to Seville for the UEFA Cup final against Porto on 21 May 2003. It is considered the greatest mass migration between nations in the history of football for a single game. During the afternoon the mobile-phone network in Seville buckled under the sheer weight of calls as people tried to contact one another. There were greater frustrations than that, but half of the Celtic fans had accepted that they would not get into the Estadio Olímpico.

No arrests were made, although with the sort of embellishment that a well-loved tale deserves, there is a claim of a punch-up between two brothers who had been thumping one another since infancy. Celtic did not take the trophy, but awards would later be made by both UEFA and FIFA. The European and world ruling bodies wished to mark the miraculous serenity of an occasion when so many people were unable to be at the match. Those fans were content and even eager to make do with watching the final in bars or on giant screens, because their overarching purpose was to mount a celebration of Celtic football club.

It was a unique episode for a club that has also been a focus of controversy and antagonism. Celtic's identity is still shaped by its origins. That can create an allure, and in recent years the club's attractiveness has been recognised with invitations to pre-season competitions. Given the Irish roots, it was rational in 2011 that Celtic should face Internazionale in Dublin. All the same, it had not been so readily anticipated that the SkyDome in Toronto would draw its largest attendance for a soccer match when Celtic took on Roma in a friendly before a crowd of 50,108 in July 2004.

In some parts of the world, after all, it is fashionable to be Irish. One study reported that far more people in the US claimed such ancestry than could possibly be the case. There was no such popularity, however, in the Glasgow of the latter part of the nineteenth century, where Celtic was founded and where its identity was forged. Celtic is a Scottish club, but the opportunities it has had and the troubles it sometimes encounters also arise from the Irish aspect.

Despite that lineage, Glasgow has always been Celtic's base and, famously, every member of the European Cup-winning side of 1967 was born within a thirty-mile radius of the city. The club appears to take strength from the belief that it is a maverick overcoming the odds, despite the fact that it draws the largest crowds in Scotland to its 60,000-capacity stadium. Celtic love to see themselves as outsiders. They have been wronged on occasion, with one episode bringing the downfall of Jim Farry, the then chief executive of the SFA. He was eventually dismissed after delaying the registration of the forward Jorge Cadete in 1996.

Farry, who died in 2010, never struck those of us who knew him as biased or bigoted, but he did seem to get locked into a struggle with the then owner of Celtic, Fergus McCann. In some senses the Celtic fans were comfortable with the notion that they were victimised. Many supporters who relish the slightest hint of outlaw chic would in any case shudder at the mere offer of a seat at the Establishment table. The standpoint, though, is a self-deludingly romantic one. Celtic's sense of commercial imperatives was keen from the very start.

Immigrants and their children do tend to be in a hurry. It is significant that Celtic's principal shareholder now is Dermot Desmond. He is an Irishman who epitomises the tensions between romance and ambition, between altruism and realism. Whatever meaning the club's heritage holds for him, he has been adamant that Celtic will eventually play in the immensely more affluent English Premiership, if not in a yet to be created European League. His spirits would have lifted in 2011 when Karl-Heinz Rummenigge, Bayern Munich's chief executive, revived talk of the latter concept coming into existence. It might have been just another bout of rhetoric, but Desmond has not abandoned hope.

In his perseverance he has an affinity with the people who founded Celtic. The heart-warming aspects of that event are genuine, but they are far from being the only truths. Brother Walfrid, a member of the Marist order, was indeed instrumental in forming the club, and he did intend that it should come to the aid of the Irish immigrant slum-dwellers in Glasgow. Charity, for all that, is often deployed to cultural and political effect. There are, to this day, Irish people who will mock someone suspected of disloyalty by saying he has 'taken the soup'. The phrase harks back to the era of men such as Walfrid, who dreaded that Catholics would abandon their faith if offered help by the charities of the Protestant church. But there were people whose aims went even further than stopping the Catholic congregations from defecting.

They had in mind an assertion of their community's worth. The immigrants were in a hostile environment, and a rallying point such as a football club was precious. Enmity to the newcomers had a variety of causes. A fiercely anti-Catholic disposition had been created by the Reformation in the sixteenth century, and it prevailed even when, before immigration, there were few Catholics in the country.

The arrival of the Irish in substantial numbers introduced more turmoil to the throes of the industrialisation of Scotland. As is the way with immigration, the new slum-dwellers were also loathed because, by working for a pittance, they were liable to drag down wage levels. They even sounded alien, and the reference to Celtic as the Bhoys, which crops up to the present day, was a clumsy nineteenth-century attempt to represent the Irish accent.

The men who were really behind the emergence of Celtic had no intention of cringing or currying favour. Other clubs were ransacked of their best players so that Celtic would have an outstanding team from the very start, in 1888. Scottish football was nominally amateur, and while that regulation was regularly infringed, Celtic broke the rules with more audacity than anyone else.

Rangers, formed in 1872, was the older club, but the brashness of Celtic quickened the metabolic rate of football in Scotland, raising crowds and nurturing the national fixation with the sport. The Old Firm rivalry was also forged. The very term 'Old Firm' is a sardonic reference to the mutual financial benefits that made them partners as well as antagonists. Little by little, however, sectarianism seeped into the relationship.

Gradually Rangers became identified by Protestants as the club best equipped to challenge a Celtic side that had won six consecutive League titles from 1905 to 1910, an achievement that prompted Rangers to sign a few Catholic players. They then reverted to the former policy of excluding such individuals, a practice that was not abandoned definitively until the landmark purchase in 1989 of Maurice Johnston, who had once been a Celtic player. Rangers could be seen to be mirroring the characteristics of Scottish society at large, where Catholics, until at least the 1950s, found their career paths blocked in many professions.

Discrimination of Rangers' sort had never been adopted by Celtic, whose most revered figures have often been Protestants, and it is a lazy inaccuracy to claim that 'one's as bad as the other'. However, Celtic have been known to wallow in their supposed position as underdog and to attribute their failures to an anti-Catholic conspiracy. There have been injustices, but victim-hood serves as a useful excuse as well. Some supporters have also been wilfully blind to their own provocativeness. There are still fans, particularly in the hard core that attend away matches, who will sing songs honouring the IRA.

This continues even in a period when the IRA has laid down its weapons. Some will argue disingenuously that they are com-memorating the struggles for Irish independence, a process of disentanglement from the UK that in other countries, including the US, is a matter of pride and celebration. This, of course, deliberately ignores the revulsion felt for the IRA of recent dec-ades, whose bombings in Northern Ireland and on the British mainland brought it scant popular support.

This matter was not confronted until the mid-1990s when Fergus McCann, a Scot who had emigrated to Canada, returned to win a takeover battle and depose the ruling families, the Kellys and the Whites. McCann radically altered the basis on which the club was run and also launched the Bhoys Against Bigotry campaign, which antagonised fans who felt that the Irish aspect of Celtic was being suppressed.

There was a period, particularly during the conflict that led to the creation of the Irish Free State in 1922, when Celtic were a worry to the authorities, who dreaded that violence in Ireland would be replicated in Scotland. In 1921 a policeman was killed in Glasgow during an attack aimed at releasing an IRA prisoner from a van. The Glaswegian version of the song 'The Smashing of the Van' is still well known in some quarters. It was in the same year that some Celtic supporters suspected of IRA sympa-thies were arrested at the club's ground and accused of having concealed weapons inside egg crates.

The feuding of the Old Firm did not lead to a wider conflagra-tion, but its effects can still be grave. In 1980 Celtic's win over Rangers in the Scottish Cup final was followed by a pitched bat-tle between the two sets of supporters on the field at Hampden Park. Mounted police drew batons to restore order.

In sporting terms, however, the Celtic experience is far more likely to be colourful, captivating and entrancingly erratic. There has always been a volatility that has no equivalent at Rangers. Considering the advantage that the scale of their following gives them, it was, for instance, exceedingly careless of Celtic to neglect to win a trophy for seven years from 1958 to 1965. In the 1950s the forward line, with a nod to Catholic theology, was referred to as the five sorrowful mysteries. In the early 1960s, as pop groups erupted across Britain, the satirists in the crowd mocked Celtic as Bob Kelly and the Easybeats. Robert Kelly was the crusty chairman of the club in that period.

Kelly did eventually come to see the need for the modernisation of Celtic, a club that had, for decades, lacked the dynamism and originality that had been the essence of its founders. Early in 1965 he appointed an ex-Celtic player and captain called Jock Stein as the first Protestant manager of the club, and allowed him complete power over all football matters.

Stein was to use that authority brilliantly. There was immense, untapped ability in the squad, and with a force of personality that complemented an acute understanding of the game, he created a side that made Celtic, in 1967, the first British club to win the European Cup. Nine of the line-up had emerged from the Celtic youth system.

The club would also contest the 1970 European Cup final. It was an era that went far towards purging Celtic of its insularity, and as the occupation of Seville in 2003 showed, supporters thereafter held onto the faith that the club belonged on the world stage. There had, however, been much to shake that confidence. It was Rangers, with the advent of Graeme Souness as manager in 1986, who were first to practise the commercialism that is the essence of contemporary football.

The Ibrox investment in players was large and, for several seasons, productive. The Celtic board, controlled by the Kelly and White families, did not possess the business acumen to react. When McCann took over in 1994, the club was on the brink of bankruptcy. He was combative, and enough fights were won to revive Celtic. By the time McCann sold up in 1999, the value of his shares had quintupled, which also showed that he had been correct in his appraisal of Celtic's potential.

Visions of a great role on the international scene were stoked during the five years, from 2000 to 2005, in which the charismatic Martin O'Neill was manager. Celtic, however, lived beyond the means to be found in Scottish football and a period of retrenchment ensued. Much as any fan will pine for money to be spent on better players, Celtic have been circumspect. They are yet to pay more than £6 million for any player, and look disinclined to do so. The contrast is stark with the period when Rangers came up with £12 million for Tore André Flo.

Nowadays Celtic aims to control its finances while seeking, through youth development and shrewdly economical recruitment, to be a respected presence on the international scene. This strategy is far from proving itself, but there never has been a plodding simplicity to Celtic. Since 1888 its affairs have carried an erratic and sometimes explosive tendency. The tantalising global prospects are real, and so, too, are the barriers to realising them.

The magnetism of the club emanates from an emotional, picturesque and idiosyncratic history of immigration and aspiration. Further journeys are yet to be made. Celtic is a tale of adventure, success, failure, exasperation and hope that will never cease to unfold.

I

JOHN GLASS

Celtic were late. The notion of an immigrants' team was already commonplace when the Glasgow club took the field for the first time in 1888. One account of the period groans about the 'superfluity' of teams in Scotland with an Irish identity. Celtic's founders understood that there was not a moment to lose. These ruthless men ensured they would begin life with excellent players by pillaging their counterparts, Hibernian. The Edinburgh club came close to extinction then, but the Irish aspect never would be a guarantee of security: Dundee Harp went out of business in 1897 and Dundee Hibernian, chasing a broader appeal, renamed themselves Dundee United in 1923.

While Brother Walfrid, a member of the Marist order at work in the parish of St Mary's, had the idea of forming Celtic, it was John Glass who set the club apart. He chaired the meeting at which Celtic came into existence and was the man whose efforts ensured it would not peter out. By 1894 *Scottish Sport* was referring to him as 'the father of the club'. Glass was a Scot of Irish descent with a knack for persuasion that was indispensable to Celtic. He was committed to Home Rule for Ireland and remained active in the cause. A generation or two earlier, a person adopting such a stance would have cut themselves off from the mainstream. Times were changing and he was one of nine people of similar background who were made Justices of the

Peace in 1902. The headline in one newspaper read: 'Catholics added to the Glasgow magistracy.'

Much had altered since 1829, when the Home Secretary Robert Peel regarded it as a moral issue that Catholics be prevented from becoming MPs if possible. Only with reluctance did he and others accept that Daniel O'Connell must be allowed to take his seat in the House of Commons after twice winning a by-election in County Clare that Parliament had insisted on restaging. The Roman Catholic Relief Act allowing men of that faith to become MPs was passed during that period. Glass's nomination as a Justice of the Peace was trifling by comparison, but it did confirm, as a single-minded Celtic had, that people of immigrant descent and their culture would have to be assimilated into society at large.

There was a greater, if informal, honour in the gratitude expressed to him for establishing Celtic so firmly. Willie Maley, player and then manager from the very first game until his forced retirement in 1940, wrote that Glass was 'a working joiner to whom, in my estimation, the club owes its existence, as he never shirked from that time till the day of his death to further the project which to him appealed as his life work'. Glass did not bite his tongue after Celtic had lost the Glasgow Exhibition Cup final to Cowlairs in September 1888 before a crowd full of animosity. 'Celtic will yet win to their proper position,' he said at the post-match dinner, 'and those who scoff today will one day have to applaud.'

Glass was entitled to such confidence since he had gone to great lengths in finding the type of footballers who would inevitably make their mark. Had he not accomplished a key task, Celtic might have been stifled at the very start. Virtually everything turned on the approach to James Kelly. Recruiting the Renton centre half was a challenge even for Glass, since other clubs had been rebuffed. Kelly had already won the Scottish Cup twice, and the latter victory in 1888 led to a challenge match with the FA Cup holders West Brom. Having beaten them,

Renton, the team from the Dunbartonshire village, were deemed world champions, at least in the eye of the Scots. The player himself would still have appreciated that the era of smaller clubs such as his was coming to an end, as the economic forces in the well-populated cities generated far more money.

John O'Hara, the Celtic secretary, had been unable to lure Kelly. Glass, however, was indefatigable and said he had 'camped on his doorstep'. The twenty-two-year-old was talked into taking part in Celtic's first match, a 5–2 win over a Rangers XI. 'No Kelly, no Keltic' became a catchphrase summary of the centre half's towering significance. 'I knew that if I could get Kelly, the rest would follow,' said Glass. That proved true, as the club signed other important players who accepted the credibility of Celtic once Kelly had joined them. The concept of an Old Firm had still to come into being and the first outing was simply a run-of-the-mill match, but the player remained thereafter. While football in Scotland was meant to be an amateur sport then, there were inducements. Considering that Kelly was soon the owner of a pub that would be worth around £150,000 nowadays, Glass had not depended solely on his silver tongue.

Resistance to a rather crass newcomer was to be expected, and Celtic were checked for a while. The club felt itself to be an outsider and encountered highly motivated opponents during the loss to Cowlairs that so irked Glass. The victors were said to have bolstered the line-up with guest players, but Celtic themselves were merciless. If they were treated as the enemy, it may have been for the ruthlessness with which financial muscle had been flexed in the search for immediate success. A hardened team had been put together in a hurry, but Celtic fans, free of any sense of irony, took exception to the opposition reinforcing its own side.

It was the losers that day who still had impetus. Those in charge did not pause. Glass barely missed a meeting in the years when the club was run by a committee, but Celtic was bound to become a limited company as the complexities and sums involved in football increased. In one newspaper report of the 5,000 £1 shares that were issued in 1897 the list is headed by Glass, who is termed a 'builder's manager'. He had been presented with a hundred of them and also an honorarium of £100. Glass gave up the presidency, although he still served as a director. He was the builder who laid the foundations of the club.

Celtic were not uniformly admired, and by 1890 there was indignation over the fact that in addition to Kelly several other players had pubs. 'On the one hand', declared *Scottish Sport*, 'the club dispenses with the lily hand of charity succour to the sick and portion to the poor; on the other hand it watches indifferently, if it does not encourage, its young men throwing themselves recklessly into a business of which every tendency is towards moral ruin.' Celtic, though, would have regarded it as essential to make the players financially secure if the club was not to wither. Amateurism became an absurdity once professionalism had been legalised south of the border in 1885, yet it took another eight years before Scottish football followed suit.

It had been a period in which individual ambition was entwined with a resolve to see Celtic thrive, and Glass had colleagues with the same outlook. There was a fluidity to the life of O'Hara. He had been little more than an infant when, in 1847, his family left County Derry during the famine. O'Hara grew up to be a shoemaker, but soon committed himself to being a trade union organiser and was to become secretary of the Operative Shoemakers' Society. Willie Maley, with a good turn of phrase, numbered O'Hara among the 'knowing novices', because these men were quick to show an aptitude for whatever they undertook. The immigrant's realisation that a chance may never come again underpinned the keen desire to embark on new projects.

The reproaches of publications like *Scottish Sport* were no deterrent. As with Glass and several others associated with Celtic, O'Hara was successful in the drinks trade and eventually bought himself an estate in Rothesay, on the Isle of Bute. He was to the fore among the business-minded people who went to considerable expense when piecing together a potent team. The club's rapid move to so nakedly materialistic a footing outraged idealists, but when the sport was already being commercialised it would have been incongruous to go on operating in a homely manner. Even so, there was selflessness in the remarkable efforts of the volunteers largely responsible for building Celtic's original ground over the course of the winter. Just two months after the club's formation, a general meeting heard in January 1888 that 'the pitch is finished, the paling well nigh up, and the grand stand – capable of accommodating from 800 to 1000 – would be begun in the course of the ensuing week'.

The completion of that project was impressive, but a far wider struggle for the betterment of the community has been sustained for centuries. St Mary's contains the bodies of some who fell in that cause. 'In 1847,' according to the church's website, 'the crypt was opened no less than four or five times to receive the remains of assistant priests in the parish who had died in the fever epidemic of that year. There are fifteen coffins there. Typhus was known (somewhat unkindly) as Irish Fever. Several of the priests who died in Saint Mary's in the 1847 outbreak had come here from Ireland to serve the people of Glasgow.'

Monsignor Peter Smith, the current parish priest, puts it even more poignantly: 'We lost four priests during one of the epidemics. There was a wee fellow, Father Bradley, who's down in the crypt here, and he was twenty-three when he died. Now, the youngest you could be ordained was twenty-three, so he arrived in the middle of a cholera epidemic and was dead from it within two or three months. That sort of cheapness of human life is beyond our thinking now. It's something we might see in Africa or after a flood in another part of the world. We once had three or four baptisms a day, and they were all being baptised on the day they were born. The families had no security that their child would live. Now we look on the death of an infant, rightly, as a disaster.'

In the St Mary's of the nineteenth century there was still a conviction that progress could come. There has been desperation and, against the odds, aspiration in the East End. Particular individuals, such as Glass, would have a far-reaching effect on Celtic, but the congregation genuinely was a community. While immigration might have been going on for generations, the Catholicism of these people set them apart to an extent, and they therefore formed many bonds with one another. A structure of mutual support allowed them to lead full lives, even if some maintained a certain distance from society at large. The zeal for self-improvement was obvious in the creation of a parish library. On another front, the craving for stability in the parish of St Mary's brought the establishment of a Penny Savings Bank.

There was a measure of fun in the parish's Total Abstinence Society, with people resisting the call of the pub to gather on Saturday night for a cup of tea and a sing-song. Behind all this was a communal urge to form a better society. Celtic itself was established with a charitable purpose, although it soon dwindled. Walfrid, born Andrew Kerins in County Sligo, reflected the Marists' focus on education. He was part of the determination in St Mary's to foster new initiatives. There was an ambition to the altruism of the parish that, to begin with, was not felt quite so keenly by others where sport was concerned.

Following Hibernian's victory in the 1887 Scottish Cup final, John McFadden, the secretary of the Edinburgh team, had challenged the Irish community in Glasgow to produce a successful side of its own. He was addressing three parishes in the East End of Glasgow, but St Mary's alone took the endeavour to fruition. Given the struggle that ensued for Hibernian, he may have well regretted the encouragement that helped bring Celtic into existence. Dynamism was already a habit in that area. Walfrid was headmaster at the Sacred Heart School, but his activities reached far beyond the classroom. His endeavours with the Poor Children's Dinner Table attempted to stave off malnutrition and starvation. Such a project was also intended to parry the efforts of Protestant soup kitchens, which might have led people away from their Catholic faith. Walfrid was exceedingly busy, and it was a kindred project that brought Celtic into existence as, in his mind, a means of raising funds for charity. Some at the club would take only a token interest in good works and had other targets in mind. Celtic succeeded in setting themselves apart by making an impact in football, but it is not simple to affect the environment of the East End.

The club had been founded in the church hall of St Mary's after Mass on Sunday 6 November 1887. The building has now been demolished and the site sold. Any development that eventually takes place in this gritty part of town would at least be a sign of urban regeneration, but bulldozing poverty or refurbishing lives running to ruin in the Calton area of Glasgow's East End is far harder to achieve. It is not so long ago that a crowd of as many as forty addicts would build up at one of the tenement closes across the street from the church when a shipment of drugs was a little late in arriving. The trade is not so blatant at the moment, and the hard-pressed police have had some effect, but it is enough of a task for them merely to make the transactions less conspicuous.

Monsignor Smith feels sorry for them since they can scarcely be expected to cure society's ills. Despite the monotony and despair, misery has its grotesque flourishes in the Calton. 'There was one guy who wanted a loan and he was willing to give his glass eye as security,' recalls Smith. 'The only time you got peace from him was when he was in jail, which was probably nine months out of twelve. He's so needy, but money's the last thing he needs. He needs a mentor, he needs somebody in the prison system to guide him, to clean him up, to take him out of his situation. Now that's a vast amount of money to deal with one guy. Society is not ready for that. Celtic's founders would not have envisaged people so far out of the community.'

For players and many fans, the East End is an area they visit only on match days. The club left the old training ground near

Celtic Park and, in 2007, opened its purpose-built and secluded facility to the north of Glasgow. None the less, the link with the traditional homeland is still strong for both footballers and the supporters who make their way to the stadium. The Calton itself is engrossing to sociologists, public-health researchers and journalists. In 2006 the *Guardian* was pointing out that the average male life expectancy of 53.9 years was ten years lower than that in Iraq. By 2008 the World Health Organisation was observing that in the village of Lenzie, half a dozen miles to the north of the Calton, the figure for a man is eighty-two. Smith's survey is conducted in regretful close-up. He waves an arm and says, 'It's fifty-three on that side of the road and sixty-three on this. Far more people are addicted to drugs there, and they're dying at thirty. That's pulling the average down.'

Anecdotes are more unsettling than statistics. In a similar parish where he once worked, Smith remembers 'a six-year-old girl who was being used to carry drugs in her schoolbag. That lack of respect for kids is endemic to drugs culture.' The general situation is the same around St Mary's. 'Many children are brought up by their grandmother because both parents are addicts with no visitation rights,' says Smith. 'Effectively, as soon as the children are born they are given to the grandparents. How are these kids going to survive? It's tragic if the parents die, but here the parents are very often still around, and they're such a bad influence that the children can't get near the parents. These grandparents are struggling to do the whole family thing again at an age when they should be sitting back and enjoying the grandchildren. There are layers of deprivation here that very often have nothing to do with money, except in the sense that the money has all gone on drugs and drink. Heart disease is another factor that pulls down life expectancy.'

Alcohol can be a bringer of havoc as well. The present is not a simple restaging of the past, but it is still easy to sense the circumstances that brought Celtic into being. As Smith emphasises, there continue to be resolute and idealistic people who are set on a better life for themselves and those around them. 'Sometimes', he says, 'a child arrives and the parents suddenly seem to realise that "This kid matters to me." They draw themselves up and become good parents. You see them rise and, for instance, become a nursery nurse when they're thirty. They climb out and the goodness within them triumphs. So it's not all doom and gloom, but the reality is that it's very hard to triumph if they've not had the right sort of start.'

Celtic's charitable work continues, but no substantial club has that as its main purpose. Even so, there is more attention paid to such initiatives now than there was in some earlier periods. Ambition has displaced idealism at times. The club was at its boldest and perhaps most materialistic towards the close of the nineteenth century. It did not fall into the trap of parochialism. Celtic, at an early stage, rejected the idea of fielding only Catholics. In 1895 a proposal that there should be a maximum of three Protestants in the team was voted down by the committee and it was decided instead that there would be no limit to the number of non-Catholics. Restrictions went against the grain. Three years earlier the club had moved a short distance from its original ground to the site of the current stadium. The motive was supposedly the rise in annual rent from £50 to £450 that they faced at their first home as the intensity of public interest, and the ensuing income, became obvious.

This was presented sentimentally as an example of a rapacious landlord exploiting the Irish. The parallel was dubious since the club was far from vulnerable and would have been foolish not to relocate to premises where they could make more money. There was hardship everywhere in Glasgow, yet an excitement over the times to come was also in the air, particularly when Celtic were settling into their first season. In August 1888 Queen Victoria came back to the city after an absence of thirty-nine years. The occasion was the Glasgow International Exhibition, which ran for six months and was reported to have attracted 5.75 million people to Kelvingrove Park in the west of the city. Its principal pavilion was in the shape of a huge mosque. Visitors were agog, too, at entertainments such as floodlit rugby, as well as the engineering prowess on display in the machinery hall. The monarch had also gone to George Square, in the centre of Glasgow, to see the City Chambers, the new municipal buildings, and accept the golden casket presented to her.

Hardship and suffering were in plain view in the city, but so, too, were enterprise and faith in a more affluent time to come. It made unarguable sense for Celtic to leave their original ground and build a far larger stadium near by. Having rented the land initially, the club spent £10,000 to buy it outright from Sir William Hozier in 1897. The ambition of Celtic in that era is striking even now. Many would have been discouraged even before they had so much as heard that high price. While the minor relocation had kept the club in its heartland, this was not an ideal site. There was, first of all, a hole full of water to a depth of forty feet that had to be filled with 100,000 cartloads of earth.

Celtic were seldom deterred. It was only by flouting the requirement for amateurism that clubs could hold on to their better players. The leading performers at Celtic did particularly well. They were paid around £3 a week at that time and knew that their value could rise further. After James Kelly had moved to the club, he was instrumental in talking the side out of its decision to go on strike at a time when payments were illicit in a sport that was supposedly amateur. Considering that he had such influence then, it was no surprise that he would eventually become chairman of Celtic, from 1909 to 1914, so initiating the role for his family in the boardroom that continued until the 1990s.

Hibernian had been one of the other contenders striving to add Kelly to their team, and he had appeared for them against Hearts earlier in 1888, but Celtic did far more than merely deny them a single player. The essential members of the Edinburgh club's team were also enticed to Glasgow, where much greater earnings awaited them. There is little to be said in defence of

Celtic. Hibernian had not appreciated the brutal and calculating aspect of a side they had mistaken for blood brothers. They had even shown benevolence towards a club with which they felt an affinity. Hibernian had played for charitable purposes before in the East End of the city, and the empathy was so marked that Brother Walfrid had to resist many of those around him who wanted the new team to be called Glasgow Hibernian. There should have been warmth towards the Edinburgh club. The official opening of Celtic's first ground, on 8 May 1888, saw Hibernian play out a goalless draw with Cowlairs, and it was not until the 28th of the month that the tenants took the field there for the game with the Rangers XI.

Celtic would get on with the plundering of Hibernian regardless of any bond, and half a dozen of their players were soon on the books. The aggrieved club was unrealistic about the changing nature of football. Hibernian would have lost members of the side in any case, but it was galling to be the victim of friends who suddenly revealed themselves as predators. The new club had equipped itself with instant heroes such as Willie Groves, a fast and stirring centre forward who had scored the decisive goal when Hibernian beat Dumbarton in the Scottish Cup final of 1887. His defection would have caused the most virulent anger of all towards Celtic. 'Weakened . . . and from the quarter least expected,' said a football official in Edinburgh. 'Better things might have been looked for from the club from which Hibernians received their blow.'

An open letter from an indignant Hibernian fan who styled himself 'Easter Road' was published by the *Scottish Umpire* in August 1888. 'Could they really think that they had the same right as you to uphold the honour of Irish football?' he asked. There is an irony to modern eyes in that charge since the Glasgow club has also been accused at times of being alien to the country in which it exists. That letter seethes over the deliberately inclusive term 'Celtic' because it is insufficiently Irish and 'may cover Welsh, Highland, Scotch, French, and all the nations of that family'. Even the club's strip was offensive to the anonymous correspondent. He was angry that Celtic had chosen then to wear 'a white shirt and edge the collar with green so that it requires a microscope to detect the colour at all'.

That derision overlooks the fact that the Glasgow club had a degree of idealism when claiming a more diverse identity for itself. If Walfrid preferred the name Celtic, it was exactly because the term embraces both the Scot and the Irishman, even if the associations with the latter were far more marked in the public mind at that time. It was not long before the club donned a markedly Irish top of green and white stripes, with the switch to hoops made in 1903. Neither 'Easter Road' nor any other Hibernian supporter could be mollified by that when a supposedly kindred club had already preyed on them.

The teams faced one another at Celtic Park in August 1888, and it would be Groves who scored the winner against the visitors. It was to be expected that a return match in October at the original Easter Road would have a menacing mood, with hundreds of Hibernian supporters eventually invading the pitch. The referee blew for full time after eighty minutes. Two of the three unanswered goals for the visitors came from Michael Dunbar, and the other was scored by John Coleman. Both men had been enticed from Hibernian.

The losers that day would eventually go into suspended animation, and did not play any matches in the 1891/2 season. When Hibernian were revived in the autumn of 1892, the chairman announced that there would no longer be a sectarian policy in team selection. Regardless of the pettiness and discrimination, Hibernian had come to see, as Celtic knew from almost the start, that it was folly to impose handicaps on themselves. Unlike Hibernian, Rangers had the means to succeed in a prolonged period of discrimination that came to a complete end only after the appointment of Graeme Souness as manager in 1986. In addition, the Ibrox club, while shunning Catholics, had been drawing on the majority of the population.

Celtic's approach was born of urgency. The conduct, admirable or otherwise, was that of people who knew there was no time to spare. They were late starters, considering that Queen's Park had become the first Scottish club upon their formation a generation before, in 1867. Those associated with Celtic also appeared to be in a hurry. If not immigrants themselves, they were often the first generation of their family to be born in Scotland. Glasgow was a seething city whose population had approached 800,000 when the club was coming into existence. Famine in Ireland played a considerable part in the city's growth. In 1841 there were six and a half million on the island. Thirty years later the figure was four million. Hunger made people flee, and projects such as the construction of the Loch Katrine reservoir in the latter part of the 1850s meant there was some work to be had in Scotland. Migrants typically rushed west to America or east to the ports of Liverpool and Glasgow. Those who are hungry and desperate cause at least as much fear as sympathy, and in Scotland there could be little enthusiasm for the vigorous revival of Catholicism in a country whose parliament had outlawed that faith after the Reformation in 1560.

The process of Catholic emancipation was not felt strongly there until the late eighteenth century. Differing interpretations of the Christian theology clashed severely in Scotland, where the French-born Mary of Guise had been regent until her death in June 1560. Papal power and the Catholic beliefs to which she had adhered were soon condemned by a Scottish parliament reflecting the Calvinism of John Knox. Some of the antagonism towards Irish immigrants was therefore a reaction to their faith, but newcomers are generally treated with suspicion and a theological issue such as transubstantiation would not in itself be the type of cause to keep a confrontation alive for centuries. People really dreaded, for instance, that the Irish would constitute cheap labour and so drag down wages even further in an era of hardship.

In 1931 Dr James Devon, who had been born in the Calton,

gave an address to the Old Glasgow Club about his experiences of that area fifty years before, when incomers were very noticeable. The mood of a time and place are evoked wryly from the Protestant perspective. 'The Irish were looked upon as an inferior race, hewers of wood and drawers of water, who should be treated with consideration but kept in their place,' he said. 'The less we had to do with them the better. Their religion was not our religion, which was the best; and their customs were different from ours, as was their speech. Doubtless there were good folk among them, but the unruly and turbulent ones showed us what we might become if we did not keep to our own people.'

The interweaving of sport and religion among the Irish immigrants gives the impression of a self-contained community, even if, in practice, there were bound to be many connections to the city at large. A correspondent for *The Bailie*, a Glasgow magazine of the time, reported on 20 April 1892 on Celtic's success in winning the Scottish Cup, its first notable trophy: 'I understand that the Cup captured on Saturday week now adorns the altar of a Roman Catholic chapel in the East End of the city. Of old, knights used to hang up the spoils of war in their churches and chapels. Other times, other trophies.' The writer was almost certainly referring to St Mary's. As late as 1949 the *Glasgow Observer and Scottish Catholic Herald* could still find a contemporary of Brother Walfrid's to evoke the interweaving of sport and religion at Celtic in the last decade of the nineteenth century, although its pious account should be treated with a little scepticism. 'In the early days,' the writer announced, 'the Celts used to go to mass and communion before major games, not to pray for victory, but because they were catholic sportsmen in the truest sense of the word and realised that the catholic concept of sportsmanship calls for health of soul and mind as well as of body.'

Community, with its bonds strengthened by church-going, was everything. In a crammed and suffering Glasgow it was otherwise a challenge for ordinary people to be at ease with one another. The conditions were appalling for those who lacked means, no matter which sort of church commanded their allegiance. Any mood of helplessness would have been aggravated by traumas such as the collapse of the City of Glasgow Bank in 1878. The institution, with 133 branches, had looked prosperous, but a general financial crisis exposed the truth and the bank closed its branches as account-holders gathered in the street. Ultimately it was the shareholders who suffered directly since they were liable for the losses. There were 1,819 of them, and only 254 escaped insolvency. The directors of the bank would be convicted of fraud, with jail sentences handed down of between eight and eighteen months. Many companies went out of business when the bank went under, and in general the late nineteenth century was insecure even by Glasgow's standards.

It would appear, technically, that the circumstances did not amount to a depression as economists understand it, but working people knew they were experiencing hard times. The historian T. C. Smout records that the first systematic census of British wages in 1886 showed central Scotland to be a low-pay area. If the Irish, as immigrants or children of them, were seen as cheap labour, then they would be treated as a cause of the suffering to the Scottish and Protestant communities. Distinctions, whether of accent or theology, were certain to be emphasised. It was hard for a workman to find security and a good wage. A Scot often earned a fifth less than an Englishman in the same job south of the border. That contrast explained, too, why shipbuilding was then such a great industry in Glasgow. The US Congress judged in 1872 that the popularity of Clyde-built vessels depended on cheapness rather than quality. That, in turn, reflected the surfeit of skilled workers who had to accept whatever they were offered in various jobs in the economy at large. The wage for a shipyard job was 8 per cent less than in England. Clydeside, from some perspectives, could easily be taken for a swath of suffering.

In 1870 Glasgow University relocated from the High Street site it had occupied for 410 years in the old centre of the city to a leafy, healthy position on a hill three miles to the west. Wise as the university had been to consider its own interests, the people who remained would have been justified in feeling abandoned. There was, all the same, far more than that to concern them. The city's Medical Officer of Health wrote a survey in 1888 of living conditions as recorded in a census seven years before, when the population was little more than 500,000. That had been bad enough. 'If a man has any rights at all,' he asserted, 'one of them certainly is the right to enough of the area of the earth's surface to afford him standing room, and enough of the cubic space thereon at least to crouch in.' To put it in more prosaic terms, the average Glaswegian in that period lived eight yards from his neighbour. There were, again on average, eighty-four people to each acre. The figure for London was fifty-one, and in the whole country the one city with worse circumstances was Liverpool, with 106 inhabitants per acre. By the time Celtic came into being, Glasgow's condition would have deteriorated further.

The rise in the population contributed to a more agreeable sort of congestion when people willingly crammed themselves into football grounds. That, in turn, accelerated the commercialisation of the game. As the sport took on a cut-throat character, money became essential. In the case of Celtic, that led to dismaying consequences. Once the Marists had moved Brother Walfrid to London in 1892, there was no one on the scene who might have been a living reproach to the new materialism. By the following year, when the club was committed to developing its stadium, Celtic could not have been diverted from their course. The *Glasgow Observer* supplied a lament, if not an obituary, for the original Celtic: 'The thing is a mere business, in the hands of publicans and others. Catholic charities got nothing out of the thousands of pounds passing through the treasurer's hands. Can we not get a club that will carry out the original idea of Brother Walfrid?'

The newspaper's reference to publicans was acute. Their association with the running of Celtic was indisputable, and while alcohol was legal, its effect on many lives led it to being treated by some as if it should have been a banned substance. That interpretation had a solid founding in reality. A Catholic temperance body such as the League of the Cross existed so that people could help each other resist an apparent means of escape from grim circumstances that might easily make their plight all the greater. On the other hand, when it was hard for them to be accepted into the supposedly respectable professions the Irish people who owned those pubs were taking one of the few routes towards success. The St Mary's branch of the League of the Cross adhered cleverly both to its principles and to the club. It had on its banner the image of the teetotal Tom Maley, who was in the first Celtic team with his brother Willie.

The issue of the club and the drinks trade lay behind disagreements at St Mary's which were covered by the *Glasgow Observer* in December 1894. There was an effort to annul the election of Joseph Cosgrove as president of the parish's branch of the League of the Cross. He was accused of having connections with the 'liquor traffic', and bad language at the meeting led to Father Murie ordering several people off the premises. The matter was then referred to Canon Carmichael, who recognised the peculiarity of someone such as Cosgrove being in such a position, even as he struggled to identify a regulation that prohibited it. Where the football club was concerned, some were clear that their stance in rejecting alcohol was untenable.

There was scant room for idealism if it barred publicans who might have the business acumen required in the sport. Football was already commercialised by the time Celtic became a limited company. It took cash to compete, and there was additional outlay on the construction of a cement track in 1897 so the World Cycling Championship could be staged at Celtic Park. That would be thoroughly outdone for oddity by the demonstration of trench warfare put on at the ground during the First World War, although it was a fundraising event for charity. Celtic, all the same, had initially been under financial strain when attempting to compete in the new environment of legalised pro-fessionalism. In the 1890s they became laden with debt because of stadium development and the growth of wages to glamorous players. The club could spare nothing for the Poor Children's Dinner Table, a cause at the core of its being not so long before. People brooded over this.

At the half-yearly meeting in December 1894, it had been Tom Maley who pointed to the complete absence of any money for the charity associated with the departed Walfrid. He drew the contrast between a striking income of £7,000 and the complete neglect of good causes. This particular Maley has a tangential yet resonant role in Celtic's history. John Glass and Walfrid, while putting together the first Celtic team, had gone to see Tom. It happened that he was out courting the girl who would become his wife. Willie was at home and, with this element of chance, embarked on his prolonged association with the club. Both brothers were well-versed in the game and had been together at Third Lanark. Willie had not achieved his aim of playing for Queen's Park, but he and Tom were in the line-up for Celtic's first game. There is no doubting that it was Willie who in every measurable way went on to make history at the club, but the relationship between the brothers was also a factor in itself. Tom drew attention readily. He, Willie and another brother, Alec, would all be managers in Scotland or England. Indeed, Alec was in charge of Clyde in 1912 and then Hibernian in 1923 when losing the Scottish Cup final to his brother Willie's Celtic side on each occasion.

Despite the trophies won, it would have been only natural for Willie to be exasperated by Tom. The latter had an effortless air about him. He might as well have been created as an incitement to Willie. Proof of that is everywhere. Tom was naturally at ease and he was, for instance, the brother who went to London for his teacher training. Even simple drawings reveal the story. A little sketch of Tom in 1903 showed a dandyish, well-kept moustache. When Willie sported one, it was more apologetic.

The contrasts are clearer still in 1931. In an overreaction, the Celtic director Tom Colgan sent a telegram asking Tom Maley to cross the Atlantic and assist with the summer tour of the US when his brother was merely unwell. A photograph from that trip presents one debonair brother living up to his nickname of 'handsome Tom', while Willie is dumpy and glum. The younger brother made the far deeper impression on the history of football, but perhaps Tom drove him to it unintentionally. Willie, incapable of outdoing his sibling in the usual course of events, was left with an obsessiveness that he put to good use at Celtic.

Tom's mind did not work in that fashion. For most of his life, he was an idealist who could keep football in perspective. In 1892 Tom was put in charge of Slatefield Roman Catholic Industrial School. He was what we would now describe as the headmaster of an establishment about a third of a mile from Celtic Park. The school took on the challenge of helping street children who were homeless or found begging, with neither parents nor guardians to protect them. The school intended both to teach them and to introduce the youngsters to a trade that might set their lives on a new course. There was instruction in shoemaking and tailoring, with the goods sold to cover some of the school's costs. When Tom was elected vice president of Celtic in June 1895, he declined the post because it would distract him from his labours in what were described as the 'inadequate premises' at Slatefield. Tom spent several years there, and when he did leave it was initially to work at St Mary's RC Industrial School.

Tom was well-intentioned, if priggish. In 1897, for instance, he gave a paper to the annual Conference of the Catholic Young Men's Society of Great Britain in which he identified 'social influences, heretical unchristian life and pernicious literature' as the main cause of irreligion among school leavers. He depicted the YMS as their protector. We can only guess how much this altruistic brother got on the nerves of the Celtic manager. Furthermore, Tom would not just make his mark in the same profession as Willie but do so in a broader football environment.

When Manchester City took the first major honour in their history with the defeat of Bolton Wanderers in the 1904 FA Cup final, he was the manager. His side were also First Division runners-up that season. Football, however, has been tarnished for as long as it has been popular, and there might even have been some *Schadenfreude* mixed up with the filial concern in Willie's heart when Tom got into terrible trouble the following year.

Billy Meredith, the winger who had scored the only goal of the FA Cup final, was found guilty of attempting to bribe the Aston Villa captain Alec Leake with an offer of £10 before a game in which victory might have made City League champions. They lost and the title went to Newcastle United, but it was the aftermath that devastated Tom Maley's club. Meredith was insouciant about his suspension from football for a year and broke the terms of the ban by continuing to turn up at City's Hyde Road ground. The FA got to hear of this and called on City to report Meredith for seeking to collect his wages while suspended. The Wales winger then turned on Maley, alleging that the manager had promised him £100 if he could bribe Leake. FA commissioners swarmed over City's affairs and learned of irregularities such as the vast sum of £931 paid in bonuses to the FA Cup-winning side. Meredith, on £6 a week, was also among the players receiving more than the £4 maximum allowed by the FA. Inevitably, the club's accounts were fraudulent. As City fell, Manchester United soared to their first championship a few months after signing Meredith in January 1907.

Tom Maley's initial punishment for the wrongdoing was to be banned for life. The sentence was commuted and in 1911 he became manager of Bradford Park Avenue, a club he took to the First Division and sustained there for a time. Maley did not leave that job until March 1923, when the side was mid-table in the Third Division (North). It would be excessive to say Maley had been disgraced by the scandal at City. Managers did not normally dictate policy at a club in that era, and there is also the usual yet well-founded excuse that City's main fault was to get caught when such practices were widespread. The club was fined £250, bans were imposed on the chairman as well as two directors, and the players were fined £900 in total. Despite not being alone in the scandal, Tom's career was affected and Willie was no longer at risk of being overshadowed within his own family.

Even so, Tom was not tarnished irreparably and his death in 1935 brought an unqualified tribute from Celtic: 'The club owes a great deal of gratitude to him as, in the earliest days, his personality and reputation did a tremendous lot in establishing the club. His promise to lend his aid . . . brought joy to the hearts of Brother Walfrid and John Glass.' There was a euphemistic accolade, too, for his ransacking of Hibernian: 'There is no doubt he was responsible for the immediate enlistment of a number of famous players who had hitherto been lukewarm in their attitude towards the venture.' Tom had been a Hibernian player for part of 1887, the year of Celtic's formation.

Despite the allure and means that Celtic had, football was not so deep-rooted as to constitute the sole possibility for the club to prosper. Various activities were tried in the hope that they might attract a crowd. If the overwhelming aim was for immigrants to make an impact, it did not matter how this was achieved. There would have been no intention of abandoning football, but efforts were made to see what other ventures might lure spectators. Motorcyclists, for instance, drew the crowds for quite a while. In his book, Willie Maley relished the memory of Harry Martin getting back on his motorbike at Celtic Park soon after a burst tyre had sent him somersaulting onto the track at Northampton and into hospital.

It was Willie who seemed to be connected to everything that had or could take place at Celtic. Tom was not consumed by the club to that extent. Willie had an obsessiveness that nobody else had or indeed wished to have. While he was distinctive, there should also be an appreciation of the sheer number of effective people to be found in the congregation of St Mary's. The importance it had to the community is reflected in its size: Glasgow's

Catholic cathedral is St Andrew's, on the banks of the Clyde near the city centre, but when it was closed for renovation in 2009 its duties were taken over by St Mary's until the spring of 2011. Father Forbes, who would become the first parish priest there, had spent three years touring Ireland to raise the money for a church that opened in 1842.

The men who occupied the pews of St Mary's in the latter part of the nineteenth century were every bit as resolute, if more devoted in some cases to the personal accumulation of wealth. While John Glass died at the age of fifty-nine in 1906, there were already others in the parish who had shown the same mettle. The capable John O'Hara became a director when Celtic was turned into a limited company. By 1894 the club was bragging that its income of £10,142 surpassed all others in England or Scotland.

O'Hara had also been the secretary of the steering committee that brought Celtic into being. There were no particularly resonant deeds, but he busied himself going from house to house while collecting subscriptions for the club in early 1888. O'Hara was an example of self-transformation. He had begun his working life as a shoemaker. While the connection with the drinks trade put him amongst a group of people thought dubious by the idealists, there was an impetus about O'Hara that had taken him far. Such men were outsiders of a kind, but it would be romantic to speak solely of the club's leaders as revolutionaries.

John H. McLaughlin, unusually for a Celtic figure, was on good terms with the football authorities, and became the first chairman of the club. The sport itself grew more complicated and someone like him, at ease with the Establishment, seemed alien to certain people. 'He never held power such as did John Glass,' said a cantankerous Willie Maley, 'and never was the aid to the club the cheery East End joiner was all his days.' The manager may have been grouchily indifferent to the fact that football was becoming tortuous and there was a need for someone who could be trusted not to get lost in the corridors of power. All the same,

Maley could not entirely disregard the sort of skills that he had: 'Mr McLaughlin did much work in the SFA and League, where his strong silent manner made him a very useful member when much thinking was to be done.' Even so, Maley declined to see the sociability in a man who had accompanied the Rangers Glee Club on the piano.

The SFA initially rejected McLaughlin's argument that professionalism must be sanctioned, and that ought to have reinforced Maley's sense of solidarity with someone who was supposedly an outsider in the Establishment. In practice, McLaughlin, a wine and spirits merchant, did make his presence felt and was never more vigorous than when challenging those who pretended that the old order could continue. 'You might as well attempt to stop the flow of Niagara with a kitchen chair,' he famously said, before making a prediction that was less than impeccable in the long term. 'With veiled professionalism players are masters of the clubs', he pronounced, 'and can go and debauch themselves without being called to account. Under the new system the clubs will be masters of the players.'

McLaughlin was determined to have his say, but free expression by others offended him on at least one occasion. He assumed the chairmanship only after the uproar caused by the club becoming a limited company. While McLaughlin was ready to deride those opposed to that change 'as corner boys and loafers', he sued Frank Havelin, a labourer who had opposed him with similar frankness. Havelin would have been ruined if the case had gone against him, but the court was contemptuous of McLaughlin, threw out the claim and awarded costs against the Celtic office-bearer. There is not much to be said on behalf of the president when he conducted himself like that, but the club was taking on a new identity as football became a commercial concern as much as a sporting pursuit. Havelin had sought to preserve Celtic in its original form. While that was unrealistic in the long term, the principled Havelin had no sooner become a committee member than he attempted to sustain the charitable purpose by moving that £50 be donated to the St Vincent de Paul Society. The proposal was defeated, but embarrassment led the club that day to give money to other good causes.

Celtic's conversion to a limited company was supposedly triggered by the costs incurred while adapting their ground for an international cycling event, despite a suspicion that this may have been a useful pretext. Although the press was banned when the members debated the issue, it was not really so great a test for a club that understood football to be an emerging business and wished to drive it further in that direction. The path would have had to be taken sooner or later. Celtic were clear-sighted if hard-hearted. Many years after the event, Tom Maley set down his memories of the meeting at which the issue of becoming a limited company was debated. The exchanges had their lighter moments. Ned McGinn was, after all, participating.

This particular supporter had secured a little fame in 1892, after Celtic took the Scottish Cup, Glasgow Cup and Charity Cup. He sent a telegram informing Pope Leo XIII of this landmark and, with no reply received, had to be talked out of demanding a vote of censure for the pontiff at a meeting of the Home Government branch of the Irish National League. At this distance, it is hard to tell whether there was a little of the humorous extrovert in this apparent hothead. Tom Maley wrote of him in his account of the inflamed meeting over the limited company issue:

> There had been mention of 'quid pro quo' and Ned, who had a great regard for good old John Glass, would not be quietened until he had his say, which was to the effect that no 'quids' would be given from the club, unless to the proper charities in the proper way. To hear and see John Glass, as he called out 'Order, order!' in his high-pitched voice was to have become infected with the laughter that he tried but couldn't suppress.

Celtic, in that era, had few moments of whimsy. There was a desire to make their opinions known on almost any topic. The practical McLaughlin also talked the SFA into using goal nets so there would be no further arguments as to whether the ball had gone between the posts, even if such newfangled technology was only permitted originally for the semi-finals and final of the Scottish Cup. Nets were an adjunct to the professionalism that Celtic epitomised, but the forcefulness of the club could cause tension within the ranks of the Irish community. Hibernian and other sides of that nature had not been as brash as Celtic. A wariness towards the club is sensed from the beginning, although there is little or no overt antagonism. People were trying to decide what to make of Celtic. After the side had lost to Queen's Park in the semi-final of the Glasgow Cup in November 1888, the *Scottish Umpire* inched towards an expression of disquiet: 'Their main objective appears to have been to get together a strong team and leave time to do the rest. Short as the season has been, during which the Celts have stood before the public, they have made a reputation and enjoy a respect which any club might envy, and while they have secured many friends their first success has also brought them enemies.'

Celtic, as moneyed opponents, had to be prepared for the craving other teams had to beat them. The club would take the League title four times in the 1890s with an efficiency that reflected the sums spent on creating a side. The first trophy that still registers now came when Celtic won the Scottish Cup in 1892. That final pitted materialism against traditionalism. Celtic beat hallowed Queen's Park at a recently expanded Ibrox, whose gates were opened four hours before kick-off as a crowd of 40,000 assembled. There was bedlam in the air and a bid to steal the proceeds had been thwarted, but no one could stop the fans from spilling onto the pitch repeatedly. After twenty minutes, the two captains told the referee that they wanted the game to be deemed a friendly.

Celtic won that day, and did so again four weeks later, with Johnny Campbell scoring a hat-trick in a 5–1 victory. The delay in staging the replay was due to the fact that improvements had to be made to Ibrox. The SFA also took the precaution of doubling the ticket prices and so halving the attendance. There had been fears that football in Scotland was losing its attraction, but a brash Celtic renewed the magnetism.

2

WILLIE MALEY

It took inexhaustible energy to fuel Willie Maley's long commitment to Celtic as footballer and manager. He was gripped by chronic restlessness. In the various accounts that he gave, there are details of compulsive travelling during his fifty-two years with the club. While his career took place in an era when a manager would be somewhat detached from the players in any case, Maley had a craving to be on the move. He reckoned, in 1938, that he had travelled 300,000 miles on Celtic's behalf. Apart from the extent of the roaming, Maley had to devote great amounts of time to it as he was largely restricted to road and rail. Commercial air travel did not expand rapidly until after the Second World War.

Even if it had been in the character of the manager to enjoy being at rest, he was uprooted by circumstance. Maley had separated from his wife Helen by, at the latest, 1901, when she is described in the census as the head of the family home, where their two sons also stayed. She and the children lived initially in Dennistoun, quite close to Celtic's ground, while Maley had settled on the other side of Glasgow, in the West End. On Christmas Day 1926 he learned of her death from peritonitis following a ruptured ovarian abscess. There had already been a hint of loneliness about him, despite the fact that he had a host of contacts and acquaintances.

While a footloose Maley was often absent from Celtic Park,

the risk of disruption was limited since, from at least 1931, he had in James Maloney an aide who relieved the workload and was also absorbed by the history of the club. A journalist of the time underlined his significance: 'When I entered the handsome pavilion I got a hearty greeting from Jimmy Maloney, who is . . . Maley's trusted assistant. Jimmy's caboose is on the right immediately you cross the threshold. In it he keeps guard over Mr Maley's sanctum, which is directly in the rear. Maloney's place contains an interesting collection of club material – photographs, old records of matches and men, reports of interesting contests.' Given so committed a member of staff, Maley could feel all the more free to roam as he pleased.

The sense of isolation persists about a man whose constant engagement with one scheme or another had a compulsive tone, as if he did not dare pause in case he became trapped in self-reflection. Prior to the First World War, the pavilion at Celtic was open to supporters on a Sunday, and Maley would generally be around to chat with them. He could be affable, even if it was not his natural state, and on the long train journey to an away match at Aberdeen there would be conversations between Maley and fans about virtually anything other than Irish politics, a subject about which his views would change gradually but greatly. To this day Celtic supporters celebrate the club's history by singing 'The Willie Maley Song', whose lyrics have been updated to include events since his death in 1958. Everyone who flourishes at the club is thus treated as an extension of his legacy. The sheer duration of Maley's tenure accounts for the reverence, yet in some respects he is far from being the embodiment of Celtic. The stereotypes did not fit him.

Fans and the club itself have been known to revel in the Irish element of their identity. Maley, who had played in the first match and was entwined with Celtic until his removal in 1940, did not seem to feel that tug of simple sentimentality. Although he was born on 25 April 1868 in what is now Northern Ireland, the Newry barracks location reflected the fact that his father, a native of County Clare, happened to be serving there as a sergeant in the Royal North British Fusiliers. The clearest sign of ambivalence over the conflict had been humane yet in grave breach of Maley senior's obligations to the army. In 1867 he allowed a man called Pat Welsh to get away from Dublin and board a ship for Scotland. Welsh would, in modern parlance, be called a terrorist, but the sergeant was convinced that his prisoner wanted to flee to a law-abiding life. Twenty years later Welsh, having established a successful tailoring business in the prime location of Glasgow's Buchanan Street, was among the founders of Celtic.

Sergeant Maley was a career soldier who spent twenty-one years in the army. Willie, indeed, was proud of his father's campaign medals from the Crimean War of 1853–6 that were barred for the battles at Alma, Inkerman, Sebastopol and Balaclava. He died in May 1896 and was buried with military honours in Cathcart cemetery, to the south of Glasgow's then boundary. His son, the Celtic manager, retained a concern for the army and was a little star-struck by the military. In August 1895 *Scottish Sport* explained that the presence of the Gordon Highlanders at the ground was due to Maley, 'who is a frequent visitor to Maryhill barracks, and popular with officers and men'.

Seven years later the *Scottish Referee* recorded that colonial troops, including 'Bengal Lancers . . . and . . . dusky warriors', marched through the city to give a display before 60,000 at Celtic Park that was 'a moving, picturesque spectacle representative of Britain's world-wide sway, and of her imperial majesty amongst the nations of the earth . . . the display at Parkhead had an educative value attached to it. Those privileged to witness it had their eyes opened to the value of military training and discipline.'

The bond that Maley senior had with the army is reflected in the fact that the manager had brothers born in Portsmouth as well as the West Indies and the Cathcart area. Willie himself had no cause to feel any specific connection to Newry, considering that he had left it by the age of two. The Irish dimension had also been scaled back at some stage in one part of the family and it was just his brother Charles, a priest, who continued to give his surname as O'Malley.

He had been born in the West Indies, but that appears only to have made O'Malley especially conscious of his roots. 'He was more Irish than the Irish themselves,' the *Glasgow Examiner* reported following his death in 1917. Another publication remembered him as a lively 'lecturer on Irish wit and humour . . . ever welcome all over Scotland'. The last few weeks of O'Malley's life were given over to the welfare of 'the large number of nomadic Irishmen' who had come to Scotland to do war work in Kilmarnock. The flags at Celtic Park, presumably on Willie Maley's instruction, were at half mast for the match with Hamilton on 10 November 1917.

The affinity between the brothers did have its boundaries, as the difference in surname would indicate. Willie Maley's views were to shift over the decades, and at the close of the nineteenth century there was an ambivalence to him. In December 1897 he and his brother Tom were listed as honorary members of the Branch O'Connell of the Irish National Foresters, a friendly society for the promotion of thrift and temperance in the Irish Catholic community. It was reported to have the backing of 'the most influential Irishmen in the city' and therefore sounded uncontentious. The purposes of the Foresters were, however, varied. In September 1898 the society organised a pageant and procession for the centenary of the Irish Rising. Around 35,000 people assembled on Glasgow Green to hear addresses denouncing England's conduct in Ireland. The band and pipers of the Slatefield Industrial School, whose governor was Tom Maley, were in the procession, although we do not know whether he or Willie went to the Green that day.

It is not simple, in any case, to establish clear divisions between the brothers and Scottish society at large, particularly when the Maleys engaged in football were committed to making successes of their lives. They did so, with Tom going on to become manager of Manchester City, while the fourth brother, Alec, held the post at Clyde (where the future Rangers manager Bill Struth was trainer). The focus tightened for all of them. In 1910 Willie had given a speech at a meeting in Glasgow of the United Irish League, an organisation established twelve years before to campaign for the right of tenant farmers to own the land on which they worked. Reports describe only one speech that was given, so it could well have been Maley who delivered a 'pointed, political address'.

By 1936, however, he would recall people who had sought an independent Irish republic in the late nineteenth century as 'foolish fellows, doing only harm to themselves'. While this had become a settled view among some of the leading Celtic figures, there were exceptions. In December 1901 Willie's brothers Tom and Alec had attended a meeting where Michael Davitt championed Home Rule in Ireland and called for an end to the Boer War, since the Boers were taken as counterparts to the Irish as subjects of British oppression. John H. McLaughlin, however, had represented another strand of opinion within the club from around that time. As president of the SFA, he had addressed a meeting of the ruling body in 1899 and denounced 'the ravings of some demented politicians, particularly in the south of Ireland'. He was referring to people like Davitt, the former honorary president of the club, who had the privilege of placing a sod of Donegal turf in the centre of Celtic's new ground seven years before.

In December 1899 the *Glasgow Observer* recorded the opposition to McLaughlin and even envisaged that the club would be split by it. 'We hear', the paper claimed,

> that a number of wealthy local Irishmen have associated
> themselves with a movement for the formation of a new Irish
> football club in Glasgow. As yet, we understand, the affair
> has not got beyond the preliminary stage. The Celtic seem to

have lost a measure of its old-time popularity, owing doubt-less to recent indifferent displays by the team, and to the vapourings of some of the officials, whose anti-Irish attitude has alienated true Celtic sympathy. Since the club was formed into a limited company many of the old guard have been excluded from any part of the management. Indeed, the affair has assumed an aspect almost purely mercantile with big dividends as the objective. For this reason the Celtic has lost much of the racial sympathy which in its early years was freely given to it.

This was a pivotal moment in Celtic's affairs. The club chose not to bind itself to the immigrant origins and saw a wider identity that it could claim. Entrepreneurial instinct was also in action since Celtic sought as broad an audience as possible so that it had the means to pursue its ambitions. The Irish strand can never be disentangled from the DNA, and even in mere busi-ness terms it would be folly to make the attempt when so much romantic appeal arises from that factor. All the same, Celtic did get its way in ensuring it was not restricted to an enclave. Davitt had already understood how the club's origins had collided with circumstances in contemporary Glasgow. In his 1892 appear-ance at the ground, he heard the sniggers of the crowd when he pronounced the name, in authentic fashion, as 'Keltic'. Celtic and the fans already had inclinations of their own.

Willie Maley had a sense of tradition, but it was not the one to which Davitt belonged. The manager had a soft spot for the status quo and, more broadly, a horror of disruption. Maley, indeed, exuded an affection for monarchy that is not normally associated with Celtic. When the engagement of Prince William and Kate Middleton was announced in November 2010, there was a spate of instant publications. An enthralled Maley would have bought all of them. He liked to suggest that he had shaken hands with Princess Mary of Teck, the future wife of George V. She had been with her parents at Richmond for England's match with Scotland in April 1893, when Maley made the second of two appearances for his country. In truth, he had been disgruntled because only the captain of the side, James Kelly, had the privilege of shaking hands with the princess.

Maley was to be introduced to her son George VI and his wife on 28 February 1940, by which time he was no longer the Celtic manager. They had come to Glasgow as part of the war effort and had visited Parkhead Forge, which was then operating as an ammunition works. In the afternoon they went on to inspect the ARP (Air Raid Precautions) depot on Glasgow Green, and Maley was presented to them. 'I waited for three-quarters of an hour in most inclement weather,' the manager reported, 'but afterwards I naturally thought it all worthwhile.'

He spoke initially about the football kit being given to the troops by the Glasgow Central Fund, but soon struck a more personal note. He told the royals about the meeting he had enjoyed at Richmond forty-seven years earlier and also mentioned the late Tom Hanick, a former provost of Forfar with whom he and the queen consort had both been friends.

Maley, awash with sentimentality, described her as 'a real, homely Scots girl with a kindly, soft voice'. He was so confirmed a royalist that the business card for his restaurant, the Bank, was the size of a postcard and accommodated a picture of that encounter with the royal couple. He had been unsettled by the death of George V at the start of 1936, and the abdication of Edward VIII at the close of that year struck him as if it had been a trauma in his own life. He had turned sixty-eight by then and a horror of disruption was to be ever more appropriate during a decade in which the causes of the Second World War took shape.

As a younger man, it would have been understandable if Maley had supposed he could dictate his own fate without interruption. He certainly strove to further his career, despite the fact that his prospects had been limited in some areas. In 1903 the sports publication the *Scottish Referee* was graciously dismissive of his efforts as a footballer prior to his retirement from the pitch six years earlier. 'Too modest to shine on the field where he always seems to be holding himself in reserve,' it pronounced, 'his light burns brightly in the council chamber.' Maley might be considered the sort of manager who has a drive born of the limitations he encountered as a player.

Forty-two years later, he was still grumbling and making excuses for the 3–1 loss to Rangers in the 1894 Scottish Cup. 'Rain!' he exclaimed in his account of the matter. 'It fell in torrents. The ground was soon churned up. The Ibrox lads revelled in the going . . . Celtic would have been wise to have played anyone but me. I had been in bed for two days prior to the final, suffering from throat and stomach trouble, and was really unfit to give of anything quite like my best.' Even so, this fast and reasonably talented midfielder had been chosen by Scotland, and Maley used those outings to underline his commitment to the country. His debut came in a 6–1 win over Ireland at Celtic Park in May 1893. Forty-three years later, despite all that had been accomplished at Celtic, he called that achievement his 'greatest football honour'. Maley's Scottishness was emphasised in other ways, too, and he had a long, amicable relationship with Rangers.

He was close to his opposite number at Ibrox, William Wilton. When the latter was drowned in a boating accident in 1920, they did not dare break the news to the Celtic manager immediately because he was ill and there was a fear of the effect it would have on him. It was more common for Maley to look invulnerable. His fondness for films was rare evidence that he could relax at all, if only in the darkness and comfort of the cinema. This endlessly industrious person may have been distracting himself from his estrangement from his wife and children. Whatever the explanation, Maley did not care to be at a loose end. Whether watching a game or a film, he created a schedule that steered him through the day.

Much of his time was devoted to developing a far-reaching network of contacts. When the teenage defender Willie McStay was on the brink of joining Chelsea in 1911, for instance, the manager was able to intervene from afar. 'Willie, as arranged, was met by a gent acting on my behalf,' Maley recalled. 'He had in his pocket Chelsea's offer and had promised to give his final answer with as little delay as possible. McStay was highly pleased to hear what my man had to say. He there and then agreed to refuse the London club's offer, return to Glasgow, and sign for Celtic, even though the terms were not as good as Chelsea's.' The manager or his representatives could not always mesmerise a footballer, and McStay was less biddable when the Celtic squad later had their wages cut during a period of economic depression. The full back, at the age of thirty, walked out on the club in 1924 with his teammate Willie Crilly because they thought there might be better terms to be had in the US.

Although McStay was soon back at Celtic, Crilly went on to play for a string of American clubs. The latter's ability to adapt might well have impressed Maley, even if he could never have said so. The manager had already displayed a similar desire to locate new opportunities, although the benefit was supposed to be Celtic's. There was a tireless originality to Maley. In 1910 he and the club director Tom Colgan were in New York attempting to arrange an American tour for Celtic, although the predicted income was not sufficient for the initiative to be taken any further at that time. There was a hankering even in that era for the club to make its presence felt abroad, and the team had played matches in Vienna and Prague during the summer of 1904, with Maley persuading the players to do without their wages for a tour in which Celtic were to receive little money. In that time, a manager would have thought of himself primarily as an employee of the board, even if he did not relish the instructions that had to be implemented. The hankering for greater horizons persisted, with Maley and his side crossing the Atlantic for a series of games in 1931. Celtic then found a new goalkeeper in Joe Kennaway, a Canadian who had kept a clean sheet for Fall River in a win over them. He arrived in Glasgow in October of that year.

That signing came the month after the death of John Thomson, the most cherished of all Celtic goalkeepers. He had raced out to dive at the feet of the Rangers centre forward Sam English in a match at Ibrox on 5 September 1931, and his skull was fractured in the collision. Thomson died in hospital that evening after an operation failed to relieve pressure on the brain. While the consequences were horrible, it was also an era in which goalkeepers enjoyed little protection. None the less, there was an ambiguity in Maley's reaction to this terrible event in a mere football match. 'I hope it was an accident,' he said at the subsequent inquiry. This might have been no more than an admission that he was just one fairly remote onlooker among 80,000 in the stand and terracing, but the remark gave unwarranted encouragement to those who preferred to take the grimmest view of Thomson's death. It left open the possibility of vicious intent by English, even though it was a period in which the sport was generally played with little concern for the well-being of an opponent.

Maley must have witnessed a great deal of harm done on the pitch because the longevity of his career was remarkable. He held himself in high regard and that would have been an element in the resilience that kept him to the fore for generation after generation. Maley credited himself with a gift for transforming even seemingly inadequate players. 'The ball looked to be more the master of him than he of it,' the manager said of his first impression of Jimmy McStay, Willie's brother. 'Our supporters were exceedingly bitter in their criticism of the young fellow. One and all predicted an early and swift finish to his Celtic career. I wondered that he stuck it out in the face of the critics. But stick it he did. Jimmy had faith in himself, as I had faith in him.'

McStay did have a sound career and went on to manage the club during the Second World War before being sacked in 1945, but as a footballer he was never to be capped by Scotland. Maley, in short, was adroit in depicting himself in the best possible light, even if the transformation of someone like McStay was not as spectacular as implied. The arts of PR have been employed ever since football became prominent towards the close of the nineteenth century. Presentational gifts should not be disdained in a sport where, now more than ever, the image that a manager projects of himself is crucial if he is to retain the trust of players, fans and employers. Maley was masterful in all respects. Footballers and supporters alike believed in him. The song in his honour declares Maley to be the 'man who put the tick in Celtic'. The club was his fixation as much as his responsibility, and that was evident even on an occasion that did not involve his team. In 1913 he was found painting the goalposts and dressing rooms because Celtic Park was to be the venue for the Scottish Cup final between Falkirk and Raith Rovers.

There was nothing at the club that was outside his remit, and he could be intrigued by innovation. In 1920 a man called Joe Gibb had been, as he put it, the pioneer organiser of the taking of the blind to football games. 'Mr Maley', he still recalled thirty-five years later, 'was the first football manager to encourage me in my life hobby of trying to brighten the lives of those blinded in the [First World] War. When I made an application the answer was, "Bring them along. We will make them most welcome." Needless to add, every football manager throughout the country followed Willie Maley's example.'

The range of his activities was broad. A postcard from 1934 survives that was written by him in reply to a man in Essex called P. Meikle. It does not appear to be a mass-produced response, although he was answering a request that must have come his way constantly. The message read: 'I have today posted you a large photo of the Celtic who are at present under a bit of a cloud but "apples will grow again" is my motto.' The manager was unflagging for most of his career, but he could not have had such an effect without a finesse that was the equal of his forcefulness.

He was also capable of springing a surprise. An eighteen-year-old midfielder called Peter Wilson had been playing for Beith Amateurs and, according to his own account, was met at the end of the match by 'a man with a raincoat over his arm' who asked if he would like to play for Celtic and then gave him £20 and a form to sign. 'The money I took home to my mother,' Wilson said. 'She wouldn't believe that anyone would give me such a big amount of cash for playing football, and put it in a vase on the mantelpiece, saying she would keep it there until somebody or other came along and claimed it. I wondered if she thought I had stolen the money.'

A long time passed until he appeared in a competitive game for Celtic. 'One day I received a postcard instructing me to report to the Bank restaurant,' Wilson said. 'I had never been in Glasgow before and when I arrived at St Enoch station I enquired of a policeman the way to the Bank restaurant. He looked at the wee country laddie and led me by the hand.' Wilson then had lunch with the Celtic players and was guided onto a bus. He was too shy to ask about the destination before it arrived at Fir Park. Wilson did have his own boots, but needed to put on a strip that was too big for him before being asked to mark Motherwell's Bob Ferrier, a leading winger of the era. The anecdote has been honed, but the fact remains that Maley had opted for a novice and perhaps spared him stress by hiding from the youngster what lay before him that afternoon. Wilson spent then spent ten memorable years with Celtic.

Maley's desire to be a Svengali figure did not prevent him from appreciating the talent of individuals. So frantic was he to secure Jimmy McMenemy, who had been on trial with Everton, that the contract was signed just off busy Union Street in the centre of Glasgow. McMenemy, nicknamed the General, plotted the path to victory in midfield as Celtic set a then record of six League titles in a row between 1905 and 1910. The manager called him 'one of the cornerstones of the club' and his composure was at the core of his impact, but Maley could also endure players of a boisterous nature so long as he was persuaded that they would have a pronounced effect on results.

Tommy McInally was the measure of his tolerance in the

search for victories. The contribution of the attacker was, in the long run, moderate, but his gifts were such that people could not stop themselves from imagining that he would make those abilities count. Maley himself could hardly bear to give up hope in a man who, in principle, had so very much to offer. The anarchic individuality had its charms. In 1928 Celtic played at Keith in a Scottish Cup tie. The match was much too easy for the visitors, but, according to folklore, McInally took it upon himself to create a sense of occasion.

If accounts penned years after the game carry any credence, the attacker, when not helping himself to a hat-trick, assisted the opposition. The tale could be a piece of myth-making, but that, in its own fashion, underlines the fascination with McInally. Having heard at half-time that any Keith player who scored would be rewarded by a local tailor with a new suit, he is said to have wheeled round to run through his own defence before setting up a goal for the hosts. He was also to take off in an unexpected direction following the match. After being ushered by Maley to his seat for the train journey back to Glasgow, McInally sneaked out of the carriage and was absent from training for several days, but the manager was loath to punish him even if the remainder of the side grumbled about special treatment for one player.

In their eyes, more than enough indulgence had been shown to him already. Stern as Maley could be, he was still ready, in 1925, to buy McInally back after his three-year interlude with Third Lanark. The player had succeeded in forcing his way out of Celtic Park to join the club on the south side of Glasgow, where better terms were on offer. It was a mark of McInally's worth that the manager was willing to permit his return. There were suggestions that the player could join Rangers, but he was a Catholic, as well as an IRA sympathiser, and the club, under Bill Struth, was stressing its Protestant identity.

The insistence of Celtic supporters that this celebrated figure of Glasgow life must return was an additional factor, but the manager also surrendered to the submerged sentimental traits that would come to the surface now and again. While McInally had no appetite for the drudgery of conscientiousness, the gifted often enjoy an exceptional licence from even the most draconian employer. Ultimately, his contribution would not be far-reaching, but he looked essential for a while and Maley declined to banish him. Following one match in which Celtic had been hapless, the manager lambasted the players and chastised the forward because he had been seen leaving a pub the previous night. 'I had to,' said McInally. 'It was closing time.'

In this case such a jest would have made Maley wince. The player was a binge drinker and the harm he did to himself was not disguised for long. His disappearance following that Keith match is likely to have involved lost days in pubs. McInally, in some ways, was fragile. The alcohol intake may not have been constant, but he could still seem like a man no longer in control of his life. The humour indeed had a desperate edge at times. There is an anecdote about him being dismissed in a match with Rangers and the referee instructing him that he was being sent to the pavilion. McInally is supposed to have protested, with a lame gag, that he would rather go to the Empire (a music-hall rival of the Pavilion). He was being expelled from the game, in any case, for having tripped the official. So incapable was he of controlling himself that one theory insists that he was apt to play under the influence of alcohol. Drunk or sober, trouble was irresistible. Having been sent off against Rangers in 1927, near the end of his days with Celtic, he then made an offensive remark to the referee, Willie Bell, upon arriving at the SFA offices for the disciplinary hearing.

McInally was skewered with the nickname of the Glaxo Baby, a reference to a chubby infant in an advertising campaign of that period. Fat and of questionable use to the team, the player was nearing the end of his days with the club. The manager had shown forbearance until then because a person of talent is not hastily discarded. In the early 1970s Jock Stein would similarly dredge the depths of his tolerance to prevent Jimmy Johnstone being lost to Celtic even earlier than he ultimately would be. McInally understood that Maley was showing a dogged forgiveness and thanked him after the regular lapses. The manager admired the decisiveness and goal-scoring of a footballer who would become more of a creator in the latter part of his career. Maley went to extremes in the matter, championing the player in defiance of the directors' scepticism, even if, as Jimmy McStay put it, he 'fairly put the hammer on Tommy when he got him in the clubhouse'. Even so, a stern approach still could never cure instability in this particular human being.

'Had the game not been so simple to him he would have taken it more seriously,' the manager would say of McInally in 1936. There would, in all likelihood, have been a streak of self-deluding pride that made Maley suppose he was equipped to reform the player. After his disappearance into what was mostly a haze of alcohol following that match with Keith, the rest of his side played a practical joke on McInally and arranged for a fake journalist to interview him on the phone. He fell for it. The player himself liked to mock others and once sat on the ball in a five-a-side tournament. There was a derision bordering on cruelty in the 1927 Scottish Cup final when his trickery was employed to torment East Fife, of the Second Division, in a game that lacked a competitive element.

All the same, he did not accept the teasing by teammates after he had been taken in by the bogus journalist following his belated return from Keith. He sulked, refused to train and was dropped for a tie with Motherwell that ended Celtic's defence of the Cup. The League title, too, slipped away. McInally's impact did tend to register, whether for good or ill. Insubordination had gone too far in a player whose free-spiritedness lost its appeal once results turned bad. He was moved on to Sunderland in the summer of 1928. Dealing with McInally would have been wearying, but Maley had striven to persist with an employee who became increasingly fat. There could have been an innate compassion, but professionalism demanded, too, that some impact should be squeezed out of a gifted footballer, no matter how exasperating he was.

Bob Shankly, brother of Bill and himself a manager of clubs such as Hibernian, once said, 'You need eleven voices for eleven players.' The adjustment to each individual on the books was not a knack particularly associated with Maley, but he would have floundered if he had lacked the astuteness to weigh people up. Intimidating as he could be, it was within his scope to be sensitive. Jimmy Quinn, one of the most renowned forwards to play for Celtic, had to be coaxed into greatness. The player was then with Smithston Albion, and Maley, having found himself on the same train as Rangers boss William Wilton and some of the club's officials, eventually had to go to the same match as them before slipping away to his real destination on the pretext that he could take no more after a hapless first half.

Although the Smithston game kicked off later, he did not get there on time and his first sight was of Quinn coming off injured. This was interpreted as an opportunity, and Maley followed him to the Plough Inn, which served as a dressing room. The Celtic manager had the skills of a physio and, having arranged for embrocation and bandages to be brought, massaged the damaged knee. Quinn was polite enough to pretend that he did not know who this helpful stranger really was. Maley thereby had the fun of revealing his true identity. Even so, the player was adamant that he was not good enough to be a professional at the top level. 'I'm to stop in the Juniors,' Quinn insisted. Maley then had to trick him into signing a registration form so, he explained, that the Celtic directors would know he had met him. The manager appreciated that Quinn could not truly be fooled into playing for the club, but he had made a start by planting the notion in his mind. In January 1901 the forward was given an invitation to join Celtic in the attractive setting of a seaside training camp at Rothesay. Quinn did then sign for the club.

According to Maley, the Celtic board wanted the forward

ditched after a slow start. 'I believed there was in this young collier chap the stuff of which great players are made,' Maley would recall in his normal self-congratulatory manner. All reminiscences end with him being vindicated, but any smugness would have been endured by everyone who worked for Celtic or supported them since Maley's faith in his own worth was well founded. The manager still had pause for thought a couple years after taking a somewhat shy Quinn to the club. The broad-shouldered player, at 5ft 8in, could look as if the chunkiness was a hindrance, and injuries were another concern at that time. The manager argued that the newcomer needed nothing more than 'patience, practice and experience'.

It was bewildering that Quinn would have some good after-noons on the wing without establishing himself entirely. Maley, having watched him as a left-winger, came to see that the power and dynamism would be overwhelming in the middle of the attack, and had even tried him there on his debut in 1901. Quinn was eventually turned into a powerful centre forward with a mighty shot in his left foot who gorged himself on 216 goals over 331 appearances. Statistics, however, dwindle when placed beside an impact that is the stuff of folklore. In the 1904 Scottish Cup final played by the Old Firm, Celtic were 2–0 down, but Quinn reacted with a hat-trick that ensured a tro-phy for his club. The winner typified his bullishness and control, with opponents rebounding from him while he kept possession and finished effectively.

Maley described Quinn as a 'robust player possessed of a wonderful pair of shoulders which he used to great advantage and more fairly than he was given credit for'. The striker had to take a pummelling of his own in return. 'Quinn was subjected to a lot of abuse in the course of his 14 years' service,' said Maley. Violence was the only answer to him from outmatched defend-ers. The forward would also broaden his reputation on the international front, particularly when scoring the clincher in the 2–0 victory over England at Hampden in 1910 after his Celtic teammate McMenemy had put Scotland ahead. 'In Quinn', the *Daily Mail* reported, 'they have undoubtedly the best centre forward in the four countries – strong, resolute and dashing, sometimes opening the game up for his wings and on other occasions going right through himself, but nearly always doing the best thing possible under the circumstances.'

In daily life Quinn was said to have had a gait that put the weight on his heels, but once on a pitch he would hurl himself at the other team. Restraint was alien to this missile of a man and he was sent off twice against Rangers. On a sodden afternoon in 1905 his team was 2–0 down in a Scottish Cup semi-final at Celtic Park when the visitors' defender Alec Craig held Quinn by the legs in an attempt to stop him. The rumbustious forward used all his force to get free and was deemed by the referee Tom Robertson to have stamped on the face of his opponent. With Quinn sent off, the crowd invaded the pitch and Celtic conceded a tie that would have been awarded to Rangers in any case. Despite a letter that Craig wrote on behalf of his opponent, the SFA inevitably backed the verdict of the official since they had no cause to undermine a man employed to make such judgements. Quinn received a four-week suspension.

The notable element in all this turmoil was Celtic's inclination to go to court over coverage of the matter. Recourse to law, whether threatened or acted upon, is a possibility that has never been far from the thoughts of a club that has quite often felt victimised. The hullabaloo over Quinn's ordering off even led the club to sue one newspaper for referring to 'violent play' by the forward. Celtic won the case, but only in a manner that made them look ludicrous. They received one shilling in damages and had to pay their own considerable costs. Even so, that period was full of satisfactions. While the Scottish Cup had the greater prestige in those days, Celtic were beginning to demonstrate a methodical prowess. The first of the six League titles in a row was grasped in May of 1905. Rangers had by far the better record in terms of goal difference and goals scored, but neither measure applied then and there was a play-off that Celtic won at Hampden.

While that band of emerging players went on to serve the club well, Maley's eye was always fixed on a more distant future. He was adept at revitalising the team over the decades and Jimmy McGrory, following the First World War, would succeed and surpass Quinn. Given the range of his activities, Maley has to be seen as a hybrid of chief executive and chief scout. The side that embarked on that run of half a dozen titles was to be extolled for its results, but Maley had an additional boast. He liked to brag that the whole line-up had cost just £200. There could also be parsimony where wages were concerned, and the inexhaustible Jimmy Hay, who formed a redoubtable half-back line with Jim Young and Willie Loney during that era, was eventually in dispute with the club. The wrangle was halted in 1911 when Celtic sold Hay to Newcastle United. A gratifying fee of £1,250 was negotiated for a man approaching his thirty-first birthday who had cost £50 from Ayr United eight years earlier.

It would also have delighted Maley to see Young thrive in his Glasgow years. He had not mustered much commitment to other clubs, where receiving an attractive wage was the main interest, yet he was galvanised once he left Bristol Rovers in 1903. Dedication swept through Hay, who would become Celtic captain and play there for fourteen years. While Maley is boastful in his memoirs, his task was an extensive one. He was typical of an era in which managers, who did not see the training ground as their natural habitat, drew up a broader agenda, but Maley went to extremes. He relished, in particular, the thrill of the search as he tracked down unheralded players who would prove valuable. As if all that did not suffice, Maley had business interests to pursue from the moment his boyhood drew to a close.

The zeal to improve himself and his prospects was endless. He had left school at the age of thirteen to work in the calico printworks of Messrs Miller, Higginbotham and Co. to the south of the city. His next step took him to the Telephone Company in Glasgow. The general manager there then drafted him into Smith & Wilson, his chartered accountants business, where Maley was a trainee when Celtic came into existence. By the time his son Charles was born in 1896, however, his occupation is given on the birth certificate as 'master draper' since he had started a gentleman's outfitters. The most notable fact is that Maley is not described on the document as a footballer. Professionalism had been legal in the Scottish game for three years by then, but it could have been tempting fate to assume it amounted to a reliable career.

He still understood the commercial potential of sport, and the SFA annual for 1894/5 carried an advert for the shop in the city centre that refers first to his role at Celtic and then to the fact that hats, gloves and hosiery are also on sale. It would not have been in Maley's nature to confine his interests to football alone. He was too animated for that. His business concerns attracted most notice for his ownership of the Bank restaurant in the centre of Glasgow. Maley continued running it until close to his death, at the age of eighty-nine in 1958. He had initially been a partner in the enterprise but owned it outright by 1926. The Celtic board were uneasy about his attachment to the restaurant, whose clientele was rather too racy for men who yearned for respectability. In that regard, there was perhaps a trace of the immigrants' desire to conform and to belong. The directors were specifically concerned about the bookies and other supposedly dubious types who patronised the Bank.

At least Maley himself would never have seemed raffish to the Celtic board. He conformed to the practices of the day by being severe towards footballers, who were seen as disposable if not quite lowly employees. Players, of course, had little or no bargaining power for much of the history of the game. It was only at the end of 1995 that the Bosman ruling established that a footballer was a free agent once his contract had expired. Prior to that decision by the European Court of Justice, clubs retained a player's registration and could demand a fee even when the contract was at an end. The temptation to despotism was strong in managers and directors.

Maley, who could be ruthless, was also bound by the policies of the Celtic board. In 1923, during a period of wage cuts, the outstanding defender Willie Cringan called for improved bonuses. In response he was dropped, stripped of the captaincy and sold to Third Lanark. As a manager in that autocratic era, Maley maintained a certain distance from the team. His duties, indeed, were not expected to entail a close relationship with his players. Malcolm MacDonald, a versatile footballer who excelled under Maley in the 1930s, would stay on the tram a stop longer so he never had to walk up to the ground beside the manager. He had no cause to believe the two of them would have a convivial chat. 'Now remember, Malcolm,' Maley used to say, 'if you don't do what I tell you, you won't be here.'

The player could not avoid meeting the manager, and if he did attempt to keep his distance he could still find himself being manoeuvred into the manager's lair. 'He was in his tower,' MacDonald once said, 'but when he came down from it you didn't wait long, you got yourself out of the road. I've never known him to come in and wax eloquent about a performance. He could always pick the Achilles heel and lambast you for doing this or that or the next thing. Some weeks the secretary [James Maloney] would come in with the wages and say to me the boss still had mine. I knew he had only kept them so I would then have to go into his office.'

MacDonald would often be told by Maley that he should release the ball sooner instead of dribbling with it, and such tips were the essence of player development. The old pros would attempt to pass on whatever insights had come from involvement in so many matches. Managers would maintain a degree of detachment. They had the flexibility to be genial and engaging when developing contacts or forming alliances, but it was a time when people in such positions exercised a near absolute power over their employees. One tale about Maley's Ibrox rival Bill Struth, Rangers' manager from 1920 to 1954, epitomises that. A deputation of players came to his office and suggested that the way in which they were paid should be altered because it would be more tax-efficient. 'Bring me the ringleaders,' was all that Struth had to say. It would not have occurred to anyone in the Celtic side, either, to imagine that their manager had any wish to engage with them in a regular and detailed manner.

Jimmy Delaney, one of the finest attackers ever to serve the club, came to Celtic in the autumn of 1933 and therefore saw Maley in the crusty, closing years of his career. 'He was physically a big man,' Delaney recalled decades later. 'When he said something you didn't talk back. He didn't talk football much to us. The only time that happened was maybe on the Monday after a game. You would be told, "The boss wants to see you." Then he would ask if everything was all right at home, and try to find out why your game might have gone off. Even the toughest players in the team quaked when they got the call to the boss. They always thought they would get laldy [a dressing down], and at the very worst be put on the transfer list.

'He never came into the dressing room. On a Friday, [James Maloney] used to come in and pin up the team sheet and we all rushed over to see whose names were on it. Mr Maley was at the ground every day, but he didn't personally supervise the training. That was left to the trainers. We met him in his restaurant every Saturday before a [home] game. It was a very famous place. We had the usual light lunch and we talked about the game among ourselves, or on the tram going to the ground. But it was never like a modern team talk.

'I thought he was one of the greatest managers ever, certainly one of the best I played under [Delaney, after leaving Celtic in 1946, had served under Matt Busby at Manchester United]. He was a great man, a gentleman. In fact, he was a father to me. I would never say anything against him. He was the greatest of a great bunch of managers – men like Bill Struth, John Hunter of Motherwell, Pat Travers of Aberdeen. They didn't buy many players. They picked them from the juniors [a term for non-League football in Scotland] and moulded their own teams.'

This frugality was often a necessity. Some believed in the 1920s that the dynamism of Celtic at the time of their formation was gone, most likely for ever. The glumness often stemmed from the sluggishness and decline of the economy. The cost of fighting the First World War had sapped the country's finances. Circumstances improved little, with growth weak, and mass unemployment led to the desperation that culminated in the General Strike of 1926. The 1930s, with its architectural striving to break loose from the grip of Victoriana, was envisaged as a fresh start, but that, of course, could be enjoyed only by those in work. It is argued that Scotland was in a worse economic state during that decade than any other country in Europe. The Great Depression dominated society and ensured that anyone in work, including footballers, would be too relieved to consider agitating for better pay. The General Strike itself was an act of resistance to wage cuts.

Despite his business interests, Celtic was the core of Maley's life and he neither accepted nor even contemplated any suggestion that he should step aside. The rise of Rangers under Struth probably seemed to justify his wish to stay in power since he would not have thought anyone else ready for the challenge. Celtic, even so, were waning under Maley. Of the ten League titles from 1930 to 1939, two belonged to his club and seven went to Rangers (the other was Motherwell's). The Scottish Cup came to Ibrox five times in that period and to Celtic Park on three occasions.

Maley was getting old, and the death of the twenty-five-year-old midfielder Peter Scarff from tuberculosis in 1933 affected him markedly. None the less, the manager still had his moments, and Celtic took the Scottish Cup in 1937 by beating Aberdeen at Hampden before a crowd 147,365, which continues to be the world-record attendance for a national cup final. It is said that 30,000 more had to be locked out. Instead of regarding that day as a culmination, the manager would have seen it as a cause to press on with his job, even if Celtic did endure their record defeat six days later when beaten 8–0 at Motherwell in a match of no significance that was still a deep embarrassment. The club could hardly bear to address the topic of their manager's retirement directly, even when it was obvious that his time had to end.

They presumed that in 1938, Celtic's fiftieth anniversary, Maley might stand aside, particularly since his team had won the prestigious Empire Exhibition Trophy, a tournament held in Glasgow. The Empire Exhibition itself was also staged in the city. It would be described now as a stimulus package since it was the creation of a government-backed body called the Scottish Economic Committee. The entire event lasted for six months and £10 million (equivalent to around £500 million now) was spent on it, directly or indirectly. The competition was a fillip for Celtic at least, since they beat Everton in the final with a goal in extra time from the centre forward Johnny Crum. In practice, that would merely have confirmed to the manager that his prowess was undiminished. In 1955 Maley explained why the victory had been so significant to him. 'It was', he said, 'a personal pride to me to see the youngsters I had developed licking the might of England as they did.'

While Celtic had been favourites to win the competition, since they had both a potent team and home advantage, Everton themselves would take the League title in England the following year. Maley's players were stretched to the limit in retaining the lead, but he was not uniformly complimentary afterwards and spoke as if the win had been essential to compensate for a home defeat by Kilmarnock in the Scottish Cup. The manager had become preoccupied by money, his own and that of the club, which were connected in any case. His team were resentful after the Exhibition Trophy because only 20 per cent of the bonus promised to them by a director had been paid. Maley would not make any appeal to the board on that topic and had no intention of alienating his employers.

Celtic did appreciate what he had done, yet were far from taking it for granted that he could offer further achievements. The 1938 line-up included a forward line that dazzled with its capacity to work in harmony, and that sophistication might have been treated as a fulfilment of Maley's career. Five days after the Exhibition Trophy final, Celtic held their jubilee dinner in the handsome Grosvenor Hotel. It was designed to feel like a landmark and Sir John Cargill, the honorary president of Rangers, was on hand to propose the toast to his own club's greatest rivals. The Celtic chairman, Tom White, presented his manager with a cheque for 2,500 guineas (equivalent to some £131,000 now), declaring that 'the triumphs of the Celtic club are the triumphs of Mr Maley'. The intention was to usher him towards retirement, and the symbolic sum, with fifty guineas for each of his fifty years with them, also implied that an era was over.

He was in a mood to reminisce and made time in his speech to hail Brother Walfrid and John Glass, claiming that 'but for the struggle they put up the Celtic club would not have survived'. It was a heart-warming dinner and those present sang 'Ole Faithful' in tribute to Maley, but the manager, while described as 'visibly moved', was not ready to give up his work or to shed his ambitions. The Celtic directors must have realised they had failed with the cheque that had just been presented when he pointedly said, 'The club has been my very life and I really feel that without it my existence would be empty indeed.' Business interests had always been pursued by Maley, and his craving for wealth had been one of the forces that sustained him over the decades. It could have been anticipated that he would not go meekly, and Maley had been described at the dinner as the 'strong but not silent man'. He reacted as if oblivious to the hefty hint of that cheque and his main response was one of annoyance because he felt that Celtic should have ensured that 2,500 guineas was the sum he received after tax. It was not until the end of 1939 that the directors steeled themselves to remove him. The then seventy-one-year-old was aghast and enraged when he left in February 1940. He would go on to lament a rejection that 'robbed me of the very tang of life'.

Regardless of that, Maley still kept himself to the fore. The journalist John Macadam depicts him at the heart of events even in the mid-1950s, just as he had been thirty years earlier: 'I doubt if football will ever see his like again. Then, even as at the moment of writing when he is more than 80 years of age, he would stand at the bar of his Bank restaurant and to him, as to an oracle, they would come every day just to listen to "the boss" talk soccer.' Macadam portrays players past and present arriving to pay tribute, each seeking a reward of sorts from Maley. The younger footballers received 'kindly advice'. Their elders sometimes needed cash. Maley showed Macadam a Scottish Cup winners medal that had been left with him as security for a loan. 'You're fond of these things,' he said to the journalist. 'You'd better keep it. I don't know where he's got to but I don't think he'll be back.'

With no place for him at the club he had shaped, Maley, who had maintained a warm relationship with Rangers, took to watching games at Ibrox. Diplomatic overtures were attempted in the hope that he would attend his old club's matches as well, but he did not do so until after the death in 1947 of chairman White, whom he could never forgive for sacking him. Even so, there were signs that his fixation with Celtic had not vanished. Towards the end of his life he was still galled that the club, in its early years, had not bought additional land on which a larger stadium could have been built. The ground then had a smaller capacity than Ibrox or Hampden, and it rankled with him that an opportunity had been missed.

The surroundings of Celtic Park did hold an appeal even after he had been forced out of the manager's job. He enjoyed seeing his image prominently on show in the tea room. The billiards room at the ground also doubled as his picture gallery. That particular display is long gone but he is still honoured in song, and even those with the vaguest knowledge of the detail appreciate that it was he who gave Celtic its great standing. Incidents from the Maley era have been summoned up, honed and savoured to such a degree that the memories feel like treasure inherited by generation upon generation.

3

JIMMY McGRORY

If ruthlessness were the key, Jimmy McGrory would never have
unlocked a defence. His humility and humanity were unflagging.
As a youngster this son of a gasworks labourer used to walk to
the Celtic ground for training, and it was necessary for his sister
to ensure that McGrory had just small change in his pocket. He
would otherwise have given away every penny he had as people
begged him for money. The years just after the First World War
made up a particularly terrible bout of economic depression even
by Glasgow's standards. Generosity of every sort came readily to
a bashful McGrory, who preferred to share the applause and so
halve the attention paid to him.

It was appropriate, therefore, that he should rejoice in taking
joint credit for one of the most renowned moments in the history
of the Scotland team. His combination with Bob McPhail for the
winner over England in 1933 is popularly stated to have created
the Hampden Roar. It is not clear what this can really mean. Is
it supposed to have set a decibel level at the stadium that challenged future crowds to strain for an even more deafening vol-
ume? In any case, the attendance of 134,710 was a record for a
football game in Europe for four years, until a further Hampden
victory over England was watched by a crowd of 149,415.

McGrory's own recollection of his winner in 1933 is as self-
effacing as feasible for the scorer. He had already put Scotland
ahead, but the visitors levelled and the Celtic attacker pointed

to the Rangers player as the man who started to tip the balance again. 'McPhail went striding through and hit a tremendous shot which just carried over the bar and no more, but the effort roused the enthusiasm of the crowd,' McGrory remembered. 'A deafening roar of encouragement came from the terracing and persisted as the play swung from one end to the other.

'With only six or seven minutes left for play, McPhail again strode through, down the middle. I cut out to the left and as Bob was challenged, a beauty of a pass came into my path. As [Tom] Cooper, the right-back, came in to intercept, I dragged the ball past him and cut in with only the goalkeeper, [Henry] Hibbs, to beat. As he advanced I lobbed the ball with my left foot beyond him and into the net. With the roar of the crowd ringing in my ears, I turned in exultation to fall into the arms of Big Bob and we both did a war dance.'

McGrory appeared to have no capacity for egotism because anyone else would have luxuriated in the fact that they had scored 550 goals in their career, a British record that is surely unassailable. The lack of arrogance will have had some connection to the knowledge he had of suffering and the precariousness of life. His parents were among the Irish immigrants in an area in the north of Glasgow that was sometimes referred to as Little Ireland. It was then known commonly as the Garngad. In apt rhyming slang, it was also called 'the good and the bad'. Such was the infamy that the place would be renamed Royston or Roystonhill, reportedly as part of a campaign by a local head-master who dreaded that his pupils would be discriminated against in the jobs market when it was known they had come from so clearly a Catholic part of town. It was fertile terri-tory for prospective footballers, and Steve Chalmers, scorer of Celtic's winner in the 1967 European Cup final, was from there.

An earlier Celtic player from the Garngad, Hugh Hilley, was part of a large family who had changed their name from Healy to try and avoid religious discrimination. Hilley, who lived to be eighty-seven, illustrated what could be achieved when people were not thwarted by prejudice. Having married an Italian wife, he followed his football career by putting money into an ice-cream and catering firm that made him rich. His granddaughter Mary Contini, a director of the well-known Valvona and Crolla delicatessen in Edinburgh, honoured him by developing a recipe for 'Celtic soup'. It was inspired by her grandfather's tales. 'Celtic taught Hugh about health in a very modern way,' she wrote.

> They looked at diet and fitness and their methods stayed with him. Whenever I stayed at Grandpa's house he would have a routine where he would get up at 6am and have a cold shower. Then he would drink warm water and jog around the block. He would have cereal and toast, olive oil and fresh orange. Hugh was fanatical about his health as a result of playing with Celtic.

The club's more celebrated native of the Garngad was part of a large family. McGrory had a brother, John, who died of meningitis when he was thirteen months old. His mother Kate was dead by 1916, when Jimmy was twelve. His oldest sister then raised him, but childhood, in any case, did not last long in the severe surroundings of a poor community of outsiders during the hardship of the First World War. McGrory's father Harry, a labourer in the steelworks, was illiterate and put a cross for his signature on Jimmy's birth certificate. The future Celtic player was something of an outsider and it can be argued that the football authorities never really thought of him as a true Scot. There is an apparent incongruity in the fact that the man who broke scoring records for Celtic was not often allowed to try and repeat such form in the national team.

The victory over England in 1933 was his second appearance against them; the first, two years before, had also been a win in which he scored. Over the course of his seven caps he claimed half a dozen goals. That was an exemplary return, yet it did not lead to McGrory becoming the focal point for his country. He was often neglected and the suspicions are bound to well up that, as a Catholic who was in the first generation of his family to be born in Scotland, McGrory was chosen with reluctance. Only a naïf would suppose that such an interpretation was unthinkable in those times.

However, those with a conviction that life is much more likely to be shaped by incompetence than conspiracy will point to the fact that a national team picked by selectors rather than a manager is sure to be confusing, with trade-offs among men whose vested interests are critical to the composition of a line-up. The XI that they alighted on would regularly include someone or other whose presence produced bemusement, if not anger. There were also valid rivals to McGrory at other clubs, and Hughie Gallacher, with twenty-three goals from twenty caps and a place in legend as one of the Wembley Wizards who beat England 5–1 in 1928, was quite a contender during his Newcastle United years. Apart from that, there were fewer appearances to be made by anyone since none of the football nations of the UK took part in the World Cup until the home internationals were used as a qualification group for the 1950 tournament.

McGrory himself was not the type to feel a grievance when he was ignored, even if he never got the opportunity to take the field at Wembley. It would have amazed him to enjoy such successes with Celtic because he had not brought self-confidence to his career. He had cause to be daunted, too, since he was an inside forward when he joined the club and, in theory, had to set himself the task of dislodging the great Patsy Gallacher. Even when the Irishman was missing, the replacement in that post turned out to be Jim Cairney. There had been no encouragement either for McGrory on his debut as a seventeen-year-old against Third Lanark in 1923, when the kind of hard-driven cross that he would feast upon when he was older caught him on the back of the head and knocked him out.

He had been with the club for two years when it was decided that he should go on loan to Clydebank. That kind of move usually proves a first step towards career oblivion, but the manager there, the former Celtic player Jimmy Hay, realised that McGrory had it in him to make an impact. At nineteen, he went on to enjoy some belated encouragement and score sixteen goals in thirty-three appearances for a team in the same division as his parent club. Indeed, one of Clydebank's rare away victories came with a 2–1 success at Celtic Park in March 1924. The winner was supplied by McGrory, who was on the left wing that day and had been relieved to find out the commanding right back Alex McNair was absent.

'The gods were on my side,' he said some forty-seven years later, with the excitement coursing through him as the memories went on the loose. 'As I ran in on the Celtic goal all that was going through my head was the thought, "Will I score? Will I score?" Well, score I did what proved to be the winning goal. As the ball went past Charlie Shaw I felt ten feet tall.' The appearance of a transformation in McGrory lasted far beyond the moment itself. That success might briefly have taken his mind off the fact that ever thrifty Celtic had cut his wages from £5 to £4 a week before the loan spell began.

Clydebank were relegated that year, but McGrory's standing had climbed. The forward himself was also given an insight into his own potential. It was badly needed because he had nothing then of the brashness of a true striker. There was a dumbfounding quality to a man who would make such an impact. He had taught himself to resist daydreams, and that must have reflected the hardship in his own life and that of everyone around him in the Garngad. 'I never expected [Celtic] to come after me but just in case they did I told myself I would have no future there,' he would recall. He had reasoned that he was an inside forward and the club had no need of new men for that position.

Oddly, Celtic had added to his insecurities when the trainer Eddie McGarvey informed him, 'You have flat feet and people with flat feet can't jump.' The diagnosis was comprehensively wrong, yet the insecurity that McGrory felt in any case became part of the force that drove him through defences. McGrory became so famous for heading the ball that he was nicknamed The Mermaid, the Golden Crust and the Human Torpedo. The obsession with his heading was natural, yet also a false characterisation. His feet functioned efficiently, as they had in that 1933 win over England, and a limited striker would not have scored eight goals in a match against Dunfermline, as he did during the 9–0 victory in January 1928 before a crowd of less than 3,000 at Celtic Park.

McGrory, in apparent seriousness, once said, 'I played my heart out for my club and was always scared of being dropped, right to the end.' That insecurity was of a rare sort since it galvanised the forward instead of inhibiting him. While McGrory was a dutiful employee, he was no cipher. He became something of a fashion plate as he adopted each new style in menswear, yet at the same time there was a sincere religious faith. In the close season McGrory would go on pilgrimage to the austere setting of Station Island in County Donegal. During the summer of 1928 he was invited by Willie Maley to join him on another pilgrimage, to the Catholic shrine of Lourdes. The train journey to France involved a night in London, and while there they were met by Herbert Chapman and Samuel Hill-Wood, manager and chairman, respectively, of Arsenal.

The offer to sign for the London club was brushed aside by the forward and McGrory either believed the encounter had happened by accident or, more likely, did not want to confront the formidable Maley over the issue. Arsenal therefore intercepted the pilgrims again when they passed through the capital on the return to Glasgow. At the first encounter, McGrory had asked Chapman for the sum of £2,000 before he would join Arsenal. It was a method of deterring him, but on the way back Arsenal, with more connivance by Maley, resumed their efforts. Celtic were to receive £10,000 as a transfer fee, and Arsenal had resolved to agree terms with the forward. McGrory would still have nothing to do with it and Chapman withdrew graciously.

'I honestly never had any desire to move,' the player would say in 1971. 'There was, and certainly still is, something about Celtic that made them different; few players ever wanted to leave. Some people say it's religious, but that's just rubbish. I think it's more of a family atmosphere, and it's always been like that.' The episode showed the clandestine conduct of which Maley, in common with most managers, was capable, although he had little option but to attempt the sale of the player when Celtic ordered him to do so. It is all but certain that he had been given his instructions by employers who needed to replace the dilapidated and even dangerous Grant stand, which was named after the club director James Grant. He had funded it under an agreement that was supposed to give him a profit share. Although it was then the only seated area in the ground, Grant did badly out of the deal.

The main stand that took its place came at a price of £35,000 and was opened in 1929. In much adapted form, it is still in use now. The cost was met despite Celtic's failure to sell their best player. Maley liked to present himself as some sort of bystander, yet he had followed his orders thoroughly when scheming to ensure that Arsenal would twice have an opportunity to woo McGrory. The manager, unable to bring about a lucrative deal, had to pretend that he could let his player chat to Arsenal since he realised McGrory would never leave Celtic. That, of course, did nothing to explain why such efforts were made to ensure that Chapman had his rendezvous with the player.

The desire to transfer McGrory was both a betrayal of the Celtic fans and proof of the timidity of those in charge, since they could initially come up with no better means of financing the construction of the stand. Between the wars the club often languished, and it felt as if the continuing presence of McGrory was all that lay between Celtic and total insignificance. Those scoring statistics would, in addition to their domination of football history, have been seen by fans as acts of mercy towards them. The goals rescued Celtic, embodied a capacity to maintain the club's standing to some degree and epitomised a man who was not primarily set on writing himself into the history books. For all the exploits, there was an air of duty to his work. When a footballer is described as a 'great servant' to a club, there can be a slur folded into the compliment since such accolades are patronising. McGrory is better seen as the protector of a side that could look overwhelmed and despondent at times in the 1920s and 1930s. As his teammate and fellow Garngad man Hugh Hilley put it, 'Jimmy played as if he was Celtic.'

In McGrory's case the Arsenal incident emphasised the strength of his attachment to his own club, but also, perhaps, his appreciation that he was not cut out to make the transition to another city very different from Glasgow. He had turned his back on real affluence. Later, his weekly wage with Celtic would be cut from £9 to £8, although that may have echoed the economic harm caused throughout the world by the Wall Street crash of 1929. More specifically, times were already hard enough for Celtic to have a gate for the unemployed at the ground. While the club has been open in some periods to the charge of small-mindedness, it is true, as well, that inhibitions might owe something to a sense of insecurity about the long-term affordability of lucrative contracts. McGrory was not the type to be affected primarily by that sort of reward in any case, although marriage would place him close to real affluence. His wife was to be Veronica 'Nona' Green, a member of a family that had become rich through the urban, and specifically Glaswegian, love of film. The centrepiece of the chain was Green's Playhouse in Renfield Street, with its grandiose decoration and carpeting, as well as over 4,000 seats. There were enticing 'golden divans' in the balcony that did brisk business with courting couples, and the cinema was claimed to be the largest in Europe at that time.

The Celtic centre forward had never known what it was to be a man of means. People in work were often the sole provider for their relations. McGrory appreciated that he, like his relatives, would have been unable to find a job were it not for the gift he had for the game. The player supported half a dozen family members and therefore was, as he insisted, 'by no means well off' at the end of his playing career. Even so, it would have been disingenuous of him to pretend that his circumstances were not favourable. The wedding itself strikes us as having celebrity overtones, much as McGrory would have detested such a thought. Celtic were returning from a summer trip to the US in 1931 and their boat approached Moville, County Donegal. Nona had travelled there from Glasgow. McGrory kept a diary during the club's tour and the entry for 10 July is touching: 'I disembarked on the Customs Officer's boat, and that morning, around 8.30am, I started off on a life-long journey. I got married.'

Having entered the extended Green family, McGrory made his home with Nona in a villa in Ayr. They also had a black Austin 16 saloon that perturbed Maley. The manager, claiming merely to be passing on the decision of the board, sent a letter informing McGrory that 'no player will be allowed to use a private motor car during the playing season. They feel that the risks of the road are too great and in addition they are of the opinion that it is not helpful to a man's physical condition as a football player.' A compliant McGrory did the commute to Celtic Park by train. He was just thirty-three when he gave up his playing career to become manager of Kilmarnock in December 1937. The decision enraged Maley since mere footballers usually had their careers shaped by his edicts.

Celtic held McGrory's registration and could therefore stop him from taking the field, but he was ready to accept that, having already accomplished virtually everything feasible in a playing career. Given his normal obedience, this bout of independent thinking came as a shock, but a Celtic director had suggested to him that experience at Kilmarnock might lead to a return as manager. The forward was not even compliant enough to finish the season in Glasgow. It turned out, all the same, that Johnny Crum, an excellent all-round attacker, switched to the central position so tellingly that he was the hero of the Empire Exhibition Trophy final six months later. Indeed, McGrory had unwittingly cut himself off from one of Celtic's most cherished feats. The attack not only coped without him but perhaps had more sophistication since there could be no emphasis on the spearhead approach when McGrory was gone. In Jimmy Delaney Celtic then had a right winger or centre forward of great impact who, to the horror of fans, would be sold to Manchester United in February 1946. The board were far too keen to rake in £4,000 and rid themselves of an employee, regardless of his brilliance, who wanted a pay rise of £2 a week. Delaney was thirty-one at the time of the transfer, but still endeared himself to his new employers and was part of the FA Cup-winning line-up two years later.

Celtic seemed to imagine that there would be an appropriate successor to whichever player was transferred. That stance was not always delusional. Gruelling as the extra-time victory over Everton in the Empire Exhibition Trophy final was to be, it showed that McGrory's move had not sabotaged Celtic. Even so, Maley continued to be angry with the departed forward for taking the job at Kilmarnock. He must have thought it insurrection for any player to presume that he could determine his own future and dictate when his days in the Celtic side were over. This particular piece of independent thinking by McGrory would have surprised most people. He was not so very old and, even in decline, had five goals in the League that season from ten matches. The statistics, all the same, will have meant less to the forward than the Kilmarnock invitation to release himself from taking part in a sport where high aggression was the norm, as were injuries such as the repeatedly broken nose that McGrory had to endure.

Such logic would only have persuaded Maley if he had come up with it himself. There was nothing to be done about McGrory's appointment except to try and make it as miserable as possible. He was no sooner in the Kilmarnock post than his side was trounced 8–0 at Celtic Park on Christmas Day. 'I don't think [Maley] ever forgave me for taking the manager's job,' McGrory would confirm decades later. He had been given a full insight into that on the afternoon of the game, when the rout had reached 6–0 by the interval. He passed the door of the home dressing room and heard Maley warning the Celtic team: 'Don't let sentiment interfere with your play.' Professionals are supposed to give of their best, but on another occasion Maley might not have felt so impelled to urge that the onslaught continue. The greatest Celtic player of that period and perhaps of all time was to be punished as a traitor regardless of the absolute devotion that he had for the club.

McGrory's lack of vanity was an asset after that. The pummelling did not break him as Maley seemed to hope. In March 1938 Kilmarnock won an away match that ended Celtic's defence of the Scottish Cup. It was not in the nature of this aspiring manager to revel in vengeance over Maley, whose stance had bordered on the sadistic during the earlier game. 'After that tie I went to Mr Maley's office to exchange pleasantries and to thank him for a sporting match,' McGrory would remember. 'All the time I was in the room he kept his eyes firmly fixed on his desk. Reflecting about it afterwards I felt I hadn't been very tactful. I should really have waited on him coming to me.' The recollection evokes Maley's boorishness even more than the chivalry of a Kilmarnock manager who would not allow himself to gloat.

Most people in McGrory's position would have wallowed in this downing of a bully whose autocratic manner became even more marked as he grew old. The victor that day did not have much opportunity to demonstrate his worth in the period that ensued. Rugby Park, the Kilmarnock ground, was commandeered as an ammunition dump during the Second World War. McGrory's wife Nona would die in 1944 of post-operative complications after undergoing surgery intended to discover why she had not become pregnant. Two years later he married Barbara

Schoning, and the couple had a son who was also called Jimmy. The relationship with Celtic was so close that she would nurse Bob Kelly when the Celtic chairman was dying in 1971, just as she had Willie Maley thirteen years before.

Although McGrory himself had come to seem like a family retainer by the 1960s, he had once radiated the aura of stardom on the field. While it is monotonously declared that he could head the ball further than most people could kick it, that does not give due credit to the excitement of his exploits. While his two goals against England in 1933 were especially intoxicating, he often made the mind swim. People could feel an emotional identification with him, too, since he had emerged from circumstances so poor that, at the age of fourteen, he had to wear sandshoes because he did not have a pair of boots. That did not prevent McGrory from coming to the club's attention while he was still in the Boys' Guild. Indeed, someone who prospers when there is little in his favour attracts all the more interest. He had overcome the odds from youth onwards and he went into a Celtic line-up that was part of tales handed down the generations and which are still retold by fans.

In 1925 one of the club's former players, Davie McLean, put Dundee ahead in the Scottish Cup final. Celtic recovered and won through a McGrory goal, but it is more appropriate to recognise the calibre of the assistance he got in that period. The leveller had come from Patsy Gallacher in the second half. He could be the most individualistic of creative attackers and, on this occasion, flickered his way past several challenges before scoring with the ball wedged between his feet as he tumbled head over heels into the net for the equaliser. Regardless of how the Dundee part of the crowd viewed that, this was a Celtic team of entertainers, even if McGrory was to the fore even then. He had the position of honour at the head of the parade of brake clubs back into the centre of Glasgow from Hampden. These were supporters clubs who travelled on horse-drawn carriages with elaborately decorated banners. 'My happiness was complete',

McGrory recalled late in life, 'when Mr Maley turned to me and said, "You can hold the Cup."'

There was an innocence in the reaction of a forward whose twenty-first birthday was still a fortnight away, but that simplicity sustained him throughout his career since nothing seemed to distract him from his purpose on the pitch. McGrory never appeared to be aggrieved. A person with the standard level of vanity would be indignant at losing his job, but when reflecting on the transfer of the Celtic manager's post to Jock Stein in 1965 he preferred to be wry. 'I was getting a bit tired and torn,' he said. The exhaustive scrutiny to which he was exposed as a famous footballer could not locate even a trace of conceit in him.

The more worldly Gallacher was the sort of figure who complemented McGrory to perfection. By the mid-1920s the Irishman's time at Celtic was moving towards to a close, but he epitomised some of the creative expression that was also emerging in a period when Scotland's forward line of five small and clever attackers would bring about the 5–1 downfall of England at Wembley in 1928. Interplay was less remarked upon in the case of Gallacher, yet he had a keen awareness of the possibilities around him that teammates were offering. Football was acquiring more sophistication, and improvements to the pitches themselves worked in favour of those who could then make their technical superiority tell. Gallacher is thought to have earned markedly more than his Celtic teammates, and there is a suspicion that he was sold to Dundee in 1926, when he was thirty-three, because the club wanted to cut its costs, although it is noteworthy that his new employers must have been ready to meet his terms.

For good or ill, football's mass appeal turned footballers into ever more noticeable stars. Gallacher himself was not cowed even by Maley, and once broke the curfew at the lavish hotel Celtic were using as a training camp by dressing as a lady. The chivalrous manager held open the door as the slightly built player escaped into the night. Despite that, even Maley warmed to a player who looked as if he would be unsuited to the hazards of a football match. Gallacher, born in Donegal although raised in Scotland, had the individuality to astonish, as he did in the 1925 final, but, critically, he was also expert at releasing the ball intelligently into space after he had drawn opponents towards him. Teammates appreciated that best of all. 'Patsy had a mind of his own on the field,' said the midfielder Peter Wilson. 'And he could impose it on colleague and opponent alike. Although he was such a supreme individualist, he was so brilliant that he could combine with any kind of player. He really believed in team-work and his individual darts and dribbles were only made when he felt nothing else would work.'

There was a match, however, in which Gallacher insisted on his pre-eminence when Wilson himself had come up with an individualistic goal. 'Get back to your kennel,' said the Irishman, 'and make sure you stay there. It's us yins up front that do the scoring.' While Gallacher would normally be characterised as a free spirit who made openings on which others would capitalise, he was not flattering himself with the implication that he was one of football's predators. He averaged roughly two goals to every five appearances for Celtic. This was a particularly rich time for the club. Much as Maley would have loathed the thought, there was also a hint of the workers' co-operative about the 1938 side.

It was essential that they paid attention to their own development since the manager could hardly have conceived of coaching his players. After they got to Celtic, those recruits learned through experience and by the passing down of the knowledge that the senior footballers had accumulated in their years on the pitch. The most to be expected from Maley was a tip about a particular flaw in one of the opponents, although he also had an overall preference for a controlled, passing style. Beyond the game itself, the emphasis was often on tracking down emerging talent. The wily Steve Callaghan, who was chief scout, merited more appreciation than he got for locating young prospects in that era.

It was he, for instance, who secured John Thomson. There is a risk that the terrible conclusion to the goalkeeper's life, following that collision with Sam English at Ibrox in 1931, blots out the success he had already made of himself. He took the danger for granted since the protection afforded by referees to the men between the posts was small. A year before his death, one match had seen him suffer a fractured jaw and ribs, while also losing a couple of teeth. A friend who visited him in hospital found that Thomson just felt it was his job to try and grab the ball even when the risks were great. He was correct since there was no viable career for a goalkeeper who thought otherwise. It was a harsh trade and those between the posts were expected to be gnarled and worldly.

Indeed, Thomson had made his debut for Celtic in February 1927, shortly after his eighteenth birthday. He was in the line-up that won the Scottish Cup against East Fife two months later. The club had been beaten in the final the previous year, when Peter Shevlin had confirmed that he was not cut out to succeed Charlie Shaw as goalkeeper. It was natural that Celtic should be looking for a replacement, but in settling on the teenager Thomson and promoting him so swiftly they were bold. While the club was rich by comparison with almost every other team in Scotland, there was a vanity or high principle that made Maley wish to flaunt his finesse as a team-builder. He was drawing, too, on the sheer extent of the talent to be found around the country. Of the line-up that took the Cup in 1927, the one footballer who had cost anything more than a nominal sum was Tommy McInally, the returning prodigal who brought out a capacity for mercy in the otherwise unbending manager.

McGrory was missing from that final because of injury, but the tournament would continue to be the setting for his excellence. There was melodrama in 1931 when Motherwell, for all their economic handicaps, had a good team with a beautifully articulated forward line. They lived up to expectations by going 2–0 in front, and Celtic were taking ever more frequent glances at the clock that then stood on the stand at Hampden. There were seven minutes left when the Motherwell players formed a defensive wall as Charlie 'Happy Feet' Napier, whose nickname came from an odd running style, rolled the free kick wide instead of shooting and McGrory tore through to score. An equaliser came in stoppage time when Allan Craig, the Motherwell centre half, headed an in-swinging cross from Bertie Thomson into his own net.

Celtic supporters saw the origins of that goal in the unnerving presence of McGrory. There were many times when everything appeared to rest with him, even if talented colleagues were in action as well. It does him a disservice to regard him as a machine, despite the productivity. Much was achieved because of an emotional bond with Celtic that meant he gave unstintingly to the club's cause in every game. As the decades shuttle past, there is a risk that someone like McGrory, if not forgotten, will be less than fully appreciated, and a statue at Celtic Park would ensure that he is honoured and remembered as he ought to be. Fans of his day knew the influence he had.

They even went looking for the forward at the Bank restaurant after the first match of the 1931 final, only for Maley to order them off the premises. Those supporters were still correct to feel that the draw was actually a decisive event. Thomson and McGrory each scored twice in the replay, with no response from Motherwell. The centre forward produced the only goal when the same opponents were beaten again in the final two years later. There was one last final to come for McGrory, and it shimmers in the mind because of the 147,365 spectators at the defeat of Aberdeen for the Scottish Cup in 1937. Perhaps a setting of that sort made him feel that the culmination of his playing career had been reached.

The next period of his career would have been disorientating. It sometimes seems that management comes hardest to those who have excelled on the field, since they do not have an intuitive grasp of what it is to be a normal player struggling with the difficulties of a football match. When a person has no aptitude for cunning, management can look wholly unsuitable as a profession. Bertie Auld played under McGrory during the midfielder's first period with Celtic, from 1957 and 1961, and the traits he appreciated in the manager are hardly typical of those who hold such a post. 'Jimmy McGrory was the most honest man I ever met,' said Auld. 'You only had to look at him to know what he was thinking.' As job references go, that is the sort of statement that would have an employer putting a firm line through his name. McGrory had more of an aptitude for the work than the simplified accounts of his career claim, but no one would see in him the craftiness and drive of, for example, Jock Stein. Auld, with his casual comment, highlighted an absence of the subterfuge that is called for here and there in management, although McGrory was not always the hapless caricature that he was assumed to be. In time he would be written off as an anachronism, but there was potential in him that was not realised in full.

He had a searing period with Celtic that has to be ignored by anyone dedicated to the cliché that he was inherently unfit for management. From the Scottish Cup final of 1951 a momentum developed that was irresistible in the 7–1 drubbing of Rangers in the League Cup final during the autumn of 1957. If there is to be any cavilling, it lies in the presence of one League title in that stretch, as part of a Double with the Scottish Cup in 1954. While becoming champions did not carry quite the prestige that it does now, there still has to be disbelief that this was the club's sole success in that competition between 1938 and 1966. The record shows Celtic, in the normal run of matches, to have been inadequate for over a generation, and that, in turn, is damning of Bob Kelly and the board. The side effect was to make the highlights stand out all the more against the normal drabness.

There were some happy distractions under McGrory. Having presided over the Scottish Cup final defeats of Motherwell in 1931 and 1933 as a centre forward, the manager saw the latest of his successors in that role apply the same kind of excellence. There was an elan to John McPhail when he delivered the 1–0 win in 1951 by beating two defenders before lobbing the goal-keeper. When Celtic completed their Double in 1954, Jock Stein was at centre half, although it had taken injuries to prise open the opportunity that he took to establish himself. When the club brought him from Llanelly (as Llanelli was then spelt), he was, at twenty-nine, intended just to help the youngsters progress, but he seized his chance fully in 1953. Stein's two years as captain of the side started after Sean Fallon, who would one day be assistant manager to him, broke his arm at the end of 1952. Mean-spirited as it sounds, there has to be a presumption that the improbable rise in McGrory's managerial career was linked closely to Stein's acumen and his knack for exercising a transformative influence over the players around him. Remarkably well paid though the centre half had been in the seclusion of non-League football in Wales, his reputation soared at Celtic.

In May 1953 the Coronation Cup was held in Glasgow to mark the ascent to the throne of Queen Elizabeth II, which took place the following month. A Celtic support inclined to republicanism liked to pretend that the prospective monarch cared who won her tournament. There is, even so, a touching quaintness to the lyrics of the song about the competition that envisage her as a keen Rangers supporter. The lyrics, of course, are those of self-congratulatory fans, as in the closing two verses:

> Said Lizzie to Philip when she heard the news,
> 'A blow has been struck to my loyal True Blues.
> Oh tell me dear Philip, for I want to know,
> How to beat Glasgow Celtic and keep them below.'

> Said Philip to Lizzie, 'There's only one way,
> And that's been no secret for many a day.
> To beat Glasgow Celtic you'll have to deport,
> The whole Fenian army that gives them support.'

Celtic were invited to the tournament because of its location, their following and the club's feats in former days. Another side with an Irish bloodline seemed better equipped. Hibernian had a dazzling forward line and had taken three League titles in the period following the Second World War. In the 1952/3 season they had lost the championship to Rangers on goal average. Eight clubs took part in the Coronation Cup, with four from each side of the border. Celtic darted out from the seclusion of a League season in which they had come eighth to dispose of the English champions Arsenal. Manchester United accounted for Rangers but then fell to McGrory's side. There was to be a final between Celtic and Hibernian, who had swamped Newcastle United 4–0. The Scottish sides may have had home advantage, but the results still demonstrated that they were teams of substance. While Neilly Mochan and Jimmy Walsh scored in the final, it was more of a surprise that Celtic had withstood the verve of Hibernian to keep a clean sheet. Stein had been at the core of a defence that conceded just one goal in its three Coronation Cup matches. His career as a player was, overall, a modest one, and he would barely have been considered for Scotland, let alone favoured with a cap. None the less, his capacity to enliven those around him was in evidence, even if no one supposed that he would one day guide Celtic so far as a manager.

The Coronation Cup win was cherished because the glint of a trophy had been supplied by a team that shone for a while. There was an element of surprise in Celtic's attacking style during the first half, but any applause after that can only have been for the doggedness following the interval on that Hampden afternoon. In view of Hibernian's prowess, it was mandatory for the Celtic goalkeeper to excel, and John Bonnar was spectacular throughout the Coronation Cup. He depended on a blend of anticipation and keen reflexes, but he had valid rivals at the club and averaged eighteen appearances a season over his ten years. Bonnar was not the sort to show strict concentration on the occasions when play was largely confined to the other end of the field. Neither did he have the height to dominate the goalmouth and so demoralise attackers, but he was a shot-stopper who wallowed in the action Hibernian generated. In addition, Bobby Evans, a player of zest and competitiveness, did as much as was feasible to aid in the quelling of the centre forward Lawrie Reilly.

Celtic, in essence, had come up with a way to win rather than establishing themselves as the most refined team in the Coronation Cup. The fragility inherent in those exploits would be exposed in the 1955 Scottish Cup final, when Bonnar fumbled an Archie Robertson corner into his net to bestow an equaliser on Clyde with three minutes remaining. Celtic lost the replay. The period was one of fluctuation for the club. In the circumstances, it appeared that improbability had been granted an extension when Celtic did a League and Cup Double the season after their scramble to victory in the Coronation Cup. By then, the influence of Stein on the side was all the more apparent and they were capable of measured, confident football that had them reacting to defeat at Hearts with a sequence of nine victories in a row. Aberdeen were their victims in the Scottish Cup final of 1954.

There had been an influx of personality, impudence and flair. The traits were entwined in the figure of Charlie Tully. For many, he was a guarantor of fun and personality during the austerity of the post-war period, which did not see rationing come to a complete end until June 1954, when meat became freely available once more. Fun was unlimited where the Belfast-born Tully was concerned. His humour was of the sort that angers opponents, as when he bounced a throw-in off the back of one of them and then crossed for a goal that led to a complete recovery against Aberdeen in the final of the St Mungo Cup, which had been a Glaswegian part of the 1951 Festival of Britain. There would be consternation as well when the notion took him to try and score direct from a corner kick. It calls for technique as much as impudence to attempt such a feat, but Tully could attend to serious duties when the mood was upon him. He was, for instance, the key to victory over Manchester United in the Coronation Cup, although he took no part in the final because of injury.

As in the case of Patsy Gallacher before him, Tully was a scrupulous passer of the ball, with more faith in the power of a well-integrated team than is commonly supposed, but the individualism of a virtuoso was so seared into the minds of supporters that a wider excellence received less comment. Given his reputation as a mercurial and intuitive player it made a sort of sense that he should be on the field for a match that freed itself from all known precedent. Everyone, after all, expects the game to be gruelling when Celtic and Rangers are locked together, particularly when silverware is at stake. It verged on the impossible that the record score for the final of a major trophy in the UK should come with a 7–1 win for McGrory's side over their natural foes.

It is futile to suggest that anything like that outcome could have been anticipated. Beforehand the most that would have been claimed for Celtic was that they were getting better. On 21 September 1957 the team had won its first League game at Ibrox in twenty-two years, just four weeks before the League Cup final itself. It was at least a fillip for a club that had come fifth in the League in each of the two previous seasons. While Rangers were beaten, the score was 3–2 and it had taken stout defending to prevent a draw. The element of the game that would take on principal relevance was the weak display by the hosts' centre half John Valentine. Even so, Celtic had no reason to assume that a burden of expectation was being placed on them.

People naturally suppose that the present will simply be an extension of the past, and few anticipate life lurching off in another direction. The relevance seemed to have gone from the Double that Celtic had secured in 1954. With Jock Stein's career ended by injury, there was much less faith in the defence. In the League Cup final the centre-half post would be filled by Bobby Evans, a vibrant player in the middle of the pitch who had learned to count on composure when selected for the rearguard. All the same, he was not at all detached in the period before the final when getting into a fight with Tully after training. It had been sparked by comments from the Northern Ireland international, who had announced in his weekly newspaper column that only two Scots would get into a United Kingdom side. Evans was not one of them. Hindsight alone determines whether such episodes are proof of strong-minded competitiveness or of the disintegration of a team.

The line-up for the final would, in the standard manner, be known only to those with a gift for anticipating Bob Kelly's views. He took fans by surprise when plumping for the popular Neilly Mochan on the left wing. In that period the Celtic chairman seemed to have a settled opposition to him. Kelly had not countenanced Mochan's inclusion for either the 1955 Scottish Cup final with Clyde or the replay. Despite being on the flank, Mochan was a potent goal scorer and, with reluctance, it has to be conceded that the chairman had come up with one of his more enlightened notions when settling on the 1957 team selection. As the result showed, all of Kelly's whims were valid that day.

Willie Fernie, originally an inside left, was kept in a deeper midfield position, apparently to his displeasure. On that afternoon, he saw space lying open in front of him and also combined well with Bertie Peacock and Bobby Collins. The 1955 Cup final had seen Collins dropped for the replay, conceivably because of Kelly's distaste for a shoulder charge on the Clyde goalkeeper Ken Hewkins. Two years later, Collins, twenty-six, was in the last phase of his time with Celtic and he moved on to Everton in 1958. The League Cup final with Rangers was not his best display, but the interplay with Fernie and Peacock injected poise into the moves. On that afternoon Rangers could not pin down Celtic.

There was no prospect of Celtic's work in midfield being mere embroidery. Billy McPhail, dominant in the air and sure of himself on the ground, established a mastery of Valentine, an opponent who had been effective against him in the past. It would not have been wise for the Rangers players to announce afterwards that it had just been one of those days, but reason alone would indicate that this was a match outside the normal run of abrasive Old Firm games. Mochan, for instance, had been overweight and out of favour the previous month, when Celtic, in principle, would have been willing to sell him to Dundee if a fee could have been agreed.

When one team swamps another, the initial disbelief rapidly gives way to the realisation that this is normality, for the length of an afternoon at least. A rout starts to appear natural and inevitable. It was like that at Hampden. McPhail set up the opener with a knockdown that was volleyed home by Sammy Wilson. The critical incident, all the same, was probably Mochan's brutal shot from an angle that got the better of George Niven at the end of the first half. After that, Rangers wearied, and the mood would not have been helped either by having the sun in their eyes or by coping, in the era before substitutes, with the injury that had the centre forward Max Murray taking a position on the left wing with his injured leg in bandages. It was, all the same, far from being the principal factor on a day when Rangers had been out of their depth throughout.

Celtic missed several opportunities but McPhail still helped himself to a hat-trick, with the other goals from Mochan once more and Fernie. The opposition intruded with a goal from Billy Simpson, but there was bottle-throwing by their supporters ten minutes from the close. A gesture is essential after so intolerable an experience, and the Rangers centre half Valentine would never be picked again by the club. The manager Scot Symon not only survived the debacle but continued to prosper with Rangers, collecting half a dozen League titles between 1956 and 1964. It was Celtic who went back to being nondescript. To the modern fan it feels peculiar that one person in particular was not viewed as the creator of what would have been thought of as an unimaginable result.

Maley and Stein properly received as much appreciation as was conceivable for their own greatest days, yet the scourging of the Ibrox side in 1957 hardly seemed to be associated with McGrory. By then, whatever credibility he held in the post had been undermined drastically by Kelly. That still did not lead to him being ditched. The chairman would not have struck anyone as being at risk of self-doubt. The outcome of that final must have reinforced his conviction that there was nothing at all amiss in the way he took personal control of every matter of interest to him. There was a pathos to it all that spread across the empty seasons to come. There cannot be a Celtic fan who regrets that 7–1 result, yet it ensured that the club as a whole would stay in a state of suspended animation for many more years.

Respect for McGrory flowed most easily from those who had seen for themselves how astounding he could be as an attacker. With the passage of time, however, memories dwindle and cease to be the critical factor. After the surge of success in the 1950s, the momentum went out of him. McGrory had little say on important subjects within the club, losing the will to keep up with the sport and its evolution. With so little power in his hands, he effectively retreated into the past to become an anachronism in manner of dress and outlook among managers. If it had been in him to rebel, this dated air could have been taken as a symbolic protest against Celtic's reluctance to give him a true purpose on the contemporary scene. The fact is that he abandoned hope. McGrory had bestowed vast excitement on the club in his heyday as a player, but by the end the promise that once lay in him as a manager had been blighted by employers who treated him as no more than a family retainer.

That was particularly poignant since his affinity with the club had been profound. His brother Harry died not long before the 1967 European Cup final, and that may have made the then sixty-seven-year-old particularly emotional in Lisbon. 'When it was all over,' said McGrory, 'I just cried like a child.'

4

BOB KELLY

When a family owns a football club, it can be hard to tell whether they are its guardians or its jailers. The Kellys had held each role at one time or another, from Celtic's formation to the 1994 takeover that would see them gradually disappear from the boardroom, along with those bearing the other well-known surnames White and Grant. If James Kelly's decision to play for the club in 1888 gave the Kellys immediate credibility, his descendants and those of the other families were denounced a hundred years or so later when they were accused of making Celtic the prisoner of their own limitations.

Few clubs are now linked to a specific clan that has held its great shareholding for decade upon decade. All the same, Bob Kelly, son of James, was not simply a prize winner in the genetic lottery. He led with conviction and, a year after Celtic had become European champions, employed his newfound status in an unexpected way. In 1968 the club was just completing arrangements for a European Cup tie with the Hungarian club Ferencváros when troops from the Soviet Union and its allies invaded Czechoslovakia. Their purpose was to put an end to the liberalisation that had occurred in the Prague Spring. Kelly was adamant that the sport could not be indifferent to such repression.

He decided that a telegram should be sent to UEFA insisting that the competition could no longer go ahead as planned, and on this particular occasion it seems that Kelly was the first to argue that sports administrators must not ignore the brute realities of international affairs. The chairman was motivated by the knowledge that western Europe had been supine over the invasion of Hungary in 1956, when, as he put it, 'only voices were raised in disapproval'. The invasion of Czechoslovakia seemed, in Kelly's mind, so intolerable that sportsmen should not pretend that the country's fate held no relevance for them. He would say later that he had been ready to withdraw Celtic from the tournament unilaterally if need be, but enough measures were adopted to placate him and those of like mind.

UEFA chose to scrap the original draw for the first round and conducted it again with clubs from East and West kept apart. Several sides within the Soviet sphere of influence, including Ferencváros in Hungary, decided not to take part. Kelly, whose knighthood in 1969 may have owed something to his stance, would have been indifferent to that. He wanted to look highminded, and his gesture may have been a minor part of a trend that saw the potency of sport harnessed to politically resonant scenes, such as the Black Power salute of the US gold-medallist sprinter Tommy Smith at the 1968 Olympics. Kelly would have cared little about any harm done to the European Cup since pragmatism was absent from his nature. He was at his most animated when there was a cause to be embraced. Kelly's defiance reached its peak when his club's identity was perceived to be at stake.

When Celtic was formed, Ireland was simply a part of the UK, but from the earliest days a traditional Irish flag, with a gold harp on a green background, was flown at Celtic Park in recognition of the club's origins. The Irish Free State, which came into being in 1922, presented Celtic with the tricolour. It came to be a key part of the scene at the ground, and when the flag was eventually seen to be in shabby condition thirty years later the club had such difficulty in finding a new one in Scotland that the manager Jimmy McGrory wrote to Eamon de Valera. The Taoiseach of the Irish Republic sent a replacement.

Following disorder at the Old Firm match in which Celtic were beaten at home on New Year's Day 1952, the Glasgow magistrates asked the SFA to ban flags that might have a provocative effect on supporters of each team. The measure was, of course, directed at Celtic. Both clubs, then as now, flew the Union Jack. Kelly valued his place in the Establishment, becoming president of the Scottish Football League and subsequently the SFA. Despite being much more a member of the Establishment than a dissident, he was forced into rebellion when, regardless of support for Celtic from the Rangers chairman John F. Wilson, the SFA Council voted twenty-six to seven that the Irish flag must be taken down. Celtic were threatened with suspension if they did not comply.

Coercing the club, however, was more difficult than it seemed, since the legal advice taken by Kelly was clear that the ruling body had no right to interfere in the matter. It was the SFA's belief that the flag was an incitement to visiting supporters, but Celtic appreciated that their suspension, even if it were feasible, would be intolerable to clubs who valued the share of the gate money from matches with them. There was little true desire to close the ground, and by the start of the following season the right to fly the tricolour was established. The Celtic chairman had prevailed over the SFA secretary George Graham, whom he regarded as an enemy.

That victory had been likely all along since Celtic were not in breach of any regulation. The episode is resonant because of the emotions and suspicions that clustered around it. Nobody could bring themselves to speak candidly about the fact that the issue had been born of the antipathy some Protestants felt for the minority community of Catholics. James Handley, who was commissioned by Kelly to write a history of Celtic, mocked the idea that the flag was intrinsically contentious, particularly since few in the crowd would have noticed its existence when there was a game to watch: 'It might have been the flag of Siam for all the attention that any spectator, supporting home or visiting team, gave to it, and if it had been the flag of Siam the SFA would pay no attention to it either.'

The tricolour, as Handley states, often went unregarded and the emphasis on the Irish strand in Celtic's genes did not normally seem so marked then. In this case the original SFA recommendation that it be taken down was made by the referees' committee, but Handley referred to an official who had been attempting for some twenty years to have the Irish flag removed. The allusion was to Graham, who would later be knighted. On this matter he happened by chance to work in tandem with the chairman of a club with similar origins to those of Celtic. Harry Swan of Hibernian was also acting president of the SFA in 1952, and it therefore fell to him to move that Celtic be given three days to comply with the order to take down the flag.

Kelly did not let himself be drawn into the labyrinthine arguments about culture and identity. He stuck to the plain truth that the SFA were attempting to dictate to a club over a matter that was not covered in their rules. Behind that there surely lay Kelly's appreciation that he was under an obligation not to betray his forebears by capitulating. The Kellys had risen in the social hierarchy, but only a generation or two separated him from the era when immigrants would have worried that such a path was closed off to them. It would have been treachery for the chairman to ignore a cause that would have inflamed his forefathers. Others on the Celtic board had been half-hearted about pursuing a matter that meant less to them, and Kelly had to hide that split while he aimed to force the SFA into a retreat.

The view of the Celtic directors who were not so incensed has contemporary echoes. Michael Kelly, the nephew of the then chairman, suggests that the club has no need to cling to icons such as that flag. 'It was deemed to be a provocation to Rangers supporters,' he says. 'That was the excuse for telling Celtic to take it down. In my era, I would have said, "It's stupid for people to think it's a provocation. They're probably just claiming that it is. But why not just take it down, for Rangers games anyway?

Then there's no excuse." Maybe that's the politician in me. But back in the 1950s maybe it would have been seen as one of the last attacks on Irish Catholicism in the west of Scotland, with the flag just an excuse.

'The founders of the club felt Scottish. James Kelly played centre half for Scotland. The community, I think, felt grateful for the welcome Scotland had given them. There were these difficulties, but still they found a life and livelihood here. Running through my time there was a feeling that Celtic wanted to give something back to Scotland. There was no real discussion in my family, or in the Whites so far as I know, of Celtic being an Irish club. They were a Scottish club and they wanted to emphasise that. There is no doubt that it was the tradition of the club. That was the intention, with the very name Celtic being both Irish and Scottish. Hibernian would have been exclusively Irish.'

Bob Kelly never wanted Celtic to be caught in any kind of ethnic ghetto and he showed deftness in exploiting divisions elsewhere. In 1952 the Scottish Football League was already peeved that nobody at the SFA had sought its opinion on the flag. It was Wilson, the Rangers chairman, who brought about the admission from Graham that he had declined to hold a meeting at which the whole matter of the flag might have been resolved. Graham also conceded that he had not told the SFA council that such a course of action was open to them. The affair was a humiliation for him, and when Graham had attempted to conduct a meeting without informing Kelly of its existence, the Celtic chairman got wind of it and turned up in any case. When the conflict was all but over, it was Graham who was absent. He called in sick while the matter was brought to an end.

Kelly enjoyed an appreciation at other clubs that none of his predecessors or successors as Celtic chairman received. He was viewed as a reformer, and he held high office not because he had schemed and double-crossed but because people turned to him. When he was due to stand down as president of the Scottish Football League, the man intended to take over asked him to stay in the post. Those among the Glasgow clubs, including Rangers, who were seeking 'renewal' in the SFA later set him on the way to its presidency.

The strength of feeling about the tricolour revealed the grip that parochial matters can take on people, but Kelly's mind ranged further afield. The European Cup draw of 1968 demonstrated most of all that he had retained the founders' appetite for what they took to be ideological and moral issues. Unfortunately, there was an attraction to the practicalities of the game as well and he was a meddler. Indeed, McGrory was probably permitted to keep the job of manager for twenty years from 1945 because of his compliance in Kelly's interference with team selection, although it was also relevant that the chairman had idolised the centre forward since his heyday on the field. It was a phase that can be looked back on with merriness only by those players who survived and ultimately flourished under Jock Stein.

'I never saw Mr McGrory with a tracksuit on,' says the future captain Billy McNeill. 'He always had his collar and tie, waistcoat, his hat and his Crombie. What he did I don't know.' There was some respite for McNeill and others from 1957 to 1960, since Stein was coaching the Celtic reserves. Otherwise, they had to make do with finding hilarity in the running of the club, when Kelly would have the final say in team selection. 'Mike Jackson tells a great story about seeing his boots with the number eight kit,' McNeill says of his friend and fellow youth signing. 'He thought that was great. He comes back in a bit later and sees the boots with the number ten. So that's OK. The next time, he goes into the dressing room with everyone else. He's looking for his boots and they weren't there at all. Mr McGrory didn't really contribute an awful lot. He was a lovely man, too. He had had a wonderful record with the club as a player, and we appreciated that. I think it's certain that Bob Kelly would give him a wee list of the team that he had to put on the park.'

Pat Crerand, McNeill's teammate until he was transferred to Manchester United, recalls interventions by the chairman that were more direct than that. 'There was an argument between me and [the then first-team coach] Sean Fallon in the dressing room at half-time in the New Year's Day game with Rangers in 1963,' he says. 'That can happen. Bob Kelly shouldn't have been there in the first place. Why should he be there? This was something between Sean and I. If I remember right he was in the dressing room quite a few times at half-time.'

The scene on the occasion at Ibrox, however, was revealing. McGrory, for instance, was in theory the club's manager, but he was either absent from or keen to stay out of the debate that afternoon. Fallon argued for a more direct style, while the midfielder wanted the priority to lie in retaining possession. Celtic were 1–0 down and went on to lose 4–0. Kelly, as was his way, took a moralistic attitude towards what he saw as insurrection, although Crerand actually had such an affinity with Fallon that he was still phoning him regularly almost fifty years later. Punishment awaited the player four days after the defeat to Rangers, when Celtic had a match at Aberdeen. As usual, the budget did not run to an overnight stay and the players travelled third class on the train, putting up with the wooden seats and the lack of a toilet. There was a greater discomfort to come for Crerand when he was left out of the team that won 5–1.

The midfielder never played again for Celtic. It is a mark of Kelly's inflexibility that he would take such a stance over a footballer whose skills he admired so much that Crerand had been the highest earner, with a basic wage of £22 a week. 'He was keen on me at one stage but why did it change?' Crerand asks. 'He was difficult to approach.' The chairman most likely thought the midfielder too rebellious, and not even his capacity to control the play compensated for that. It turned out that United already had first option to buy Crerand, which would suggest that selling him in due course had been Celtic's intention all along. The fee of £56,000 appealed to the club. Remarkably, it turned out that there was such a surfeit of talent in the squad that, once Stein was manager, they could still do wonderfully well without a superlative passer of the ball such as Crerand.

It seems that the chairman also took the decision to get rid of Bertie Auld in 1961, when the then winger was sold to Birmingham. Kelly saw him at the time as being far from a model professional. The disenchantment had been noticeable for years. 'It was down to whether or not the chairman liked you,' Auld says. 'I felt I was progressing enough to get a run in the team, but instead what happened was that I played in every round of the League Cup but was dropped for the 7–1 win in the final [over Rangers]. For someone who had a passion and love for the club that I had it was hard to take. On the day that Big Jock and his Dunfermline team beat us in the 1961 Scottish Cup final, I was playing at Tannadice [against Dundee United] in a reserve game.'

He moved to Birmingham City, although Celtic were at least to buy him back before Stein became manager. Interference by the chairman was normally more subtle. His nephew Michael Kelly, who has gone on to become a prominent figure in Scottish life, had a place in the directors' box while still a youngster. He tones down rather than denies the reports of his uncle's meddling. 'I sat in the second row,' he says, 'and there was never ever a note or a message passed down. The directors sat in the front row and watched the game. I don't think there was any need [to pass a message]. Bob Kelly would have made his instructions pretty clear before the game. The main thing was team selection, like the 1956 Cup final defeat to Hearts when he put Mike Haughney [a right back] into the forward line [although he scored] and Billy Craig made his Cup debut on the right wing.'

This may have been the nub of the matter. Dabbling in team affairs was then commonplace for directors and chairmen throughout the sport. Injuries had a part in the readjustment of that 1956 line-up, but the propensity of Bob Kelly to impose his wishes is not in dispute. He could also be eccentric in his meddling and will be remembered for the whimsicality of his reaction when he looked out the window of the team bus and saw

Willie Goldie, a back-up goalkeeper, walking to a game with Airdrie as a supporter, with a Celtic scarf round his neck. The bus was stopped and Goldie made his sole appearance for the club that day. 'We all thought it was crazy,' says Crerand. 'And what was the manager Jimmy McGrory doing? He was just a figurehead.' Goldie's errors in the match led to a 2–0 defeat. That tale, indeed, shows perfectly the harm done when a concoction of whimsy, Corinthian spirit and sentimentality makes people light-headed. The chairman felt a strong attraction to such an approach.

'I thought he kept Celtic back for a long, long time,' Crerand says, yet he also believes that Kelly's conduct was in keeping with the practices of the time. 'I think every club was like that. Matt Busby must have been one of the first, when he became manager of Manchester United, to have the strength to control the club. I think the same sort of thing went on at Ibrox as it did at Celtic.' If Kelly stood out, it was because his interventions could be wildly experimental, as if he hoped to demonstrate that he possessed an insight that was superior to plain common sense. Between 1955 and 1963 Celtic appeared in four Scottish Cup finals and lost them all. In each case the team selection was controversial.

There was a wistfulness to the meddling because Kelly can only have been frustrated by the manner in which his own hopes of becoming a footballer were denied. As a child he had been hit by a tram car, and the nerve damage weakened his right arm. By his own account, he was still an effective tennis player, but his father James was against his playing professional football. The argument was that opponents would be inhibited by concern for him. An unusual halo of chivalry hovers above the game in this depiction, but the nephew was persuaded by it and the seeds of his lingering idealism may have been planted then. Kelly was open-minded in some respects and there was, for instance, an appreciation of the need to develop ideas about the game when Jimmy Hogan was appointed as coach in 1948.

The Englishman had been coaching on the continent since before the First World War, and many believe that his influence was far-reaching in Austria and Hungary, with the principles he inculcated underlying the style of those national teams in their heyday. He was, however, sixty-five by the time Celtic turned to him and no longer so transformative a figure. His arrival in Glasgow did still underline that the men running Celtic were not necessarily parochial, and neither were they without a yearning to galvanise the club, even if realising that ambition was beyond them.

Kelly had a job at the Glasgow stock exchange in the period before all such trading became located in London, but Celtic was his true purpose. He joined the board in 1932, was appointed chairman in 1947 and died in 1971. As with many families, there were stresses whose origins could barely be recalled, let alone explained. Michael Kelly was therefore taken aback one day simply to hear from his uncle, even before he found out why he had got in touch.

Every club that lasts, regardless of its size, becomes, to use the Barcelona slogan, more than a club. Connections run in all directions, and Michael enjoyed the benefit of them to get his true start in political life, even if that help took him by surprise. 'There was a fall-out between two sides of the family,' he says. 'My father [David] and Bob did not get on. They would meet at family things, but they didn't talk to each other. It spilt over onto me. Bob treated me in that same way, which was very peculiar because it had nothing whatsoever to do with me then, when I was thirteen or fourteen. It was inexplicable, not talking to one another over decades. The woman Bob married was not someone the rest of the family got on with, and she may have been insulted earlier on. These sorts of things can happen in any family.'

It is also known that there was a great disagreement in 1950 when Bob resisted David's wish to try and replace McGrory as manager with Matt Busby, who was already at United by then,

but that may also have been a reflection of the general antagonism between them. 'I never understood it,' says Michael, 'and I
don't know if Bob did either. When I first decided to stand as a
councillor for the Labour Party, I went up to try and get a nomination in Anderston [to the west of Glasgow's city centre]. That
would have been 1971, when I was thirty-one. The phone rang
and it was Bob, who had never phoned me in his life before. I
had never had a social conversation with him. He said, "I understand you want to stand as a councillor for Anderston. I've just
had a call from 'Needles' McCafferty, who is chairman of the
Anderston Labour Party. He used to be chairman of the Celtic
Supporters Association. He was just phoning to check out that
you were my nephew."

'Bob then said, "Do you want this nomination?" I said, "Yes,
of course I do." He said, "OK, I'll speak to Needles." I was
very brave in that conversation and said to Bob, "Why is there
this tension between different members of the family?" He just
blanked it and said, "I don't know. Would I be phoning you if
there was any tension?" I remember him as being a very remote
figure. I would say I only ever had a proper conversation with
him on two or three occasions. He was a formidable personality
who didn't really encourage me to speak to him. You depended
on him for entry to the games, which meant you weren't really
going to confront him over various things. I think he portrayed
that power and remoteness to the players at the club as well, in
that despotic, authoritarian manner.'

Michael Kelly would make the most of any small assistance
from his uncle or anyone else. He has led a successful life. Apart
from his involvement with Celtic, he would be well known as,
amongst other things, the Lord Provost of Glasgow in the early
1980s, the period when the city began to revive in a burst of
stone cleaning and marketing that both highlighted its Victorian
architecture. The 'Glasgow's Miles Better' campaign did its work
as the locals smirked at what they took to be a dig at Edinburgh,
while the city fathers soberly explained that it merely referred

to the improvement in the place. The culmination came when Glasgow was selected as European City of Culture in 1990.

Kelly was also an economics lecturer at Strathclyde University who went on to start his own PR consultancy. He might well have had a stimulating effect on Celtic had he not been restrained by the wish to protect his relatives in the boardroom. He was convinced that bloodlines bound a club together. 'In the first Celtic team [in 1888] there was not only [his grandfather] James Kelly,' he says, 'but also my great uncle Michael Dunbar. So I do feel a great association with that team.'

While that pride is honourable, the batch of Kellys and Whites who were at work in the late 1980s and early 1990s had no means of dealing with a bold Rangers who were at least looking to the far horizon while also keeping Celtic under their thumb. Efforts were made to bring new blood into the boardroom, but that led to the sort of divisions that saw Brian Dempsey, a property developer, being ousted not very long after he had been co-opted.

All of that had overtones of the directionless, if much less newsworthy, period immediately before Stein's return in 1965. In a witty if lugubrious reference to the sort of pop groups coming to notice at the start of that decade, some supporters renamed Celtic Bob Kelly and the Easybeats. The breadth of Michael Kelly's career had shown him to be a more dynamic presence than any of his relatives since Victorian times. None the less, his sense of loyalty to tradition and to family restricted his scope for making the break with the past that a sluggish club needed so badly. He is deft in evoking Celtic as it seemed to him. Kelly speaks knowledgeably and evokes the forces that shaped both the club and himself.

The average fan might not have any forebears who played for the team, but the tale of the Kellys still assumes a broad familiarity for many when he muses on his grandfather James, the centre half in that first Celtic side: 'His father, David, is recorded in the 1840 census as being a blacksmith in Renton, Alexandria. James was an apprentice carpenter, a working-class guy. His father, of course, came over for economic reasons.' In twenty-first-century Glasgow, Celtic fans are sometimes taunted with the chant, 'The famine's over, why don't you go home?' One response might involve pointing out that societies stagnate if there is no immigration, but Kelly makes a more matter-of-fact point. 'People', he says, 'tend to forget in this current "Go home" controversy that Ireland at that time was part of the United Kingdom. People were moving from one part of the UK to another.'

Where Celtic are concerned Kelly puts an emphasis on continuity that is only natural, since it enfolds the club in family history. 'I thought', he says almost ruefully, 'that all supporters thought, like me, of the traditions and community roots of the club and the fact that there was this broader responsibility. There was this Scottish institution that had done so much for Scotland, and which Scotland had done so much for.'

That type of rhetoric implies it would have been better for the ownership of Celtic to be kept along the traditional lines, but that, for instance, does not take into account the badly needed money and entrepreneurial innovation that Fergus McCann eventually had to provide. Jock Stein, in his typically intelligent way, also engineered a radical shift. He nudged Bob Kelly into giving him the manager's post at Celtic. There was no sectarianism about the then chairman, who had not hesitated to appoint non-Catholic captains, as Stein himself knew from direct experience as the leader of the Coronation Cup-winning side of 1953.

If Kelly was to be a prominent office-bearer in the Scottish Football League and SFA, it was because of his trustworthiness and efficiency. As with many individuals who are thought to be aloof, the Celtic chairman was affected by inhibitions that inclined him to maintain a distance. 'He was difficult to know, introverted and sensitive to a degree that caused people to sometimes regard him as an abrupt man,' said an obituary in the *Scottish Catholic Observer*.

That observation goes to the heart of the matter. If others

were uncomfortable in Kelly's presence, it could well have been because he himself was ill at ease. Bob was not the eldest son and therefore might have been surprised to find himself the leader of Celtic and, ultimately, of that generation of the family. The position belonged in theory to Frank, a chartered accountant and trainee stockbroker who was with the Junior club Blantyre Victoria before being taken by Celtic on a continental tour in the summer of 1914 that saw him play in Leipzig and Berlin. He turned out, too, in some games with both Celtic and Motherwell towards the close of the First World War. Frank was still a soldier when he died of his injuries in the spring of 1919 following a train accident in France.

The second son, Jim, had been killed during the war itself. In theory, Charlie Kelly was next in line to fill the family role at the club, but he was a shy person who did not even take part readily in conversation. James Kelly, who became chairman of the club in 1909 and served as a director after that, seems to have transferred the expectations gradually to Bob, who was just sixteen at the time of Frank's death and would not normally have looked cut out to be in the public eye. There was a reserve to a man for whom religion was the core of his life. Bob's devotion to Catholicism was no mere conformity to the values of his family.

The sincerity was embodied in his habit each day of stopping at a church and attending Mass before he got to the office. Faith was much more than a cultural matter for him and he would have been betraying his beliefs if he had resorted to squalid tribalism. Indeed, a future manager had witnessed Kelly's determination to ignore religious allegiance. 'He gave me the biggest compliment of my life, by his decision to appoint me, a non-Catholic, as manager of Celtic,' Stein said. 'He firmly believed that Celtic should keep an open door to sign anyone that suited them. As far back as when I was chief coach he once rebuked me for signing too many players from Boys' Guild sources. He thought we should cast an eye a bit wider. I don't think anyone has given more of their life to any club or done as much for any club as he did for Celtic.'

None the less, turning to a Protestant manager for the first time was a further step by Kelly. Stein metaphorically led him by the arm to ensure that he took it. The then Hibernian manager called the Celtic chairman in 1965 on the pretext of seeking his advice as to whether he should accept a job in England, where Wolverhampton looked ready to appoint him. Any idea of Stein being in need of such counsel was absurd, but the conversation served its purpose by flattering Kelly while also compelling him to come to a decision.

The chairman would have much preferred to impose an idio-syncratic policy. He even tried to talk Stein into being assist-ant manager to Fallon, a stalwart in his playing days who was cut out for no more than the post that Kelly was trying to foist on the then Hibernian manager. Stein was already too powerful a figure in Scottish football even to consider such a proposal. It can only have been stubbornness, with stupidity as its side effect, that led to Kelly persevering with another version of his scheme, but Stein had no need to consider being joint manager with Fallon. He knew the value of popular feeling and not even Kelly could quite dare to make enemies of the Celtic support by terminating discussions with Stein. Instead, a dialogue that had started months before was slow to reach its end. Pat Crerand, then at Manchester United, had an inkling of Stein's appoint-ment months before it was confirmed. 'We played Everton in the Fairs Cup at Old Trafford in January of 1965,' he says. 'Jock used to come down to a lot of the games. He'd bring rolls and square-sliced sausages. There'd be a fight amongst the players, particularly me and Denis Law, to get them. Neilly Mochan [the Celtic coach who had been a teammate of Stein's] said, "He's got great news for you, but I can't tell you." I said to Jock, "You're going back to Celtic Park, aren't you?" He wouldn't say a word, but later on that year a journalist told me Stein was getting the job and asked me, "What do you think will happen?" I said,

"Celtic will win the League six times in the next seven years." I was wrong.'

Stein took the title for nine seasons in a row, starting in 1966. His appointment met with delight as well as disbelief from Michael Kelly. 'I saw it all happening,' he says. 'There was a speculative story in the *Sunday Express*, and that was the first time I ever phoned up a news desk. I asked if it was true that Jock Stein was coming. It just seemed unbelievable. There had been such a lack of success and attendances had fallen off so there was an economic imperative. Something had to be done. It was quite clear that Stein was the guy. But the fact that Bob Kelly sacrificed all the control that he did took me aback. It was a volte-face. He had been impervious to criticism.'

At Hibernian, Stein's team had played with a flourish that would have been alluring to any chairman, and his negotiating position was formidable, as Kelly understood. The principal difficulty for him was not so much Stein's religion as the surrender to the manager. But Stein was soon in charge, with McGrory retained on the payroll out of loyalty as a supposed public-relations officer. Sooner or later there had to be a set-piece confrontation to confirm that new arrangements genuinely were in place.

The right back Jim Craig was sent off in a Cup Winners Cup quarter-final with Dinamo Kiev in January 1966 that was a mere irritant since the home leg had already been won 3–0. The match was staged inconveniently in Tbilisi, Georgia, because weather conditions in Ukraine were too harsh. There was much resentment that the Soviet authorities had forced Celtic to break their journey in Moscow, and tempers were further aggravated by a disrupted trek back to Glasgow. People were short-tempered that week and Craig, despite Stein's urging, had declined to apologise to Kelly for the dismissal because the defender was sure he had been the innocent party. The squad got home in time for a Friday training session at 11 p.m. Craig, by order of the chairman, was not in the line-up for the game against Hearts that Celtic lost the following day.

Attitudes, however, were evolving and director Desmond White, later to be chairman himself, argued at a specially convened board meeting that team selection must be the sole preserve of Stein. The manager was even brought in to confirm that, given the chance, he would have picked Craig. Kelly had, in effect, been stripped of the right of veto that had mattered deeply to him. So far as the side was concerned, his main means of control had been taken from him. As the chairman would have understood wryly, Celtic's domination made his standing look great just when he was at last being shackled. He had sometimes intervened, as with the Craig case, in what he took to be issues of principle. The high-mindedness reflected a pride in being above the ugly compromises that others might make. Winning matches, however, is the purpose of a team, and a supposed moral superiority does not lift a club above others in the League table. In any case, there was not really a dichotomy. Stein's sort of football was idealistic in its own way. The occasional player would, like Craig, be sent off, but his teams were more commonly associated with enterprise and excitement.

With the boardroom examination of the Craig affair completed, Stein assumed full authority as Celtic's leader, but it was also a conclusion that formalised a trend that had been growing irresistibly in any case. Bob Kelly took it hard from the start that he was no longer sure to be the arbiter of team selection, even if he had seen the immediate rewards for this sacrifice when Stein's Celtic won the 1965 Scottish Cup. All the same, the chairman, too, had felt the cost of the lack of professionalism in the management of the team, which he had not only tolerated but actually prolonged by his continuing endorsement of McGrory as manager. The downturn can be said to have lasted twenty years from the end of the Second World War, regardless of some unforgettable victories.

'There was a lot of unrest,' says Michael Kelly. 'Rangers were so strong. Most of that time it was men against boys in games with Rangers. Rangers were a mature, professional, cynical team. Celtic were just immature lads running around. You might win the occasional game, like the first League game or an early League Cup game. But when it came to the crunch – the New Year's Day game for example – I never remember winning that, or games against them in the later rounds of the Scottish Cup. It was a hardness of attitude by Rangers.

'There was great discontent. The people I was mixing with remembered the Celtic of 1938 winning the Exhibition Cup. Then the war came and after that Celtic were almost relegated in 1948. They had to win a game in Dundee to guarantee staying up. I went up to the chapel in Blantyre to pray during it. They won 3–2, having had three goals chalked off.' Kelly jokes that it is important for a Celtic fan to keep the chip on their shoulder.

His uncle had excused himself much too readily when asked how the club could find itself in such a predicament. 'The answer', said Bob Kelly, 'is that the war had practically wiped out our playing resources.' Celtic did little more than keep itself in existence and, three years after the end of hostilities, had still not accustomed itself to genuine competition. The situation that the side faced against Dundee had been ignominious and the thrill of a hat-trick by Jock Weir, signed from Blackburn Rovers for £7,000 two months before, did not alter the mood.

'There was a lot of unhappiness,' says Michael Kelly, 'but people didn't think they could do anything about it. They would turn out and shout abuse at the directors' box from the enclosure in front of the stand but there was no feeling that anybody could actually make a difference.' Kelly is too astute not to notice the irony of his then dissatisfaction with the state of club being echoed by protesters inveighing against him and the others on the board two generations later.

By then fans had seen, in Stein's time, what Celtic could achieve and therefore believed that they could not only complain but also insist that only the owners stopped the club from succeeding. In his youth, Michael Kelly himself was annoyed by Celtic's failure to live up to its past or its potential. For him, the victory in the Coronation Cup and the 7–1 defeat of Rangers in the 1957/8 League Cup final have to be termed 'consolations', even if they were of a spellbinding type. The generally indifferent form also made people turn away from the field itself and, in his case, the family felt that Celtic were being victimised.

'Certainly,' Kelly says. 'There was, of course, the incident with the flag. I remember things that my father would quote to me as a wee boy that were before my time. There was a riot at Ibrox, so they closed Celtic Park. Try and work that one out.' He is referring to an occasion in 1941 when the stadium was indeed shut down for a month by the SFA, and it is also the case that the disorder had occurred at Rangers' ground. However, the bottles thrown had been hurled by Celtic fans peeved that a penalty had been missed after Rangers delayed the taking of the kick. Bob Kelly himself thought that the SFA had 'acted according to the rule and within their right'.

Ultimately, the chairman did stand opposed to the ruling body. The referee, Jim Callaghan, was suspended by the SFA for two months in the autumn of 1969 because he had failed to send off John Hughes of Celtic for a foul on Willie Johnston in an Old Firm League Cup tie when he had already been booked. Kelly felt that the official was being subjected to a special punishment that would not have been applied if a lesser game had been involved. It rankled with him that Rangers had made a written complaint to the SFA and seemingly got the desired effect. As soon as Callaghan's punishment was announced, Kelly resigned from the SFA's referee committee. The club's chairman, none the less, had largely thrived in officialdom because he was clear and firm.

Regardless of his progress, paranoia did not wholly account for the belief among Celtic fans that they were treated unjustly. 'We had just come through an era in which Catholics were quite severely discriminated against,' Michael Kelly says of an earlier part of the twentieth century. 'Weir of Cathcart [a large engineering firm] wouldn't employ Catholics. There were all sorts of barriers. The Conservative Party, or Unionist Party as it called itself in Scotland, was very anti-Catholic. There was a whole series of institutions in the west of Scotland that quite clearly wanted to discriminate against Irish Catholics. A lot of accountancy and law firms simply wouldn't start Catholics as apprentices. If you were living in that environment and had suffered that kind of discrimination, it was quite natural to assume that the football authorities and the referees were as discriminatory as the rest of society.'

Bob Kelly had a forbidding air, but the fascination with the sport was open-minded and almost innocent. There was a time when he was incapable of even walking past a football match being played by youngsters in a park. According to his own calculations, he saw hundreds of games a year then. Kelly was the type to start rearranging the cutlery at lunchtime while he attempted to recreate a goal. It did not even matter which club had scored it. There is a description of him becoming animated as he attempted to summon up the piece of play with which Bobby Walker scored for Hearts against Celtic before the First World War. Fans accused him, with some cause, of holding back the club, but they must also have understood his passion since thousands of them lined the street outside St Columbkille's Church for his funeral, with a congregation of 1,500 present at the service itself.

He was, after all, a fellow supporter. On one occasion he received a letter complaining that a volunteer agent for Celtic Pools, a body that raised funds for stadium development, had not received his customary ticket for the next European match. The reply from Kelly contained two tickets for the Milan game in 1969 and a handwritten apology in green ink, the colour of which expressed his fixation with the club rather than a broader instability in his mental health. If he was prone to interfering with football issues, it was, aside from any high-handedness, a reflection of his fixation with the sport and its future.

That trait gave him a modernity in some respects, even if he did cut a most traditional figure. Kelly was so keen to broaden the horizons of the Celtic players that he sent them to Wembley for Hungary's historic 6–3 win over England in November 1953. It has to be stressed that he was cosmopolitan enough to realise that in an era when Britain was especially conceited and insular, this was a side in the process of changing our very conception of the game. There was, all the same, another sort of romanticism that was a hindrance. A year after that outing to Wembley, he said, 'It is important to remember that Scots football has still one big advantage. The Hungarians, the Uruguayans and the rest are undeniably good but in a drilled, mechanical way. They have reached a point where they always do things to pattern.'

Lurking behind the statement is the old Scottish delusion that their race has an intuitive connection to the game that scarcely exists in other lands. That outlook was still alive when Scotland set off for Argentina in 1978. One reporter raised the stakes by asking the manager what Scotland would do after winning the World Cup. 'Retain it,' Ally MacLeod barked unhesitatingly, even if he must have known he was playing to the gallery. Kelly was not afflicted by deluded bravado to that extent, and although he had become an obstacle to Celtic by the early 1960s, if not before, there was a severe idealism to him.

The chairman turned into a paradox. He was to be an obstruction, yet he had the best of intentions and nobody can ever have accused him of taking too little interest in the club. The youth development to which he was committed was sincere, and some of those prospects were known as the Kelly kids. However, that nickname was discarded as soon as they helped Celtic become a force. By then they could only be associated with Stein. There was an implicit indictment of Kelly in that since the contrast with what had gone before could only be explained by saying that he had been out of his depth. In the ten seasons that followed the completion of the Double in 1954, Celtic took just the League Cup, on two occasions.

For all that Kelly wanted the best, he often ensured that it could not be attained when he kept absolute power in his own inexpert hands. By the end, the chairman flexed his muscle most notably as a moralist. When Celtic had a spate of orderings off in the decider with Racing Club for the Intercontinental Cup in 1967, Kelly fined every player £250, although that was the equivalent of over a month's basic pay for each man. It was a draconian act, too, since the general income would not even ensure that that they had sufficient savings on which to draw.

He did like to exercise his principles, and that habit had charm when it touched on his love of the game. The tendency was as marked as ever towards the close of his life, when he was asked how defensive tactics could be eradicated from the sport. Kelly proposed that results, as such, should not matter and that the League title must go simply to the club that scored the most goals. It was a startling thought, and although that sort of notion might inflict a one-dimensional quality on the football, he was clearly not a curmudgeon. His absorption in the game was itself a terrible disadvantage to Celtic since he could not bear to allow independence to his managers. Or not, at least, until Jock Stein took the job.

5

JOCK STEIN

It was never Jock Stein's plan to be fashionable, but success drags people to unexpected locations. After Celtic had knocked Ujpest Dózsa out of the European Cup in March 1972, Richard Burton sang 'I Belong to Glasgow' at an impromptu post-match party in Budapest. He and his wife Elizabeth Taylor were in the city while filming *Bluebeard*. There was an incongruity to such an occasion, but it did reflect the increasingly cosmopolitan and alluring nature of football. The game was capable of transporting people further than ever from their roots. Hollywood could pull off that same trick, and had been doing so for much longer. Burton, the son of a coal miner, had an affinity of sorts with Stein, who had worked in the pits. The future Celtic manager used to get scratches on his back as he squeezed a bulky torso into those confined spaces.

Stein was marked by his circumstances and still wished to retain the spartan tone of those times when he was back in the daylight and spotlight as a figure of global renown. No manager draws up a team selection without producing a self-portrait. His experiences, fears and hopes must be revealed whenever he plumps for a particular group of footballers. Stein went further in his efforts to see a younger version of himself on the pitch. He held an ideological view of haircuts and ensured for much of his time as Celtic manager that the players, with their short back and sides, would look as if they were doing their national service, despite the fact that conscription had ended in 1960. Stein himself had been spared a stint in the armed forces because as a miner he was exempt. As a part-time centre half for Albion Rovers, he had needed another job. Stein favoured working underground and spent twelve years at Bothwell Castle pit. That decision was made because the pay was less in the carpet factory where he could have had a job. After his father suffered a cerebral haemorrhage, Stein's wage packet was critical to the family, and the centre half could not have assumed that there would one day be a transfer to a club such as Celtic to improve his income.

His circumstances were unremarkable, but they made him wary of esoteric notions. He was loyal to his community and was seen cramming bank notes into a collection can during the miners' strike of 1984–5. Sir Alex Ferguson remembered Stein's anger at that time when meeting scab drivers who brought in coal from Belgium. 'He looked at them', the then Aberdeen manager remembered, 'and said, "I hope you're proud of yourselves. You're doing people out of a living."' During the Second World War there had also been a strike and Stein handed over to the union leader Mick McGahey the £2 a week Albion Rovers then paid him so that he would be no better off than his workmates. He was never to forget what it was to make a harsh living underground. It even impelled him to a stark lyricism when he strove to describe that life to the journalist Hugh McIlvanney. 'There's nothing as dark as the darkness down a pit, the blackness that closes in on you if your lamp goes out,' he said. 'You'd think you would see some kind of shapes but you can see nothing, nothing but the inside of your head. I think everyone should go down the pit at least once to learn what darkness is.'

Anything he interpreted as affectation would be banned and the trends of the 1960s were resisted regardless of their acceptance elsewhere. George Best could follow the Beatles, going from mop top to the beard and straggly hair of the band's Maharishi Mahesh Yogi period, since Old Trafford was permitted to reflect the summer of love and psychedelia. Matt Busby, the United manager, had also emerged from the Lanarkshire coal-mining community but adapted himself to the cultural upheaval more happily than Stein. When the Celtic manager later had the opportunity to take charge at Old Trafford, he rejected the offer ostensibly because his wife Jean refused to leave Glasgow. His accountant, Gerry Woolard, said that Stein would have seen his wages tripled or quadrupled if he had left for England. It may be that the manager, despite his open-mindedness, felt at his most authoritative in the environment he had known all his days. Following his departure from Celtic in 1978, Stein became manager of Leeds United, but spent just forty-four days there before taking charge of Scotland.

Once more this was popularly explained by reference to Jean's parochialism. It is not in dispute that she was attached to Scotland and the family home near Hampden Park. Even so, Stein would not have been the type to be confined to the west of Scotland if he had really craved a management post elsewhere. Pat Crerand signed for Celtic as an eighteen-year-old in 1957, at the same time as Stein began to coach the youngsters there, and they were still in touch in 1978. By then Crerand was long established in England, where he was at that time a scout for Manchester United, the club he had served so well after leaving Glasgow in 1963. The move south of the border was not so simple for Stein.

'I remember he phoned me up from Leeds,' says Crerand. 'Morton were playing at Oldham [in an Anglo-Scottish Cup tie]. Mike Jackson and Benny Rooney were the joint managers of Morton. They were two pals of mine, and I was going to the game anyway. Jock came and picked me up, and it came onto the radio that Ally MacLeod had been sacked as the Scotland manager. I turned to Jock and said, "You know something? It's a certainty they're going to ask you." He never really said anything. I told him it was the most sensible choice the SFA could make. I don't think Jock was ever really happy at Leeds United.

He was always a bit of a home bird anyway, Jock. He must have been bored out of his tree because he came to collect me that day and then turned round to go back to Oldham.'

A balance had been struck in the Celtic years as Stein made a global impact while never having to break his bond with a place and its people. Glasgow, in his lifetime, had the note of working-class conformism to which he was attuned. By the early 1970s the dress code for Stein's squad was marginally more flexible, but the manager still insisted on austere, purposefully uncomfortable conditions to somehow offset the glamour that his successful team increasingly relished.

Billy McNeill, the captain in that era who would later manage the club in two separate spells, had known little else in any case. As a young prospect the defender was drawn to the excitement of the sport, but no one felt any financial allure. 'I was a part-timer for a few years,' he says. 'I was working with J. B. Noon and Company, a firm of insurance brokers in Glasgow, and was office manager. I liked my work there. The firm's directors were extremely good to me. They taught me a great deal and were most considerate when it came to getting time off to play for Celtic. I thought very carefully about going full-time. It seemed such a big step at the time, giving up a secure and worthwhile job to do nothing but play football.'

The austerity concocted at Celtic has stayed clear in McNeill's mind. The then training ground, Barrowfield, which was half a mile from the stadium, had dressing rooms that were off limits. 'We still changed at Celtic Park,' McNeill says. 'Stein wouldn't allow us to use tracksuits. On the cold winter days we had to run up that road and get there quickly. He did all these things just to keep us on our toes.' Scratchy training tops were still in use, with first-team players alone permitted to wear a football jersey beneath them. Those yet to make the breakthrough could be identified by the rash on their chest. The favourite gag claimed that if you whistled, the top would come bounding over to you. At least Stein himself could point out that his own working conditions were modest, if not spartan. He had a tiny office at Celtic Park that was just off the foyer.

Puritanism came to a halt on the pitch. Stein encouraged a luxuriant attacking style that reflected his sense that the game then was the fixation of people who wanted a release from the chafing circumstances of everyday life. The road to the football stadium that the footballers resentfully ran along was an escape route for supporters who longed to relish a sense of occasion. While he would never have acknowledged it, the social liberation of the 1960s and the growing affluence in society had an indirect impact on Stein. There was a breezier tone and an aversion to deference. Stein himself sensed the trend and was so fully aware of his rising status that he could politely stop short of letting the chairman Bob Kelly know the precise line-up he intended to pick. Such conversations in the past had often seen Jimmy McGrory, Stein's predecessor, behave like the family retainer he was and make the changes Kelly stipulated. Stein, none the less, was too much the realist to suppose he could prosper without reaching an accommodation. He had been on friendly terms with the chairman ever since taking the Coronation Cup round supporters clubs, as captain, with Kelly in 1953.

That might have smoothed the transition in the club's affairs once Stein was manager. 'Jimmy McGrory had been a magnificent servant to Celtic, as a manager and player,' said Kelly in 1969. 'But like me he was getting on in years. I had always been close to the players. The ones in the teams of the twenties and thirties were my friends. I could still talk to the players in the fifties, the ones when Jock played. But by the sixties they looked on me as an old man. We needed someone who could talk their language, and we needed to make the change when we had a chance of success.'

Kelly never entirely got over matters such as John Hughes, originally a centre forward, being turned into a winger, but he knew where to stop with his new manager. Stein appreciated that and, following Kelly's death, said, 'It was to his credit that for the six years we worked together as chairman and manager he kept his side of the bargain. He always had opinions on players, and he would give me them. But he never once insisted I should pick someone for the side or, just as important, drop anyone.'

If Stein had the benefit of an ally in a position of great power, there was greater craving in the boardroom for anyone who could release the club from a torpor broken only by sporadic success in knockout competitions. There was the glint of power about Stein because he had already flourished elsewhere, turning Dunfermline Athletic into the 1961 Scottish Cup winners with victory over Celtic in a replay, and making a promising start at Hibernian, who had strong hopes of a League and Cup Double before he returned to the East End of Glasgow. He would already have known well how primitive arrangements were. Despite being on the Celtic backroom staff for three years after his retirement as a footballer in 1957, he had not had the seniority to introduce a thoughtful approach to training throughout the club. All the same, the youngsters he coached understood the difference he could make.

As a midfielder, Pat Crerand appreciated innovations that honed the specific skills he already had. 'If you spoke to all the players at Celtic Park, like Billy McNeill,' he says, 'they'll tell you they were going nowhere until Jock Stein came. I was very fortunate because when I came to Celtic Park Jock was running the reserve team. He was brilliant and he had these little training exercises. He'd get these wooden benches and put them on different areas of the pitch and you had to hit them. It was great for your passing. He did little things like that. Jock was way ahead of his time. You only have to ask Sir Alex Ferguson and he will tell you that.'

There were glimpses of Stein's craving to release Celtic from the clutches of the past. For instance, he sent the reserve team out in the 4–2–4 formation with which Brazil had taken the 1958 World Cup. While Stein was no theoretician, he was alive to the potential benefit of any new approaches to football that he came across. His former Celtic teammate Bobby Collins recognised the cunning. 'When Big Jock runs into the forest,' he said, 'all the foxes run out.' The craving for innovation emerged from Stein's personality, but the restlessness was also influenced by his medical history. Discomfort from the ankle he had damaged severely during an Old Firm match in 1955 probably explains why he hardly appeared to sleep. It was his habit to drive to midweek matches in England, and especially Manchester United games, before turning the car round so he would be at training the following morning. That trip to Old Trafford and back was no cruise since the road network was underdeveloped and the motorway did not run all the way from Glasgow to Carlisle until 2008. It was, too, a compassionate errand since he often brought those Scottish rolls and sausages for Crerand, who had been born in the Gorbals.

Football then was poised between two eras. Its ties to local communities were still strong, even as the sport was also developing a global reach so that South American stars would move to mainland Europe, if not yet Britain. The Internazionale manager in the 1967 European Cup final had been a walking prototype. Helenio Herrera was born to Spanish immigrants in Argentina, moved with his family to the slums of Casablanca when he was three, and ultimately made a career in French football before going on to manage in that country, Spain and Italy. Few could be quite so cosmopolitan as that, but Stein had a yearning for the knowledge to be unearthed elsewhere. In 1963, while with Dunfermline, he and Willie Waddell, who was then in charge of Kilmarnock, took up an offer from the *Daily Express* to go and watch Herrera at work with Inter. So brief a visit did not transform either man, even if Stein began experimenting with a sweeper system when he got back to his club, but the curiosity that saw the pair make the trip to Milan was an asset. Waddell would follow the Celtic manager in bringing a European honour to Glasgow, when his Rangers side won the 1972 Cup Winners' Cup.

The week before Celtic won the European Cup, Waddell reflected on that visit to the trendsetting Appiano Gentile training ground four years earlier and confirmed, of course, that the Inter manager had not let slip any secrets. Stein left instead with a sense of Herrera's key attributes. 'He saw a wee man with the burning ambition to be top of the heap,' Waddell said. 'He saw a man absolutely dedicated to the game, with the single-mindedness and driving urge to get the best out of the players at his disposal. At the same time their courses were so far apart. Inter was backed by a fortune. Nothing was too expensive in facilities. They could search the world for the best players. That was the Herrera route to success. Stein had to be so different. He had to develop wee Scots lads. Dunfermline had to be run on a shoestring. Even at Celtic Park the money does not run into the thousands and thousands of pounds that Inter toss around. But rich or poor the approach is the same. The man at the top must himself be ruthless in his demands and ambitions. The high standards he wants from his players must also be within the boss. He must lead the way.'

It was Stein's feat to take the game in a new direction. Until his breakthrough, the eleven European Cup finals had been won by Real Madrid, Benfica, Milan or Inter. By 1967 the Spanish club had lifted the trophy on half a dozen occasions. Nowadays, people deplore the concentration of football power in a few countries, but there had been even less diversity in Stein's time. The combination of pride and the wish to tease the looming neighbour to the south saw Celtic hailed as the first British club to take the trophy. Stein himself would consider the landmark and its ramifications in a more measured way. 'What Celtic did in 1967', he observed towards the end of his life, 'was worth an awful lot because it brought something new to the game and created new targets. British clubs got to the European Cup final after that because they knew it was possible. We didn't think it was possible until we began to get nearer and then we started to think that anything could happen. But it was us who opened the door.'

Official recognition of Stein's coup was restricted. He was not to be knighted, although Matt Busby received that honour once he had taken the trophy with Manchester United the following year. Of course, Busby was also hailed for all that he had done, whether in helping rebuild Old Trafford after its devastation during the war or in assembling a new team after the tragedy of the Munich air crash in 1958, which ultimately caused twenty-three fatalities, eight of them players. The discrepancy with Stein arose, too, from the mayhem of the Intercontinental Cup, in which Stein's European Cup winners faced the holders of South America's Copa Libertadores. Celtic won 1–0 against the Argentine side Racing Club at Hampden before losing 2–1 in Buenos Aires. In the latter game, the veteran Ronnie Simpson was struck on the head before kick-off by an object, sometimes said to be a brick, and had to be replaced in goal by John Fallon. Since away goals did not apply, a third match was needed. Celtic lost it 3–1 in the neutral setting of Montevideo, Uruguay. The Scots, much as they felt wronged and cheated, had four men sent off, with two leaving the field early for Racing.

In 2007 papers released under the Freedom of Information Act confirmed that Stein had originally been denied official recognition because of those scenes in Montevideo. His name was taken off the New Year Honours List for 1968. Stein got a CBE two years later, while a knighthood had already gone to the club's chairman, even though Bob Kelly had achieved far less. The manager is saluted best and most lastingly in the appreciation of what he brought about in football. Stein's victory over the conservatism that had been in vogue led to a broader liberation. Within seven years of the Scottish triumph in Lisbon the trophy would go not just to England but to the Netherlands and West Germany as well. Stein suffered for that awakening, since Feyenoord would beat a jaded Celtic in the 1970 European Cup final.

For a stimulating period, it had been his side that made iconoclastic history. The future centre half and captain McNeill was signed in 1957, the year that Stein stopped being a player. As a youngster the notion of modernity and even revolution would have seemed preposterous to McNeill at a club that plodded along and unthinkingly did whatever it had become accustomed to doing. There was also a lack of thoughtful training, although Stein was on the backroom staff for three years after his retirement from playing the game. Arrangements were rudimentary. 'You wouldn't become a full-timer until you were maybe twenty-one or twenty-two,' says McNeill, who joined Celtic as a seventeen-year-old. 'I used to meet some of the boys and get the number 9, Auchenshuggle tram [from the city centre, where the player then had his day job]. On the winter nights there were two lights, one on the corner of the main stand and the other on the corner of the Jungle [north enclosure]. You basically ran round the track and up and down the terracing. There was very little emphasis on ball work. You seldom saw a ball. They would say, "Aye, you'll get a ball on Saturday." We'd say, "We'll no know what to do with it." The ball wasn't a permanent part of training until big Jock came as manager [in 1965].'

Stein was the first non-Catholic to hold the post at Celtic. Although a completely sectarian employment policy would have been an absurd self-erected barrier to success in a country where Protestants are in the majority, there were sensitivities. The manager's office and directors' box had been occupied solely by Catholics until then. Stein's widow Jean did not think that Bob Kelly, despite being on good terms with him, had really waved the then coach off to Dunfermline as part of a masterful scheme that would ready him for the post of Celtic manager. Nobody who was well informed believed at the time that there was such a plan. The key intermediary in the appointment, the journalist Jim Rodger, had been used to sound out Stein, and he had no inkling that any grand, long-term strategy was being pursued. All he told the Celtic coach was that the manager's job at Dunfermline was already his since the board at East End Park had settled on his appointment and only wished to get acquainted with him.

When Stein was brought back to Celtic, it was plain desperation that prompted the outbreak of open-mindedness.

The west of Scotland's divisions were normally so profound in that era that they looked permanent. After Stein had come from Llanelly to join Celtic as a player in 1951 there was a silly, persistent rumour that he had a tattoo of King Billy on his chest. The joke lingered and a couple of decades later there were mischievous players who liked to refer to this supposed decoration on their manager's torso when they knew fans were eavesdropping. The cultural and religious tensions had not been so comic at the time Stein was signed as a centre half. His father was in a quandary on the day of matches against Rangers. 'I hope it's a draw,' he would say.

The son was not cut out for compromise. Celtic needed him badly when he was appointed in March 1965 because despair over the decay of a club without a trophy since the rout of Rangers in the League Cup final of 1957 had encouraged an exodus. At the beginning of the 1960s a young McNeill felt almost abandoned as senior players departed. 'In quick succession Bobby Evans, Bertie Peacock, and Willie Fernie all went,' he says, 'but there was no formula for developing youngsters. We were just going round that track. The actual practicalities of football weren't dealt with.

'Myself, Paddy Crerand, Mike Jackson, John Divers and Bertie Auld, who was a bit older than us but still in the same category, got a lot of games in the first team but there was no real development.'

McNeill spent a year or two resisting the temptation to jump ship from a becalmed Celtic, who were particularly affected by the switch to Everton of the hardy yet deft midfielder Bobby Collins. 'I was very close to going to Liverpool and to Tottenham,' McNeill says. 'Maurice Norman was the Spurs centre half and he was getting towards the end of his career. Bill Nicholson [the manager] got in touch.' Dave Mackay, the Scotland midfielder who had already moved to White Hart Lane, told McNeill pointedly that he had been as mad about Hearts as the centre half was about Celtic, but had made a realistic decision all the same.

McNeill resisted the approaches. 'Liz and I had just got married,' he says. 'I was happy as Larry. Celtic was where I wanted to be. The money didn't seem that important. If I had had any sense it would have been, because what they offered, in comparison to Celtic, was massive. It was four times what I was getting at Celtic.' Over the following year or two disillusionment did begin to creep over McNeill. 'I had made up my mind that I had had enough and that I would move on. I was twenty-five. Then Big Jock came back. When he went in 1960, all the ideas left. I was very lucky. Jock had a car and he used to drop off myself, John Clark and a lad called Jim Conway after training. He was great. He would talk to us about football. He would talk to the younger players about what they should and shouldn't be doing. He took an interest in us. But then he went off to Dunfermline and we were back to square one. When he came back I knew good things would happen. If I had gone all that glory would have disappeared. It would have annoyed me.'

For all Stein's relentlessness, there was warmth and fun when appropriate. It was the practice in those times for sides to spend the night after an away match in Europe at their hotel, and players would generally hit the town. If there was little or no reporting of this, it may have been because the travelling press were also socialising and, in any case, would confine their coverage to the matches themselves. The team also tended to know where the limits lay. Stein, at the height of his powers, could let players develop until they had a confidence that did not normally topple over into self-indulgence or rebellion.

A mere disciplinarian would have floundered when dealing with Jimmy Johnstone at Celtic. The winger's errant ways had an oddity to them that made him perhaps the most cherished of Scotland's cast of miscreants. After a night's drinking with other members of the national team in 1974, he was pushed out into the Firth of Clyde in a rowing boat that lacked oars. Johnstone had to be picked up by the coastguard, but he himself was so well equipped to rescue others on a football pitch that the manager, Willie Ormond, kept him in the Scotland side. He was the key to the defeat of England three days later. Stein himself was shrewdly tolerant where a precious asset was concerned, and the winger's value meant that the manager had to be careful not to punish himself with ruinous emphasis on perfect discipline. Getting rid of Johnstone for breaching a rule would have ensured an early close to his time at the club that would have hampered Celtic as much as the winger.

Stein did everything he could to monitor him, and Johnstone was amazed that the manager's intelligence network kept him informed of his activities in the most obscure and shabby pubs. On occasion, Stein would put on a fake accent when calling a particular bar where his player was drinking and ask to speak to him. A fiery blast followed when Johnstone put the phone to his ear. Given the prolonged attention needed to keep the winger under some degree of control, it felt as if he was in constant rehabilitation, but Johnstone was easy to pardon because of his uncanny gifts. His jinks, those twists and changes of direction that threw opponents off balance, seemed always to come as a fresh shock to defenders regardless of how often they had suffered them in the past. It was a simple trick that kept on flummoxing opponents, and that artistry made him a prime target.

The danger was constant. Then, there was an unspoken agreement that those of exceptional talent could be subjected to extreme violence on the pitch, as if a balance was desirable in the ancient encounter between virtuoso and brute. Johnstone, who had feared that he was too puny ever to be become a professional, had pulled on his father's pit boots when he went running in the field behind the family home. He understood that it was essential to put more muscle on his legs if he was to get clear of opponents who were momentarily off-balance. It is briefly startling to realise that the virtuosos only reached such status with the aid of sheer doggedness. By his own reckoning, Johnstone still came close to rejection. Celtic farmed him out to the Junior (non-League) side Blantyre Celtic. The winger believed he was being jettisoned gently. A Celtic trainer called Jimmy Gribben told him that he would never have been brought back to the club had it not been, ridiculous as it is to our ears, for his display with the Central League Junior team against a select side drawn from the Irish B League.

Gribben's effect on Celtic's affairs was profound. The trainer's influence had been great when Jock Stein came back to Scotland from Wales in 1951 because his wife was distressed by a break-in at the family home in Lanarkshire, where she was still living. Celtic turned out to be his destination merely because of Gribben. The trainer kept insisting to chairman Bob Kelly and manager Jimmy McGrory that a 29-year-old journeyman of a centre half steeped in the realities of the game would be of use. Gribben was an unseen hand in Celtic's affairs. He also argued constantly that the club had to believe in the young Johnstone no matter how weak and inappropriate for professional sport the winger seemed as a teenager.

Gribben, a man in a little-noticed post, was not forgotten by those who saw his impact at close hand. Jim Craig, right back in Celtic's greatest team, illustrated the real status of this employee when he described the homecoming after the glories of Lisbon in 1967: 'Jock Stein carried the European Cup off the bus and once inside turned left towards the boot room, where old Jimmy Gribben, the former assistant trainer [who was also sponge man and scout in his time] got the first feel of the trophy.' When a testimonial game against Liverpool was played for Stein in August 1978, three months after he had left his post at the club, the manager made sure that Gribben was saluted in the match programme. 'Jimmy', he wrote,

> was my mentor, the man responsible for Sir Robert Kelly bringing me back from Wales to Parkhead. Jimmy was one

of the real backroom boys, a good player in his day, an able coach. Never in the public eye, he did a remarkable job at Celtic Park. No one knew more about football than Jimmy Gribben. He was my friend and my advisor. Jimmy is long gone now, but I will never forget him. He taught me much, especially in my apprenticeship days as a coach and manager.

While Gribben was a boon to the young Johnstone, it is also true that the winger would prove he properly belonged on the grand stages of the sport. Humbled opponents could become eloquent in their disbelief. Nantes, easily beaten by Celtic in the first round proper on their way to the European Cup final, marvelled, and their defender Jean-Claude Suaudeau said that attempting to mark Johnstone was like trying to pin a wave to the sand. Opponents who had been overwhelmed and humiliated could feel fondness for him once the match was long over. He was hard to forget in any setting. Robert Duvall played the part of the manager of a lower-division Scottish club in the film *A Shot at Glory*, which was released in 2000, and got to know Johnstone during the filming. The player died of motor neurone disease six years later, but he was still prominent in Duvall's mind in 2010. 'The most interesting guy I ever met was the ex-soccer player Jimmy Johnstone, from Celtic,' said the actor and director. 'What a character: the voices, the rhythms, the speech patterns . . . and he'd sing to me like Neil Diamond. He'd drink and come on to women. I named a dog after him.'

There was certainly a spontaneity to Johnstone. In retirement, he never was the type to be the curator of his own career. Only Johnstone could have got confused, as he did in one conversation, and suggest tentatively that Celtic had been beaten by Aberdeen in the 1967 Scottish Cup final. No other player or fan has forgotten that the club won every trophy it went for that season. Johnstone was free of solemnity, but there was, too, a meagre supply of responsibility. Stein was proud of keeping the player in the top flight for so long, yet the achievement was relative. Johnstone was just thirty when Celtic released him in 1975, and he did nothing of note while meandering downwards through clubs of diminishing significance as he gradually ceased to be a player.

His popularity could not flag purely because he had gone. Children, indoctrinated by their parents, would flock to Johnstone when, in retirement, he came to Celtic Park. A statue of him now stands near the main entrance, but solemnity would be exactly the wrong tone in which to commemorate him. He embodied sheer fun when he embarrassed opponents who had so much height and power to pit against him. Johnstone was as uncontainable on the field as he was in his private life. Nothing deterred him and, despite standing a mere 5ft 3in, there were occasions when he would score with headers from corner kicks. However the irrepressibility manifested itself, Johnstone was impossible to subdue when fit and motivated.

Stein got the very best out of him on a November night in 1968. Johnstone had a terror of flying and was promised that he would be excused from boarding the plane to Belgrade for the return leg of a European Cup tie with Red Star so long as Celtic won by at least a four-goal margin. Some teammates, who had not known about the deal, were baffled when Johnstone celebrated the last goal in the 5–1 win by screaming 'I'm no going' as he ran back for the restart. This showed a curious ignorance of popular newspapers, considering that the manager had revealed the arrangement in his regular *Sunday Mirror* column three days earlier. Special treatment was wise where the winger was concerned. Despite the courage Johnstone displayed on the field, he was also riddled with insecurities. He was mired in the reserves when Stein was appointed, and just before a second-string match with Hibernian the new manager walked up to him in the dressing room and said simply, 'What are you doing here? You're too good for this.'

It was a plain remark that struck deep, and Stein had more luck than most in getting through to Johnstone. The key to

Celtic's impact on the field was often Bobby Murdoch, a wonderful passer whose lack of mobility became less of a handicap when Stein assigned him a deeper role than he had previously held. Murdoch, in particular, was essential in getting the ball to Johnstone, but he always felt that he had to supply compliments as well as passes to maintain his teammate's confidence over the course of a match. Johnstone was at his most buoyant on the spacious Hampden pitch when overwhelming the England left back Terry Cooper as Celtic beat Leeds United in the 1970 European Cup semi-final. The opposition would have been unpopular even if they had not been English, and their manager Don Revie, viewed as a cynic or worse, was widely disliked. The Leeds squad had been assembled at far greater cost than Celtic's, and that deepened the contrast further, although the extraordinary impact of the Scottish club's youth-development programme had cancelled out the economic imbalance.

If anything it was Leeds who suffered, because of the populist dislike for their affluent cynicism. Given the various factors, the tie was irresistible and, with the return leg moved to spacious Hampden, the record attendance for a European tie was set in Glasgow, with an official total of 136,505. Celtic had already won 1–0 at Elland Road with a goal from George Connelly after forty seconds of a match in which Johnstone had been at his most elusive. While no one spurns an away victory, it can leave a team in a quandary as to how they should approach the second game. The dilemma was soon lifted from them, even if gratitude was not the immediate reaction when the outstanding Leeds side tied the aggregate score with a long-range drive from their Scottish captain Billy Bremner. If Celtic had to start all over again, it meant at least that the match had been simplified. They merely had to pull level and, for safety's sake, take the lead. They did so in the second half, equalising with a header by John Hughes before the low drive from Murdoch that defeated Leeds.

It is an occasion still gloated over now, even by those who happen not to have been alive at the time. The Leeds players were sportsmanlike, but the admission of, say, the respected Cooper that he had been powerless to deal with Johnstone merely intensified the glee. There was an eventual wish that the game at Hampden could overshadow everything. The 1970 European Cup final itself, after all, is an occasion that the club would much prefer to plunge into perpetual darkness.

Celtic were ultimately beaten 2–1 by Feyenoord in Milan. The Scots had led through Gemmell, but were helpless against the passing and movement of their opponents. Defeat did not come until a winner from the Swede Ove Kindvall three minutes from the end of extra time, just when it seemed that Celtic would survive for an unmerited replay. There was a fad for blaming the outcome on complacency in Stein or his men, but that is too comfortable a conclusion since it carries the flattering implication that their reduced level of performance had been the key element to the outcome.

Feyenoord paved the way for the 'total football' that made Ajax European champions three times in succession from 1971. Celtic's breakthrough in 1967 had been a moment of liberation. Stein captured the tone of his team with complete precision when he said, 'We must not be too clever . . . we must only be clever.' The 1967 final was, too, a turning point in the history of the game because it made precautionary football look like a folly. Inter did not just suffer a defeat in Lisbon, they were brought to the end of a time in which their efficiency cowed opponents. The side had taken the trophy in 1964 and 1965 before going out to the eventual winners Real Madrid in the semi-finals the following year.

Such relentlessness is bound to have an underpinning of authority, and Helenio Herrera was among the first to swathe the post of manager with the mystique that is now associated as a matter of course with people at the peak of the profession. He was born in Argentina of a Spanish mother and a father of North American descent. As such, he could virtually have been genetically engineered for a sport that was beginning to appreciate its global standing. A modern audience can understand him best by seeing him as the forerunner of José Mourinho, who himself accentuated the resemblance when becoming manager of Inter in 2008 and going on, two years later, to take the European Cup back to the club for the first time since 1965, when Herrera was in charge. The latter might not have had the sulky charisma of the Portuguese, and neither was there a worldwide media to be held in thrall. Even so, the manager devised an identity for himself.

His widow Fiora kept his handwritten notes and drawings before publishing a selection of them in 2010. She also told the journalist Marcela Mora y Araujo that, while recovering in hospital from a broken leg, he had been struck by the notion of holy men retreating into the wilderness to find spiritual renewal. This supposedly led to him becoming committed to '*il ritiro*', the withdrawal of a squad to a secluded location before key games that once seemed a particular preference of Italian clubs. The wish for control is normal in a manager, but in the case of someone such as Herrera it is virtually a fixation. He had an aura of command that was encapsulated in aphorisms such as, 'The worst thing is to make a mistake with someone else's ideas,' or, 'He who plays for himself plays for the opposition.'

The latter insight underpinned his conviction that the triumph of the team calls, to some degree, for the subjugation of the individual. 'Style is in limitation,' Herrera insisted. It would be a travesty to deny that his team could play to a very high standard when necessary, and Herrera had not wholly become estranged from the joy of the game. 'Touching the ball is good for the mind,' he asserted with endearing simplicity. None the less, Herrera was the type of manager who dreams of dictating victory, detail by detail, from the sidelines.

Subterfuge was part of the repertoire. When he came to see Celtic play Rangers as part of his preparations for the final, he had suggested that Stein fly back with him in a private jet for Inter's match with Juventus the following day. At the last moment Herrera announced that this would no longer possible. There were apparently only three passenger seats, two of them already reserved for the sons of the then Inter president Angelo Moratti (one of them, Massimo, is the current head of the club). Stein had been too wise to cancel his original booking and made it to the match, even if a wearisome journey entailed changing planes in Rome. On arrival in Turin it emerged that the promised arrangements had not been made, yet Stein and the accompanying Scottish journalist, John Mackenzie, still got into the Stadio Comunale with the brandishing of a press card.

The difference between the Celtic manager and Herrera was fundamental. Stein, too, was a sly character who laid down tactics and unquestionably imposed his will, but leeway was almost always allowed for impulse and self-expression from his men. There was a subtlety to a manager who knew the harm he might do by issuing a torrent of instructions from the sidelines. He did not forget what it is like to be a footballer caught up in the maelstrom of a match. Stein once explained the delicate nature of a game and how it can be damaged by an unwarranted intrusion, particularly when the only people within earshot are on the wing closest to the dugout. 'You might get the message over to a player, who is playing well, to pass on, but it might put him off,' he said.

The manager was counting on players who had developed their identity in games played in the streets and public parks long before any club took control of them. Scottish football, to its occasional and heavy cost, has always been in thrall to the daydream of untutored virtuosos who trounce the doltishly diligent foe. Stein, all the same, was lucky in his timing. His zenith as a manager coincided with the last phase in which Scotland could hardly stop itself from producing accomplished footballers. In England, with Denis Law at his most glamorous and potent for Manchester United, the leading Scots were forerunners of the exotic stars from mainland Europe and other continents who are now vital to the status of the Premier League. That still left an abundance of excellence north of the border.

The return of Stein to the East End of Glasgow took him to a club where a torrent of talent thundered through the ranks. Football still mesmerised the city and surrounding areas, but the 1960s also introduced a free-spiritedness and iconoclasm. That was of use to Stein since the rebelliousness was certainly not going to be a danger to him. This, after all, was still an era in which a player remained the property of a club even when his contract had expired. Footballers enjoyed no freedom of movement and could, in theory, have their careers destroyed by being both dropped and denied the right to switch to another club. A player's bargaining power lay mostly in the harm done to his transfer price if left to moulder on the sidelines.

It was the promise of great achievement that did most for stability at Celtic. The side finished eighth in the League in 1965, but there was time for the newly arrived Stein to draw an indelible line between his era and the bumbling days that had preceded it. His side won the Scottish Cup that year to bring the club its first trophy since 1957. The manner of the success was at least as significant as the prize. Celtic had to come from behind twice against Dunfermline, and the winner was supplied by Billy McNeill when he headed in a Charlie Gallagher corner.

The defender got into the habit of making that same impact at the critical instant. In the quarter-final of the 1967 European Cup against the Yugoslav club Vojvodina, who were the most tenacious team the Scots met that season, the aggregate score was 1–1 as the return leg at Celtic Park entered the last minute. Penalty shoot-outs had not yet been introduced, and a third match at a pre-arranged neutral venue would have been required. 'It's going to be bloody Rotterdam,' Stein grumbled to his assistant Sean Fallon just as McNeill climbed to head in another of those Gallagher corners to beat Vojvodina. The manager explained his attitude afterwards: 'I thought of all the fixtures we still had to play. I was crushed by these 75,000 folk up in the stands and on the terracing. And I thought, "I've let them down."'

That could be regarded as a crass remark made in a blaze of manipulative populism, but the affinity with the audience was simpler to maintain in those days. Although he was comparatively well off, Stein was part of an era in which a manager would bet on racehorses but not actually own them. His days as a Celtic defender also meant that the relationship with the crowd had been so sustained that there was an intimacy to it. Stein could certainly flatter those fans, but he also recognised a need to lead and even reproach them. In August 1972 Stein waded into the midst of the visiting supporters at half-time during a League Cup tie with Stirling Albion at Annfield and rebuked them for sectarian singing. He did not attempt to deflect attention from the matter either. 'Surely there are enough Celtic songs without introducing religion or politics or anything else?' he said. By and large, success was Stein's best way of lifting supporters out of a type of parochialism.

Celtic's passage into the 1967 European Cup semi-finals, where Dukla Prague were eliminated with a 3–1 victory in Glasgow and a goalless draw in Czechoslovakia, was one more step away from the claustrophobic obsessions of west of Scotland life. McNeill, whose goal took the side past Vojvodina, was one of many assets who had been waiting to demonstrate their worth. Stein, to some extent, was lucky because the difficulties at Celtic lay in outdated coaching and the interference in team selection from the boardroom. He would not have come back to the club without ensuring there would no longer be such hindrances. With those matters settled, Stein could rejoice in the luck he had in inheriting a fine squad, several of whom he already knew from that stint as a Celtic coach at the end of the 1950s. Of the line-up that won the European Cup, Willie Wallace alone had been bought by the new manager.

Despite the means at the club, a side had still to be assembled with care and even humility. After all, it was Stein, while with Hibernian, who had felt that Ronnie Simpson was dispensable when he sold the then thirty-three-year-old to Celtic for £2,000 in October 1964. The goalkeeper did not become first choice at his new club for another twelve months, when Stein appreciated what the veteran had to offer in the different environment that had come into being. Building that line-up was a prolonged exercise in common sense and a reminder that few managers stay above the clamour of events for long enough to take a balanced view. Simpson's age had turned into an asset when the Celtic line-up was generally callow. Finding himself outside his penalty area in the European Cup final, for instance, Simpson resolved the problem with a back-heel to John Clark, one of the centre halves. The pieces of this team snapped into place as a perfect fit for one another.

Clark was included for his reading of the game but, at 5ft 8in, would have been a liability in the middle of defence had McNeill not enjoyed such aerial command. Additional height was supplied by the strapping full backs Jim Craig and Tommy Gemmell. At the core of the midfield, Bobby Murdoch was paired with the former winger Bertie Auld, a tough character with intelligence in his passing who was rehabilitated when he came back to Celtic from Birmingham. The roles of the individuals Stein had inherited were redefined in many cases, and the swift Bobby Lennox, once regarded as a winger, was to turn into a prolific scorer when employed to hurtle at defences from deep positions where he could only be marked with difficulty.

When a manager is at his peak, he comes up with the right answer repeatedly as the unending questions roll towards him. Lisbon was the ideal moment for Stein and his men. He himself looked wholly at ease, even if he would have been working furiously to convey the relaxed air. Idealism also underlined the contrast with Herrera, and was designed to hone Celtic's appeal to neutrals. 'If you're ever going to win the European Cup,' he said, 'then this is the day and this is the place. But we don't just want to win this Cup, we want to do it playing good football – to make neutrals glad we've won it, glad to remember how we did it.' It was the ideal moment for Stein and his men, yet he also needed to keep those players at ease since that was the best protection against a stage fright that was less likely to affect the professionals of Inter.

Stein could hardly have been sure of the truth about the opposition, but, in retrospect, it does seem that Inter might have been too battle-worn by then. Given his record, Herrera's methods cannot be ridiculed, but the isolation gnawed at his men to an unusual extent in the build-up to the final in Lisbon, perhaps because they suspected that their best days at the club were behind them. As usual for such an occasion, Inter booked an entire hotel. It was on the coast, half an hour from the city. 'There was nobody there, except for the players and the coaches,' said the right back Tarcisio Burgnich. 'By that stage, even we had reached our breaking point. None of us could sleep. I was lucky if I got three hours a night. All we did was obsess over the match and the Celtic players. Giacinto Facchetti [the left back] and I would stay up and listen to our skipper, Armando Picchi, vomiting from the tension in the next room.'

It had not been all that long since their manager had sounded fully at ease. Before the second leg of the quarter-final with Real Madrid, he had said: 'I am quite sure we will win the European Cup. The only team, apart from Real, that gives me any concern are Celtic. They are very fast, very robust and quite ruthless when their opponents make a mistake. But I doubt whether they would beat us in the final in Lisbon. After all, we would only need one goal to win.'

By the time of that match Inter had started to feel embattled because of a rising unpopularity. On the Sunday before the final McNeill had been playing golf near the club's Ayrshire base and was taken aback when an Italian cameraman wished him luck in Lisbon. The person was not necessarily a Milan fan. Distaste for Herrera's approach to football and his arrogant manner was on the rise, with plenty of antipathy left over for the petroleum-magnate owner Moratti. There was indignation, too, for the allegedly favourable treatment accorded to Inter. Herrera's men had advantages, but the contempt shown towards them was taking its toll.

Such an account has its element of retrospective excuse-making for Inter, but the contrast with Celtic was indisputable. The match happened to take place on the feast of Corpus Christi, a Holy Day of Obligation, when Catholics are obliged to attend Mass. Churches were bound to be busy given the presence of an estimated 10,000 Celtic fans in Lisbon. It was all splendid source material for Stein as he maintained an easy-going tone. 'Tell me,' he asked Hugh McIlvanney, 'the nine o'clock and ten o'clock Masses are all-ticket?' The manager could switch suddenly to an earnest and even principled discussion of the match to come. 'Cups are not won by individuals,' he said, 'but by men in a team who put their club before personal prestige. I am lucky – I have the players who do just that for Celtic.'

Without being bombastic, Stein conveyed pride in the side and its readiness to outdo Inter. He was not to be diverted into comment on Luis Suárez, the opposition's playmaker, who was then struggling to get over an injury. 'That's not my problem,' he said, despite fearing that the Spaniard was actually in fine fettle. The Celtic manager was willing to record his appreciation of the opposition, its tactical acumen and its stars such as Facchetti and Sandro Mazzola, but these were detours in a speech whose destination was always an affirmation of his own men as an exceptional force whose moment had come. The Belgian newspaper La Meuse quoted Stein's trust in a Celtic line-up 'capable of bringing any side to its knees; they're fearless, they're Scotsmen'.

The afternoon was so perfect that even adversity served his side well. They conceded the opener after eight minutes, when Sandro Mazzola converted the penalty awarded for Jim Craig's foul on Renato Cappellini. That opener had a liberating effect. It was now essential that Celtic follow their instincts and attack with energy and gusto. The Inter side, for their part, knew they were coming towards the end of a spell of ascendancy in the club's history. Suárez did indeed miss the final, but even if they had been free of hindrances Inter would still have followed their habit by shunning risk as they sought to negotiate their way to the full-time whistle in Lisbon. That strategy could hardly have been more foolish since it invited Celtic to settle down into the rhythmic attacking which suited them best. Their boundless energy was a concern for Herrera's men, who lingered in the dressing room at half-time while their punctual opponents had to stand in the sun and await the start of the second half.

Nothing could have drained the energy from Celtic then. Inter concentrated on blocking Johnstone, but that left space for others to run free. It epitomised Stein's side that they should equalise with a goal concocted by the two full backs. After sixty-two minutes, Craig strode into the penalty area and, with the opposition probably anticipating a shot, pulled the ball back into the path of Gemmell. The left back connected with his customary power and the drive soared past the goalkeeper Giuliano Sarti. By then Inter were in despair as an exhilarated Celtic tore through them. Burgnich saw and heard the anguish: 'I remember Picchi turned to Sarti and said, "Giuliano, let it go, just let it go. It's pointless, sooner or later they'll get the winner." I never imagined my captain would tell our keeper to throw in the towel. But that only shows how destroyed we were.'

Glory was inevitable after Gemmell's goal, and Stevie Chalmers, who had been with Celtic for eight years and knew how down-at-heel the club had become, had the honour of scoring the winner. He was a forward alive to the randomness of the penalty area, and when Murdoch miscued a drive in the eighty-fifth minute he reacted to turn it into the net. Happiness radiated to virtually every corner of Europe. If anything, Celtic may not have understood the impression they had made in country upon country. Across the continent, newspapers reported that a Scottish team had set football free from Herrera's prison.

1. Patsy Gallacher was one of Celtic's greatest entertainers, but he had a tactical intelligence to complement the individualism.
2. Jimmy McGrory leaves the field after the 1937 Scottish Cup final victory over Aberdeen. It was the last winners' medal of the prolific striker's career.

Clockwise from top left: 3. John O'Hara did much, as secretary, to establish Celtic. He was a trade unionist who later became wealthy in the drinks trade. 4. Willie Maley was with Celtic as player and then manager for 52 years. He relished his absolute authority over footballers. 5. Bob Kelly. The steely and idealistic Celtic chairman from 1947 to 1971 was a meddler in team matters until Jock Stein's appointment. 6. John Glass. He was the most determined of the founders, paying leading players well to join Celtic in a supposedly amateur era.

GLASGOW   28TH FEBRUARY. 1940

7. Jock Stein. The club's greatest manager did so well at
Dunfermline and Hibernian that Celtic had to give him complete command.

8. Willie Maley was a passionate royalist. Soon after being
forced out of his job at Celtic in 1940 he was introduced to
King George VI.

9. Flax Flaherty, newspaper seller and close friend of Jock
Stein, holds the European Cup won by Celtic in 1967.
10. John Cushley, Bobby Murdoch and Jimmy Johnstone (left
to right) in Red Square, en route to a 1966 match with Dinamo
Kiev played in Tbilisi.

11. Billy McNeill returned as Celtic manager in 1987. Maurice Johnston, seen here, left for Nantes and later signed for Rangers.

12. Fergus McCann. The owner who rebuilt the ground in the 1990s did not always get a fair hearing from fans, but his impact was great.

13. Gordon Strachan. After winning three League titles (2006–08) and making an impression in Europe he was still undervalued by some.

14. Paul McStay. He often suffered because of mediocrity around him, but excelled in the Double-winning centenary year of 1988.

15. Henrik Larsson. The club and the striker, who cost just £650,000 in 1997, galvanised each other after both had been in the doldrums.

16. Martin O'Neill. The manager who took Celtic to the 2003 Uefa Cup final inspired excitement with a side containing some high-profile players.

17. Neil Lennon. In his first job as a manager, he has been reshaping the squad while enduring death threats. A suspect package was intercepted.

It was Inter who entered a dungeon. They returned to Italy and lost their Serie A title a week later with a defeat at Mantova, where Sarti, who had been flawless in Lisbon, conceded a goal to a cross-cum-shot. The goalkeeper's reaction to the miscalculation was to bash his head repeatedly against the post. Herrera ought to have yelped, too, since he had sneered, not all that long before, that Juventus had more chance of winning the national lottery than Serie A. For the sake of completeness Inter were then knocked out in the semi-final of the Coppa Italia by Padova, a lower-division side. No one spared much compassion for Herrera and Moratti.

The suggestion that Inter would never be quite the same again until the advent of Mourinho might be taken as a piece of Scottish self-satisfaction were it not for the fact that the club's followers felt a keen and lasting hurt over Lisbon. Gianpiero Lotito, co-author of a 2006 history of the club, said that his most enduring memory where Inter are concerned is of the loss in Lisbon, when he was an eight-year-old: 'I just could not bear to carry on watching the match on television. I went down to a courtyard below my house to play with a cloth ball. My mother came to the window from time to time to let me know the progress of the match, right to the end.'

In 1967 the Milan-based *Gazzetta dello Sport* had not concentrated on a lament for Inter's loss in Lisbon. The 'boundless vigour' of Celtic was saluted, and any accolade for the losers was presented to Sarti for preventing a rout. In Germany, the *Stuttgarter Zeitung* detected climate change in the sport's environment: 'Celtic did the biggest service to football on this continent since Real Madrid's heyday by showing to a football public of millions that attacking football pays.' In France, *Le Parisien Libéré* acclaimed an 'extraordinary spectacle' and declared that the tournament had never seen 'such an explosion of joy' as the one that detonated inside the thousands of Scots at the Estádio Nacional.

Celtic were in the ideal, and transient, state where talent, zest and know-how converge. Without a thought having been given to the matter a balance was struck between the achievement that set these men apart and the background they had in common with their fans. They were feted as the trophy was flaunted on a lap of honour at Celtic Park, but the vehicle from which the players waved to the crowd was a builders' lorry that belonged to the local firm R. D. Stewart. It just happened to be around because some work was being carried out at the ground, and the man behind the wheel was a former player, John McAlindon, who had a job at the club as a maintenance man.

While Celtic would barely have understood then that their success rested on spontaneity, a German journalist marvelled at the players in the San Siro dressing room following a goalless draw with AC Milan in 1969. He understood that they were free of the regimentation and neurosis associated with some of the more august clubs. 'Look at them, they are the most feared team in Europe yet they are as happy as schoolboys,' he murmured in similar terms to so many of his counterparts on the continent. No fan or footballer wanted to walk away from the homely ecstasy that saw the European Cup on board a lorry, but nothing could be precisely as it was after the glory of Lisbon. At a team meeting before the following season, Stein said, 'For some of you football will never be the same again.' He may have intended to challenge the squad to prove him wrong, but the manager had actually spoken the plain truth.

None the less, Celtic did win nine consecutive League titles from 1966 to 1974. In addition, more youngsters of uncanny ability continued to arrive. There was keen anticipation over the prospects of some players, such as Vic Davidson, a midfielder who turned out to lack athleticism, or Paul Wilson, who eventually proved inconsistent even by the standards of wingers. However, Celtic could afford to be philosophical about those who did not make the grade when others were startlingly effective. Danny McGrain became one of the best right backs in the world and spent twenty years as a player at the club, partly because a fractured skull, a troublesome ankle injury and the diabetes diagnosed in 1974 seemed to keep him out of the marketplace. George Connelly, who was just twenty when he walked the ball round the Rangers goalkeeper to score in the 1969 Scottish Cup final, became a sweeper who could utilise his long passing from a deep position.

He was a loner and his dislike of the top-level football environment was clear to the public from the moment in 1973 when he chose not to board a plane taking the Scotland squad to a match with Switzerland. Connelly was destabilised in various ways. His friend David Hay was sold to Chelsea in 1974, and Stein's efforts to counsel Connelly failed. The manager was powerless in the face of a player who was reported to have insisted that he would prefer to be a lorry driver since he wouldn't have to put up with any more training sessions. More recently Connelly has claimed that any such remark was intended as a joke, but he had been dissatisfied with his wages. The player's final appearance for the club came in the autumn of 1976, when he was twenty-six, and he drifted to lower levels that saw him end his playing career at non-league Sauchie.

The abundance of prodigies made even such episodes tolerable. Lou Macari was a sharp-witted goal scorer, even if he could not be prevented from going to Manchester United as a twenty-three-year-old in January 1973. One of the most prominent figures in Celtic's history was in far less of a rush to be gone, although it may be that the club made an exception in Kenny Dalglish's case by offering the sort of improved terms that were not open to others. He was no devotee of the club and as a young man his passion for Rangers was so intense that he cut short a trial with Liverpool so he could get back to Glasgow and watch an Old Firm match at Ibrox. Dalglish was none the less a player to consider matters carefully. After being signed by Celtic, he was insistent on remaining a part-timer until he had completed his apprenticeship as a joiner that would ensure, if need be, an alternative profession.

Dalglish and his peers were in no position to take anything for granted. Macari grew up in Largs, on the Firth of Clyde, and as a youngster needed a fifty-minute trip by rail and two bus journeys so that he could train with Celtic on one night a week. Delays were feasible, but not tolerable to Stein. 'You had to make sure you weren't late because Jock would be there,' Macari says. 'He would go mad if you were late. It was just the case that you had to be at Celtic Park for half past six. No excuses.' There was no delusion for Macari either that he enjoyed a special favour when a decision had to be taken after two years over whether he should be signed. 'It was quite a daunting prospect when they called you in because there would be no parent or agent with you in those days,' he says. 'You're punching the air when you make it but little do you know that you're not on a road to stardom, you're just on a road.'

Macari's perspective differs from outsiders agog at the spectacle of so many emerging players. For him, there was no inherent reason why, say, Dalglish should go on to win three European Cups with Liverpool, as well as 102 caps for Scotland. There is a distaste for hindsight, and Macari puts the emphasis on the improvement to the young players that Stein planned and supervised. He makes the point by recalling the early version of Dalglish, which had a basic flaw. 'If he had a deficiency then,' says Macari, 'it was his goal-scoring ability. Jock used to get him take a bag of balls out onto an empty park and smash them into the net and go through the routine of a goal scorer.'

Macari is even more scathing about the inadequacies at that age of a band who would in the end be remembered as the Quality Street kids: 'If it hadn't been for Jock, his methods and what he demanded, none of us would have made it. I back that up with my own case. I wasn't strong enough to go and do battle in England. That's for certain. I wasn't ready at all. I remember having to battle for Scotland schoolboys at Southampton. The pitch was heavy, the ball was heavy, the England team was six foot. I never got a kick and I was hopeless. If anybody had been watching me, there was no way they would have considered taking me to a football club.'

Delusions had, in any case, been outlawed for Celtic's youths. 'Jock was always there, and discipline was the priority. Nothing was held back and they let you know that this was going to be no easy ride. You'd be at Celtic Park at 9.30 in the morning to get all the kit ready. On the Monday after a Saturday game we'd get the brushes and clean out the whole ground. The terraces would be full of all sorts of crap. If you managed to get it finished by lunch-time your reward was a little training session in the afternoon behind the goals at Celtic Park on the bit of grass there. It would be five-a-sides and everyone was busting a gut to get the cleaning done. The senior players would come back from training and you would pick up their kit, get it to the washroom, clean their boots.'

During the rest of the week he would join the squad in running down to Barrowfield with boots in hand, because they needed their trainers for the pavements. 'Then you would be going about a training session with the Lisbon Lions,' Macari says. 'I don't think the younger players considered that there was a career in front of us. You'd ask how it was going to be possible to make it when these European Cup winners were standing in your way. There's a downside to joining a team that's doing well. Your chances are slimmer. On the other hand, what better way to develop than to be with them and play with them? There was no need for academy systems. You just needed a strict manager who would get you to do your best every single day.

'As a result of that sort of simple method there were hundreds of players coming out of all parts of Scotland in that time. After a couple of hours at training, with no pulling out of tackles, it was back on with the training shoes to run to Celtic Park as fast as you could. Jock would be coming along in his car, and if he thought you were jogging a bit too slow he would wind down the window and tell you to get a move on.'

Bystanders who witnessed such scenes knew for sure that

football truly was part of the community then. Macari himself understood that he had work to do, too. 'I used to get onto the track, put my spikes on and build my stamina,' he says. 'Because of the system at Celtic I was built up and got stronger, quicker. I do believe it was simply down to Jock's direction that I made the grade because at that age you're looking for guidance.'

Macari is also impressed that he received so much assistance, too, from the European Cup-winning players. 'To a man they were superb,' he says. 'Their attitude was brilliant. They were so helpful. Even though you might one day be taking their place, they genuinely wanted you to succeed.' Under Stein, Macari was brought to the fore. He was an unused substitute when Rangers scored a late equaliser in the 1972 Scottish Cup final. A dissatisfied Stein put his squad on the bus to go back immediately to their base at Seamill and begin preparations for the replay, although with no mobile phones it was hard for the players to tell their families where they had gone.

Events worked in Macari's favour. 'There was no indication that I would be picked on the Wednesday night,' he says. 'The thing about announcing the team an hour before kick-off is that it doesn't give a player all that long to crap himself. It was a shock, but Jock had a habit of pulling off these surprises, and the player he brought in usually did something. I scored the opening goal in the 2–1 win. It was the best night of my life until then.'

All the same, the economic trends in the sport were already militating against such simplicity by January 1973. 'I was happy to sign as a Celtic supporter,' says Macari, 'but I got married, there was a kid on the way, I had lost my father and I was helping to support my mother. I was on £50 a week, and when I went in to see about a new contract Jock told me it would be £55. That was after he'd told me how well I had done. I just couldn't afford to accept it. Times had changed, but Celtic hadn't. They probably thought nobody would leave. We were all happy there and the thought of moving never entered your head, but then circumstances change. You go with the Scotland team and people talk about earning £250 a week, while you're getting £50. I think I was looking for £65 or £70. I told Jock I wouldn't accept £55 and that I was going, although I didn't know where.

'I was just pissed off. There were no agents. I was just put in a car and told I was going to England. I didn't ask exactly where. Sean Fallon was in the car and he wouldn't tell me. I was going to Liverpool but I didn't have a clue. We stopped at Southport and it really confused me, never having been in that area. A couple of hours later I was going through the gates at Anfield because there was a game on with Burnley. Bill Shankly was very similar to Jock and quite scary, but Manchester United people happened to be there. Pat Crerand was in the directors' box with Tommy Docherty. They said they'd take me.'

Shankly covered for the bungling that day by claiming that Macari would not have made his starting line-up in any case, but United were happy to spend £200,000 on him. A trend developed, and the sale of Dalglish to Liverpool four years later was inevitable, but Celtic were much less adept by then at identifying and bringing through new players. Indeed, a post-war phase in which Scottish talent was constantly replenished gradually came to an end. Stein, in addition, no longer had the dynamism to overcome handicaps as frequently as he had once done. There were still flickers of dexterity as late as the autumn of 1976, when he bought Hibernian's outstanding midfielder Pat Stanton, who was almost thirty-three, and made him the captain and sweeper in a Celtic team that won the Double that season. Dalglish's ominous departure in the summer was the true landmark. The side went on to finish a humbling fifth in the League the following year, a decline that brought Stein's gleaming era at Celtic to a lacklustre close.

It was understandable that Dalglish would wish to experience football at Anfield, but there was a quantifiable appeal as well. The pay gap between Scotland and England was, and remains, a grave matter. Jim Craig remembers that full-timers received £40 a week in 1966. When he left Celtic six years later, the figure had risen to £52, after the most glorious seasons the club had known. Win bonuses, of course, added substantially to the income, but Billy McNeill wryly points out that only a fool would have banked on receiving them regularly in the early 1960s. It took Stein to make such financial planning feasible. He also began to deal with Celtic's affairs by proxy and used an intermediary to ensure that a player who had been at the club before was persuaded to return. 'Bertie Auld knew, ahead of most of us, that Jock was coming back,' says McNeill. 'There was a man called Dougie Hepburn, a Hearts fan, that big Jock used to sound out people. He went down [to Birmingham] and sounded out Bertie. He told Bertie he would be going back up the road in the next wee while. That was Big Jock planning already what he was going to do.'

There was cunning and the necessary ruthlessness about Stein, but he was nuanced. While the members of his squads would all admit to having been a little afraid of him, a simple tyrant cannot inspire people. There has to be flexibility and humanity before a group can achieve its full potential. Barriers could be lowered, although it took a very special occasion before a player dared to snatch Stein's sun hat from his head and pretend that he was about to throw it into a swimming pool. That happened at the hotel the day after the European Cup was won, and the culprit was the scorer of the equaliser, the bold Tommy Gemmell. The individuality of Stein's men was never quashed because their essential audacity would have been crushed at the same time.

It is the critical and largely unseen task of a manager to create an environment in which everyone can make the most of themselves. While Inter were famed for retreating into a sombre regime at their training ground, Stein, at times, went with the grain of exuberance in his men. It was the custom for Celtic to base themselves at Seamill on the Ayrshire coast while readying themselves for critical matches, but there was fun to offset the solemnity. Within seven weeks of Stein's appointment, Celtic won the Scottish Cup, their first piece of silverware in eight years. On that occasion the preparations took place at another seaside location, Largs. 'We were training at the coaching centre and at night we played all sorts of daft games,' says McNeill, 'so there was serious stuff and relaxation. We won the final and that was the start of it all.'

The last years of his life were spent as Scotland manager. He was slightly past his peak by 1975, when Celtic had finished third in the League, and sustained grave injuries later that summer when a car, travelling on the wrong side of the road, smashed into his. The manager was behind the wheel of a car that belonged to his friend Tony Queen, a bookmaker who was even more badly damaged in the collision. Stein himself was out of football for a year while he recovered and subsequently looked diminished, even if he did complete the League and Cup Double with the club in 1977. That, all the same, may be a formulaic conclusion. His secretary during his stint as Scotland manager, which began the following year, was Marjorie Nimmo. She wisely suggests that he had actually developed a sense of proportion since the crash on the A74. Former 'enemies' such as the SFA secretary Ernie Walker became friends, and Stein also liked to lean his backside against a radiator and revisit old disputes in the company of the former referee Jack Mowat. There were glimpses then of a knack for establishing bonds. He was often heard before he was seen in the SFA offices as his voice drifted out from the lift while he sang some Sinatra standard.

He had scope, too, to express a light-heartedness. When asked to write to a boy who had broken both arms while pretending to be Tarzan, Stein's letter proposed Kenny Dalglish as a safer role model. There was also a demonstration of a knack for fellowship. While driving to work one day he heard on the Jimmy Young programme about the minneola, a cross between a tangerine and a grapefruit. Some of the staff would not believe there was such a thing, so Stein popped out of the office and came back with a bag from the grocer's. Those who had trusted him were presented with a minneola; sceptics had to make do with an orange. In such simple scenes there was an illustration of Stein's ability to forge bonds with and among a group.

He died of a heart attack in 1985 at the end of a match with Wales in which he made the inspired decision to introduce the artistic Davie Cooper when the pace of the action had waned. Cooper himself converted the penalty that secured the necessary point to keep Scotland on course for the World Cup finals. So close to the end of his life, Stein's urgency ensured that his instructions would register, yet his wisdom was, as it always had been, the indispensable factor.

6

'FLAX' FLAHERTY

A man who sells newspapers can have better connections than the people who write for them. Jim 'Flax' Flaherty had a place in the heart of Glasgow life because of his pitch at Queen Street station and the acquaintances that it brought him. He was one of Jock Stein's closest friends and had known the manager when he was still a player. It was more feasible for football figures to mingle with the public in a time when their fame was not accompanied by extreme wealth. Flax, in any case, made a sound living in a period when it was taken for granted that newspapers were a vital source of information.

In the 1950s there was a readership in Glasgow that sustained three evening titles alone. Flax had others who worked for him, and he was free to set off for Celtic Park each lunchtime and bring the players whatever magazines or other publications they wanted. It was particularly urgent that the *Noon Record* should be delivered to Neilly Mochan well ahead of the afternoon racing and betting. Mochan was a Celtic player of the 1950s who came back to the club as a trainer and coach in 1964.

Flax, who ran a supporters club in the north of Glasgow, fitted in well. At the station he was near to the newsagent's owned by the Celtic midfielder of the 1950s Bobby Evans. Stein, as centre half, reserve coach or manager of the club, would have passed through Queen Street for decades. Indeed, the meeting with the chairman Bob Kelly that led to him becoming Celtic manager in 1965 took place in what was then called the North British Hotel, beside the station.

Stein had often lingered in the area since he preferred to bet on the horses at a bookies in Dundas Street, close to Evans's shop. He was part of a little community, and when Real Madrid met Eintracht Frankfurt in the 1960 European Cup final at Hampden Park Stein came up with a ticket for one of the men who worked in the train station. As a Celtic player and then reserve-team coach of the club who was dependent on public transport, it was natural that his job would take him through that part of town. Later, Celtic provided Stein with the Ford Anglia in which he gave lifts as far as Bellshill Cross to young players who lived in Lanarkshire, such as Billy McNeill.

The car must have been off the road when Flax instead drove Stein to Fife for the formality of the job interview in 1960 that brought him his first post as manager, at Dunfermline Athletic. There was an opportunity for Flax to become part of Stein's circle, and he even acted as an unpaid employee of Celtic. The club, at the practical level of day-to-day business, was more or less run then by the office secretary Irene McDonald. On a Tuesday she would go to the Glasgow Cross branch of the Bank of Scotland and take out the money to make up the wage packets. If footballers were paid in cash nowadays, it would be proportionate to have off-duty members of the SAS for company, but McDonald would still have been carrying substantial sums. Yet her escort back to the stadium was Flax, a man who looked in shaky health, was affected by an eye problem and walked with the aid of a stick. It was gallant of him to fill that role, but the Glasgow of the time must, in daylight at least, have been a bit safer than was supposed. There was little that Flax would not undertake on the club's behalf, and he was also an agent for Celtic Pools, which was launched in 1964 as a means of raising money towards stadium development.

If footballers and fans were once closer, it was because there was not such a gulf in income between them. Pat Woods, a historian of Celtic whose father was the Queen Street station employee who received that 1960 European Cup final ticket from Stein, senses a tipping point. 'I have long held the theory', says Woods, 'that Celtic's Lisbon triumph represented a last hurrah for the "Old Glasgow" – the grimy, industrial city which by the mid- to late 1960s was in economic decline, particularly in shipbuilding and engineering. Glasgow was in the throes of redevelopment. It resulted in the virtual flattening of tenemented districts such as Anderston, Townhead and Cowcaddens to make way for high-rise flats and the inner ring road. I had been brought up in Shettleston, in the shadow and sadly the twilight of Parkhead Forge. It closed in 1976.'

The Celtic feats nine years before were watched by people caught up in a time of change for the city as much as the club. There is a picture of a fan at Glasgow airport who had just come back from Lisbon. This toothless man is wearing a heavy coat and a bunnet. A workmate subsequently wrote to the *Celtic View* and identified him as Jimmy McKinlay. He was the gaffer of a Glasgow Corporation demolition squad who specialised, where necessary, in taking down some of the old buildings by hand. 'He never had his teeth in,' John McTigue said of his old boss. 'He kept them in his pocket along with a pipe he always smoked, but for the life of me I don't know how he coped in the heat of Lisbon with his "Paw Broon" outfit on.'

McKinlay caught the eye then, and, for good or ill, fans are indeed more than bystanders. That was been the case for over a hundred years. The replay between Celtic and Rangers of the 1909 Scottish Cup final, to take one notorious instance, ended in both a draw and a riot. Communication was poor and the crowd was under the misapprehension that there would be extra time. In practice, an additional thirty minutes would only have been played after a second replay, but there was to be no further encounter because the trophy was withheld following a pitch invasion. This may have been a unique event since it saw Old Firm fans launch into acts of violence aimed at the authorities instead of one another. The story goes that whisky was used to fuel the fires intended to burn down Hampden.

Willie Maley, the Celtic manager that day, gave an account of the episode forty-six years later. 'In my judgment,' he wrote,

the cause of all the trouble was a man. He was a wee man, with a dark moustache, a stubby chin, wearing a dark blue suit, a white muffler and a 'hooker-doon' [cloth cap]. If that wee man had remained in his place or cleared out in an orthodox way there would have been no riot. But look at him – he leaps the barrier directly opposite the stand, crosses the track, is halfway across the pitch, running and shouting before he is followed by hundreds more. And so it goes on, sheep-like, till the arena is swarming with thousands of spectators.

Meanwhile the wee man is prancing close to the stand, shouting for extra-time. The standites laugh and cheer. So far there is no ill-temper. The oncoming mass of humanity from the terracing is not yet inflamed. The invaders are interested in the wee man. They want some fun. But then happened that which turned an invasion meant to be harmless into a sanguinary riot, which caused dire destruction and gravely imperilled many lives. A man took violent objection to the busy wee man's activities. He gave him a clout on the head. That clout was as a spark to [a wick]. The whole show was ablaze in a minute. In less than five a full-blooded riot was in progress.

The crowd was furious. Police reinforcements – horse and foot – were rushed to the scene. The fire brigades were called out. The defence of the pavilion taxed to the full the energies and courage of the police and their civilian helpers. It was the aim of the rioters, after grievously damaging the ground, to fire the pavilion and so complete the work of destruction.

Blood flowed freely. Casualties were many. Heaven knows what came of the wee man, whose barrier leap had been a prelude to a disastrous Saturday afternoon. I say the wee man was responsible for it all. Little did he think when he leaped the barrier and hurried over the verdant turf that his act was to lead to bloodshed and to the destruction of over £1000 [equivalent to £100,000 now] worth of property. They set fire to the pay-boxes [turnstiles] and pulled down the entrances.

Any temptation to risk a further replay can only have been feeble.

The next riot at a Scottish Cup final came in 1980, and there was no alliance whatsoever between the fans after Celtic had scored the only goal against Rangers in extra time. It had been decided that, as in earlier occasions involving a fixture of this sort, the police would leave the ground at the end of the match. This was intended as a non-confrontational approach that would see them concentrate on patrolling the streets.

While there was nothing particularly new about this policy, the Celtic fans saw that they could get onto the track and join the celebrating players, who were parading the trophy. Youngsters went first, followed by adults. There was nothing to stop Rangers supporters from advancing to confront them, and the two groups then fought and threw missiles on the pitch. Mounted police had to come back into the ground and onto the field to carry out what was reputedly the first baton charge by them in the city since the General Strike of 1926.

Beer cans were amongst the objects hurled by fans, and the fact that the contents had already been drained intensified the recklessness. One consequence of the riot would be certain provisions in the Criminal Justice (Scotland) Act 1980. The banning of alcohol from football grounds was among them, although care was taken to exempt the match-day entertainment packages that generate income for the clubs. In lounges or executive boxes, with curtains drawn, boozing still takes place before and after the game. It would be a comfort to think that denying booze to the great majority of the crowd will in itself drain away the hostility of fans.

That is not the case. The death threat made to Neil Lennon in 2011 was of a different order to anything faced by his predecessors as Celtic manager. It was taken so seriously for a while that he was warned against entering his own home unaccompanied. 'There were phases when I was getting twenty-four-hour security around the house,' he says. 'And then they were revamping the security system inside the house. There were security guards walking me in. It was a bit of a distraction, but they just felt it was the right thing to do. Hopefully it was a tipping point and things will settle down again.'

The club's former midfielder had been in charge of the young reserves until the sacking of Tony Mowbray led to his appointment as manager in the spring of 2010, originally in a temporary capacity. Lennon's first full season saw him produce a team that played appealing football, even if he had to make do with the Scottish Cup while Rangers retained the League title. His most obvious problems, however, had no connection to the matches themselves.

There is often a peculiar formulation employed when the hostility shown to him is being discussed. After an expression of disgust at such treatment, people, using precisely the same wording, will add 'but he doesn't help himself'. It is not simple to wrestle sense out of this. What were Lennon's offences? He was certainly the kind of footballer that fans detest unless he happens to be in their team. If there was a confrontation, he would be the type to put himself at the centre of it. Nor would he hide his glee when getting the better of any tormentors. As a manager he still does not blend into the background.

Even so, none of that begins to explain the scale of the animosity and the wish to do him grave harm. Lennon is the sort of person who flinches at the idea of hiding himself away in a secluded housing development. Following an Old Firm match he was attacked and severely hurt in September 2008, with two

Rangers fans subsequently jailed for two years, but he goes on living close to the cafes, restaurants and night life of the area around Glasgow University. 'I was very lucky,' he says. 'People told me that if I hadn't been as fit as I was at the time I could have been seriously damaged. I was unconscious and I don't remember much about it.

'Those two guys served time for it so it was a pretty serious assault. It shakes you up for a while. And then there was all the stuff that happened last season. You have to try and get into their heads to understand why they do it. Why do they single me out? Or why do I get so much abuse at every ground? My background plays a part in it – there's no doubt about that. Maybe they just see me as a threat to their sort of happiness. In a way that motivates me. In a perverse sort of way you take it as a backhanded compliment.'

It is hard to deter Lennon, although he did give up his international career with Northern Ireland in 2002 after a death threat. The midfielder had forty caps, and appearances for his country had not seemed a cause of hostility until he moved to Celtic. Lennon remained with the club because it is there that he had an outstanding opportunity to enhance his career and, in addition, it does not come easily to him to back down. Indeed, he is more passionate than ever about where and how he leads his life with partner Irene and son Gallagher.

'I love living here,' Lennon says. 'There's a great energy to this city. I had a time out when I left and played in England in 2007 [with Nottingham Forest and Wycombe Wanderers, before joining the Celtic coaching staff in April 2008] but I missed it. I missed the excitement of it all. I enjoy going to football dinners in England and to the Premier League games, but this club offers me as much if not more than those clubs. We are not spoiled by the corporate side so there is still a raw energy to the atmosphere. You go to some Premier League clubs and, while it's a decent atmosphere, it's not at the decibel level you have with the Celtic fans.'

When not in the grip of a football match, Lennon is reflective and eloquent. He points to the flaws in the notion that his troubles are wholly self-inflicted. 'Everyone said that it is because of my aggressive style of play,' Lennon notes. 'But then Paddy McCourt and Niall McGinn [two wingers on Celtic's books] got sent bullets in the post and you wouldn't say they were aggressive types of player. They have the same background as me [Catholics from Northern Ireland]. People try and bury their head in the sand sometimes and hide from the reality of it. They're just afraid to write about it.

'I love what I do. It's not being stubborn. If I gave it up, what else would I do? The next best thing to playing is coaching or managing. I am very fortunate that this job fell into my lap so early in my life [he was thirty-nine when he became Celtic manager]. I know I've got to get it right. You don't get much time in Glasgow because it's such an unforgiving environment. If I am here for three or four years, then I will know I have been successful. We're going in the right direction, but ultimately you're gauged on winning championships. All the other stuff should not be part and parcel of living in Glasgow, but it was here long before me. I stand up for what I think is right and fair.'

In May 2011, with Celtic on their way to victory, a Hearts fan came out of the stands at Tynecastle and reached Lennon, although stewards then seized him. John Wilson was subsequently charged with breach of the peace and assault, both offences aggravated by religious prejudice. The jury rejected the religious prejudice aspect. He was convicted only of breach of the peace, with the other charge found 'not proven', and was sentenced to eight months in prison, as well as being banned from football grounds in the UK for five years.

Late in the evening after that match Lennon had tweeted: 'I don't walk alone.' That was poignant, but it is also normal for a manager to find himself in an antagonistic setting. Supporters stump up to be there and, within limits, can show animosity. All the same, a callow manager does not find it simple to gauge how he should react, assuming it is not in his personality to stay in the background.

Managers underestimate the hypocrisy of most fans, regardless of which club they support, when there is a riposte to their behaviour. Following a goalless draw at Ibrox in April 2011, Lennon cupped a hand to his ear in mockery of a home support that had gone quiet. Indignation ensued from some of those fans. 'That's something called humour,' Lennon argued, to no avail. In practice, it is wiser in Glasgow to savour a pleasing outcome privately and avoid giving anyone an excuse for taking their anger onto the streets.

Lennon had already made his club uneasy in March 2011, during the aftermath of a 1–0 victory over Rangers in the Scottish Cup. There was a confrontation at the close of that match with Ally McCoist, who was managing the visitors that day as part of his preparation for succeeding Walter Smith a few months later. It was claimed that Lennon had been provoked by a remark, but the Celtic chief executive stopped far short of exonerating him.

'Neil reacted to a particular situation he didn't instigate in a way which he regrets,' says Peter Lawwell. 'He immediately apologised to the board and the matter is now closed. We do not condone his behaviour. The reputation of Celtic is something we hold dear and if someone tarnishes that, action will be taken. In terms of mitigating factors you need to understand what is going on in his life. He is a man who is under the normal pressure as Celtic manager to win games. But other than that he's got to put up with live ammunition being sent through the post, death threats, twenty-four-hour surveillance and security measures. So it's quite a lot to take on at the moment.'

Bigotry is also stimulated by certain football results themselves, and Lennon picks out one match as a turning point. 'It all started when we began to turn things around and beat Rangers 2–0 in the January [2011] Old Firm game. This was when the packages started to come. It snowballed from there.' In April of that year parcel bombs had been intercepted that were addressed not only to Lennon but also to two Celtic supporters, the QC Paul McBride and Trish Godman, a former deputy presiding officer of the Scottish Parliament. McBride had confounded the SFA by exposing flaws in their disciplinary regulations to reduce a touchline ban imposed on Lennon. So far as the bombs themselves were concerned, two men from Ayrshire were charged with plotting to assault and murder Lennon, Godman and McBride.

The animosity towards Lennon in some circles intensified the allegiance to him felt by the Celtic support. With the 2011 League title all but certain to go to Rangers, the final home match of the season became a demonstration of solidarity with the manager. The 4–0 win over Motherwell was all but incidental, with the most intense reaction of the afternoon coming after the game when Lennon addressed the crowd of 57,294. 'This isn't the end, this is just the beginning,' he said. It was no fault of Lennon's, but the threat to his life had taken Celtic's matches even further away than usual from a normal sporting occasion.

Politicians could not keep their distance. Alex Salmond, first minister of the Scottish Parliament, is a nationalist seeking independence, yet the notion of Scotland as a modern European country, ready to determine its own destiny, is undermined by tribal divisions. The Old Firm matches may aggravate the situation, but they also mirror squalid antipathies in society that exist regardless of sporting events. In March 2011 Salmond announced plans for anti-bigotry legislation that would carry jail sentences of up to five years for offenders.

He was bold a few months later when predicting the impact. 'If this legislation is passed by the Scots Parliament,' Salmond said, 'we shall face down any sectarian displays at football matches and they will be finished, over, done with. That's the determination we have and we are supported by, I think, 99.9 per cent of people in Scottish society who are fed up with it. And that includes, of course, the vast majority of fans, not just of Celtic and Rangers but other clubs as well, who recognise that it's high time we stamped this out as a sort of parasite on our great game of football. We're not going to have it any more and that's going to be an end of it. I'm not saying it will be easy, I'm not saying it will be done in one match or one season, but it's going to be done.'

This was quite a pledge, but Salmond bowed to pressure from MSPs and the Old Firm clubs when abandoning the bid to see his proposal become law in time for the 2011/12 season. Critics believed that the bill, which covered the conduct of supporters at games, in the streets and even online, had been drafted in haste and needed more discussion. As in all such cases, there is a potential dilemma, since the right to free speech must be protected. The challenge of drawing up workable legislation is a steep one, despite Salmond's hopes of dealing with the country's divisions, particularly as they manifest themselves in the west of Scotland.

Followers of Celtic and Rangers tend to be more than rivals. While church-going may be in decline, allegiance to the tribe that each faith represents is still vigorous. Opposing fans have a habit of seeing one another purely as caricatures. If Rangers' supporters are regarded as fascists, the Celtic fans are classed as terrorist sympathisers, if not active backers. Some do still sing in honour of the IRA, even though the Good Friday Agreement was signed as long ago as 1998. Regardless of the stereotypes, the fans, for much of the time, are the same as those anywhere else in their principal desire to see their side to win.

Antagonism springs up naturally in sport. The proximity of notable clubs puts police on the alert, and security is, if anything, a growing issue when Liverpool and Manchester United meet, particularly now that the Old Trafford side has broken the Anfield record with a nineteenth League title in 2011. In Turkey, an encounter between Galatasaray and Besiktas can spark rioting in the streets of Istanbul. The clashes between Celtic and Rangers contrive to seem more raw still, with murders having been committed in the aftermath. It sometimes feels like a regular facet of Glasgow society, rather than the monstrous aberration it should be. There is a sense, too, of an ingrown city overly preoccupied with its own tensions. It has not been possible to develop or even sustain fully the cosmopolitan ambience generated when it was European City of Culture in 1990.

Five years after that event a young Celtic fan called Mark Scott was stabbed to death in an unprovoked attack as he walked past a pub particularly associated with Rangers supporters. Subsequently, his girlfriend Cara Henderson started the anti-sectarian charity Nil By Mouth. Society is now more diverse than ever, whether through the process of immigration or through the turning away from monolithic bodies such as the mainstream political parties. Football games are unusual in still bearing the potential for mass expression, although the messages they transmit can be disturbing. Protest marches do continue and, for specific causes, will occasionally attract large numbers, but there is no doubt, too, that people find it more of a struggle to detach themselves from the comforts of the modern home. Raw emotion, however, is still vented at matches, and anyone misguided enough to assume that political expression in the stands was disappearing entirely would have been taken aback during a match with Aberdeen at Celtic Park a week before Remembrance Sunday in 2010. A banner was unfurled by home supporters at half-time, with its message directed at the armed forces: 'Your Deeds Would Shame All the Devils in Hell. Ireland, Iraq, Afghanistan. No Bloodstained Poppy on Our Hoops.'

This version of military history is selective in neglecting the defeat of fascism in the Second World War, as well as, on a far smaller scale, the retaking in 1982 of the Falklands, which had the welcome side effect of bringing down General Galtieri's dictatorship in Argentina and paving the way for a return to democracy. In the latter case, the Green Brigade, a group of fans who enliven the atmosphere with their visual displays, preferred, on their website, to denounce the circumstances in which the *Belgrano* was sunk during that conflict. More specifically, there are strands to Celtic's identity that concern pride in the military.

A supporters club from the Gorbals is named after James Stokes VC, who was killed in Holland by machine-gun fire in March 1945 while charging a series of buildings occupied by the enemy.

A club of substance carries within it a variety of traditions, including those of the Green Brigade. So far as the poppy issue is concerned, it was inevitable that Celtic would join the other clubs in having one woven into their shirts for their match on Remembrance Sunday 2010. The controversy arose most keenly from the consciousness of Ireland and its struggle with the British army, both during the achievement of independence for the southern part of the island and in the period before the Good Friday Agreement in the north. When Lord Mountbatten was assassinated in 1979, some of the Celtic fans sang, to the tune of 'Old MacDonald Had a Farm', 'Old Mountbatten had a boat, ee-i-ee-i-o/ And on that boat there was a bomb, ee-i-ee-i-o . . .' The ensuing furore would have been what they wanted since it brought a form of attention. Scotland, then, also had faint parallels with Northern Ireland in the widespread belief among Catholics that they were regularly passed over for promotion. No one doubted that a football ground still had the potential to be a centre of deep feelings that surged far beyond sport.

In plain football terms, the Green Brigade is a boon to Celtic, a generator of excitement and noise in a ground that, like so many others, has grown quiet for the time being as spectators see themselves as customers as well as devotees. Even so, the potential for volatility in Celtic's dealings with their fans looks high. The club came into existence suddenly, with no homely story to tell of modest origins. There was much at stake immediately and, while Celtic have been in the doldrums for periods, the tendency towards melodrama is never far from the surface. The tale does have resonance. Irish immigrants came to Scotland and other countries, such as the US, out of desperation. In their own birthplace, disease, famine and the necessity of emigration reduced the population of the entire island from 8.2 million in 1841 to half that number at the start of the twentieth century.

None the less, Ireland, as it is now, continues to be a stronghold for Celtic. There are more than eighty supporters clubs there and, apart from the basic arithmetic, Celtic is enhanced by the richness of that Irish dimension. It brings texture to the tale, making Celtic more than a side from a city with a population of 600,000. In hard, business terms, this gives the club an additional means of projecting itself to other countries and continents, despite the fact that its home is in a backwater. Without that extra dimension a summer tour to Australia in 2011 would have been unlikely. A substantial number of good players have emerged there, but it is still a country where football is far from being the dominant sport. The capacity of Celtic to draw crowds of 20,000 to mere friendlies was therefore noteworthy.

In the Glasgow of the nineteenth century, people of Irish birth or background also gave the club impetus. Immigrants, with their usually slim resources, are typically people in a hurry who are also determined that their children will flourish. That strain of impatience characterised Celtic at the start, and a version of it can be sensed in the descriptions of their fans in the 1890s. They were far from acquiescent and did not wait long before at least attempting to establish their power. These fans would travel to matches on horse-drawn brakes and had soon banded together in the hope of putting themselves in a position to negotiate. They wanted a group discount on season-ticket prices, but Willie Maley replied that the board 'cannot see their way to make any reduction'.

Just nine years after the club's first game a fan accused Celtic of abandoning their original principles. This is an allegation that has rung out in each generation. There has to be scepticism about the idea that Celtic ever were pure and innocent. Professionalism, first covert and then rampant, made sure that football would be crammed with materialism and dubious conduct. At a meeting of the brake clubs in 1897 a certain Mr Flaherty thought that members 'should not bother with the tickets for next season'. It is a threat made every decade, and the refusal of the club to capitulate does not vary either. There was disdain of the board as well in the 1890s since there were directors in the drinks trade, whereas some of the supporters were members of the League of the Cross, a temperance body. Those who favoured sending a deputation to hold talks with the board were accused of 'crawling to the Celtic directorate'. One member left, declaring that the fans should start a new club and that he had a promise of £5,000 for that very purpose. Nothing happened.

In practice, it is hard to turn seething emotions into an effective programme, and the takeover of the club in the 1990s was unprecedented. Turmoil, whether or not it has any function, comes naturally, but Celtic, more or less breaking even, are relatively stable these days. One boon has been the advent in the UK of the all-seater stadium, and the increased revenue it brings. That requirement was forced on clubs at the higher levels of the sport after the Hillsborough disaster, when ninety-six people were crushed to death at Sheffield Wednesday's stadium during the 1989 FA Cup semi-final between Liverpool and Nottingham Forest. Rebuilt grounds, such as Celtic's, offer a virtual guarantee that there will be a clear view of the pitch. As a consequence, women can go to matches with some confidence that they will see the game clearly instead of having to peer round generally taller men. The remaking of Britain's grounds was born of tragedy, but it had the side effect of opening up a greater audience for football. The presence of women was a contributory factor in allowing Celtic to have an average attendance of nearly 50,000 for home League games in the 2010/11 season, despite the fact that the title went to Rangers for the third season in a row.

Fergus McCann, the owner of Celtic for five years from 1994, would have been heartened to hear that women continue to make up a noticeable part of the crowd. Apart from the commercial aspect, his instinct was to open up Celtic. After he had come to power, an older member of the Croy Celtic Supporters Club recalled McCann's determination to alter attitudes decades before. 'Even at the age of sixteen and seventeen he was dictating new policies to stalwarts of the club who were in their late fifties,' said Jim Lochrie. 'As early as 1961 he was proposing that women should be allowed to join the club, and in those days that took a bit of doing. When that was passed, he stood against the motion that they shouldn't be allowed to travel alone on the bus.'

The sexism that McCann challenged was more likely to arise from misplaced gallantry than blatant misogyny. The sensitivity about swearing was greater then and, with alcohol still allowed on supporters' buses, there was an assumption that the whole atmosphere would be distasteful to women. The term 'ladette' did not enter the pages of the *Concise Oxford Dictionary* until 2001. McCann, however, had long been comfortable with the concept of female fans. He was uniquely equipped, as well, to make arrangements on behalf of his supporters club since he is said to have been the only member of it, in 1960, to have had a telephone at home. The young McCann had business cards with the number on them: Kilsyth 2361. He was intent on making an impression. A respect for equal rights must have mingled with the appreciation that the presence of women would bolster the attendance. Pragmatism and principle were entwined in McCann.

In earlier times it took doggedness for a woman to watch matches regularly, considering the obstructed view they were likely to have. Margaret Gilmour was among those who were not deterred. The hairdresser disliked the idea of watching a game seated and relished the enclosure then known as the Jungle, even if some procedures were unfamiliar when she first went there. 'I just wish somebody had told me to jump up and down when Celtic scored,' she said in the 1988 edition of the then annual publication *Playing for Celtic*. 'I was nearly flattened, and that's my clearest memory of that game.' Gilmour also used to cut the hair of Tommy Burns, the Celtic player and future manager. Someone had to give him a trim, but it is still noteworthy that one of the more prominent footballers at the club would be happy then to go to an ordinary salon.

Players have the opportunity now to become vastly richer than those who watch them. The risk is that they live only in the opulent but enclosed society of football itself. It is likely that links to the outside world were more extensive in the past. Tony McGuinness, as a successful businessman, was not quite an ordinary person, but one wonders if anyone from outside the hermetically sealed environment of the game now could be on such close terms with someone like Jock Stein. In the closing years of the Scotland manager's life McGuinness was often with him when he drove south of the border to watch matches. When Stein collapsed at the end of the win over Wales in 1985, McGuinness was with him in the little treatment room at Ninian Park where he died.

The businessman had seen Stein before the centre half moved from Albion Rovers to Llanelly, but retained little memory of the defender when he played for Rovers against a visiting Celtic side in a 3–3 draw one afternoon in September 1948. That day 25,000 people were jammed into the Cliftonhill ground. Getting to the game was more memorable than the match itself. 'We got a tram-car from Glasgow Cross,' McGuinness said. 'I don't know how long it took but it seemed like an hour and a half and when we got there the gates were closed. We had to climb over the wall, and they had put soot along the top to keep people out. We were manky by the time we got into the ground.'

The result on that occasion was symptomatic of Celtic's then mediocrity. On the other hand, the difficulties of either member of the Old Firm also illustrated the diversity of the game in Scotland. In the 1950s the League title went not only to Celtic and Rangers but also to Hibernian, Aberdeen and Hearts. Dundee United and Aberdeen would impose themselves in the 1980s, but the League title has been the sole preserve of the Old Firm since 1985. The repetitiveness has not yet seen fans of the dominant clubs turn away in boredom. Having been fixated with one another for so long, the unwavering command of Celtic or Rangers in the League looks simply like confirmation of the financial advantages they hold. The era when players' wages could be artificially restricted and the right to a transfer was not guaranteed even at the end of a contract can only be denounced as unjust and unsustainable. Those rules, however, had at least protected diversity, ensuring some prospect of success in the League for clubs beyond the Old Firm.

Given that Celtic and Rangers are now much less open to challenge in Scotland, it is remarkable that supporters are so engaged. Activist fans have become a distinctive force in the game. Where Celtic are concerned, many were galvanised in the 1980s by opposition to the way in which the club was run. The fanzine *Not the View* has its origins in a Glasgow pub, on a day in 1987 when the side had just lost at home to Falkirk, a result followed by the sacking of the manager, David Hay. The larger topic was the financial domination by Rangers and the inability to counter it while Celtic was a hidebound institution.

The fanzine's name reflected the scorn felt for the official publication, *The Celtic View*. 'There was a whole load of us in the Horseshoe,' says Gerry Dunbar, the editor on course to bring out the 200th edition in 2012. 'It was the day Celtic lost to Falkirk. That was Davie Hay's last home game in the League before he was sacked. People tend to forget, but that season was a nightmare. The talk got around to the *Celtic View*, and we were all saying that the £10 star letter in the next week's edition would be "Hats off to Jack McGinn" [the then chairman]. So somebody came up with the idea that we should do a publication of our own.'

The innovative and often hilarious *Not the View* was part of the broad fanzine movement, but there was a particular relevance while the family-run Celtic floundered. The nature of clubs and their financing presented the Kellys with a challenge they were unable to meet. Supporters were not convinced by the board of that time, even when the Double was won in 1988. 'People were coming out of the Scottish Cup final,' Dunbar recalled, 'and everybody was saying, "This is a chance for them to kick on if we get two or three players in." But if that was going to happen we'd have had to sell four first of all. That was the story with Celtic for decade after decade.'

Such frustration was all but universal in a support that cherished the satire and the forum for protest. 'To begin with', says Dunbar, 'it was a bit of a trickle, but by the Christmas issue in 1990 we were selling 12,000. People were sending things in anonymously, which were very helpful, so we had inside information. Or they would send us the accounts, which were hard to come by in those days. Or George Shanks [a fellow founder] would go down to Companies House and get the microfiche.

'The circulation was a pretty steady 10,000 for a couple of years. The Christmas edition was in colour and it was double the price. Happy days. Davie Jarvie will tell you. Him and four or five of the guys that sold it – who were all his student buddies – went back to his flat in Thornwood Avenue. They used to pool the tips, so when they got back they threw the money on the bed and began bouncing up and down like some crazy movie scene. They'd never seen that amount of money in their lives. They were on 20 per cent commission. Good money for three-quarters of an hour's work. They must have been selling a thousand each: £200 a man in 1990. That was a good Christmas all round.'

Not the View is still being published at the unflagging rate of eight editions a year and also exists on the Internet, even though it cannot have the impact or circulation associated with a particular period of tumult at Celtic. The fanzine has been a constant throughout the phases of Dunbar's life. 'When the babies came along, it was a nightmare,' he says, 'but, then again, you're up all night anyway. You could have the baby on one arm and type with the other.'

Dunbar cannot detach himself from *Not the View*, even though the men who ran Celtic in the 1980s were removed long ago and replaced by people who do not provoke such rebellion among the crowd. 'I like to think it is a bit similar to Peter Cook at *Private Eye*,' Dunbar says of his persistence. 'He could have done anything he wanted, but he kept it going for long enough because he enjoyed it. *Not the View* has been a chore at times, but it's good to see it there still.'

Fans were attracted to *Not the View* for its satire and piercing realism. There was particularly great interest in 'They Embarrassed the Hoops', a feature about the worst players to have turned out for the club. It did present the odd difficulty. 'I got an email', Dunbar recalls, 'from a woman in Australia who said she had heard that her great uncle was in *Not the View*. She mentioned the name. He was in "They Embarrassed the Hoops". I had to tell her the edition was sold out and there weren't any spare copies lying around.'

Not the View and fanzines at large stimulated interest in clubs, with the satire and campaigns assisting the movement that saw fans become activists. A closer watch than ever is kept on the boardroom now. There is, in addition, a general scrutiny of the games themselves born of technology, whether it arises from television coverage or something more unusual. The referee Dougie McDonald mistakenly awarded a penalty to Celtic in a match with Dundee United in October 2010 but, realising his error, explained his change of mind by claiming that his assistant Steven Craven had used the microphone system that links officials to point out that he was wrong. Craven then resigned because he had done no such thing.

Lennon was indignant because he, too, had been misinformed and wanted an apology. 'I don't like being lied to,' he says. The SFA strained to protect McDonald and merely issued a warning to him, but the pressure did not drop and the referee eventually resigned. 'It was not of my making,' says Lennon. 'The delegate asked me to go and speak to the referee and I wasn't even that bothered. And then they proceeded to tell me a small lie. It just snowballed when the linesman came out a few days later and said, "Look, that isn't strictly true. That isn't really what happened." And in the end these two guys lost their job and people were pointing the finger at me. The point is, if they had done that to me then how many other managers had they done it to? I think that is what the inference was.'

Hugh Dallas, the head of referee development, had put himself in difficulties by supporting McDonald's version of events. He left the post in late November 2010, however, because of accusations that he had used his official email account to circulate an image of the road sign warning of children crossing that had the words 'The Pope is coming' added. The email, alluding to child-abuse scandals in the Catholic Church, was sent around the time of Pope Benedict's visit to the UK, including Scotland, in September of that year.

After losing an initial appeal against his sacking, Dallas reached an out-of-court settlement with the SFA in July 2011 following a conciliation process involving ACAS. The SFA also confirmed that three of the four other members of staff who were dismissed over the email had been reinstated. It would be preposterous to claim that Scotland is unchanged, but the episode invited the conclusion that divisions, tribal more than genuinely religious, are still marked. In addition, people once again found themselves wondering if any other country in Europe would be likely to experience a scandal of this nature.

Referees, furious at a supposedly widespread animosity towards them embodied in the McDonald episode, had gone on strike at the end of November 2010, although scab officials from the continent and Israel then took charge of the major fixtures. While those events were unprecedented, it was generally a time of change. Following a review the SFA streamlined itself in June 2011, cutting the board from eleven members to seven and setting up a semi-autonomous judicial panel.

The era is one of reappraisal on all fronts, with both Celtic and Rangers understanding that the outlay that got each of them to the final of a European trophy in the 2000s was no longer sustainable. In this period crucial issues have, more than ever, turned fans into commentators and analysts. The effects register strongly on the Internet. In Celtic's case, websites have emerged that are stimulating and informative. Paul Brennan, by creating and developing celticquicknews.co.uk, has contributed markedly to the understanding of financial matters and the impact they have on the field.

Brennan, a computer-network consultant, was moved to create the site in 2004 because of exasperation over the lack of understanding about the club's finances following Celtic's appearance in the UEFA Cup final the previous year. 'The Scottish media', he says, 'couldn't get over the "Where's the Seville money?" question. The accounts were plain to see. In the Seville season Celtic had lost £9 million, and in 2004 they were losing over £7 million. It was obvious why they weren't spending. The club couldn't continue to lose money at that rate, but the story wasn't being told. I was speaking to a Rangers pal of mine, and he said, "Well, why don't you start a blog?" I didn't even know what a blog was, but he got me started.'

A greater number of fans are ready now to study the annual results in earnest. CQN contributes to that. It appears that the club, existing as it does in a small country, also recognises that it can best retain support by creating at least some sense of community. Irritating though criticism will be to a club, people are maintaining a bond with it even if they also happen to be frothing at the mouth. The popularity of a website is measured in page impressions, a count of the total number of requests made to the server for particular pages. 'On a quiet day,' says Brennan, 'if I'm not there and I haven't posted anything, there will be 20,000 to 30,000 page impressions. On a busy day it'll be over 100,000. In the early days it was scary.'

People are no doubt better informed and realise, for instance, that the value of assets in the accounts must be written down. Brennan remembers fans accusing Celtic of a scam, as if amortisation was a trick to sneak actual money out of the bank account. It was prudent and even essential for the club to maintain links with websites and fanzines that may eventually shape opinions as much or more than the mainstream media. Brennan was one of the people who came, for example, to know and communicate with the chief executive, Peter Lawwell.

Celtic's position is precarious. With no access in sight to the major football markets, the revenue from domestic television coverage will be modest. There is no cause either to assume that there will be sustained runs in European competition. While astute signings can be made, as Lennon showed when buying the Israeli midfielder Beram Kayal, the odds stay unwaveringly against a manager of limited means. Given that context, it must be a greater priority than ever to reinforce the bonds with the fans. The target must be to bring about even more of a community, where a sense of belonging motivates people to keep coming through the turnstiles.

It would be foolish of Celtic not to take note when posters on CQN and other sites raise issues. Brennan sensed the shift in habit one day. 'I got an angry Peter Lawwell on the phone,' he says. 'Eventually people began to understand what was going on and wanted to work the system. He began to work the system and speak to as many websites as possible who were willing to engage with him. It wasn't easy before that. I had to write and write again because the initial letter wasn't responded to.'

There is no panacea to put the club on the same financial footing as clubs in more lucrative leagues, and the frustration was apparent in 2011, when Lawwell made reference to Swansea's promotion to the Premier League. The implication was that there should be no logical objection to Celtic playing in that same competition. As Lawwell appreciates, however, the presence of a Welsh club in the top flight is a historical accident. Actively choosing to draft in a member of the Old Firm now is a different issue entirely.

So it is that supporters are left toiling to shore up the standing of Celtic and Rangers. Those fans have more means of expression and, if need be, dissent. 'Twenty years ago,' says Brennan, 'you really had the *Daily Record* and Radio Clyde to stand between the Celtic support and the club. If Celtic could manage that relationship between those two outlets, to some degree they could manage the support, but the messages that the club now has to deal with comes from all angles and new angles. It's a difficult job for the club to manage that effectively.'

Celtic, indeed, can seem to be passive over issues. Supporters were resentful when there appeared to be no reaction to the chants of the Rangers crowd that mocked them for a supposed obsession, in their fondness for a song such as 'The Fields of Athenry', with the devastating Irish famines of the nineteenth century that sent emigrants to Scotland and other countries.

'Celtic fans leave a Rangers game having listened to that and come on to CQN to complain bitterly,' says Brennan. 'And then they complain that "The club is doing nothing. It doesn't speak out." I know the club cares deeply about that, but the message I get is that they need to build influence and can't do that by grandstanding. It has to be done through indirect channels, and it's going take longer than today and tomorrow.'

The unwavering truth is that each set of fans feels morally superior to the other. This is a by-product of the fixations that consume them when, at the worst periods, the clubs can think only of one another. 'So far as the SFA is concerned,' said George Peat, the then president in 2008, 'it's got to be stamped out, and we'll be having a meeting soon with the Scottish Premier League and the police to see what we can do about it.' Subsequently, it seemed there was little to be done since extreme measures such as playing certain matches behind closed doors were not favoured.

Alex Salmond and other politicians in the Holyrood parliament are aware of the severe divisions and their longevity. With no indication that Celtic and Rangers can be released from one another's grip, the clubs face the danger of being locked in an ever more severe struggle that holds ever less interest for anyone outside the west of Scotland.

There have been well-intentioned campaigns in the past, with Celtic launching 'Bhoys Against Bigotry' and Rangers calling for 'Pride Over Prejudice'. They may do some good, but the time is unlikely to come soon when each club is regarded purely as a sporting institution. The Reformation that took place in Scotland had a far more ideological and theological impetus than its counterpart in England. Several clubs south of the border also emerged from one church or another, but it is a factor that ceased to define them long ago. In Glasgow, religion is manipulated into a cause of conflict.

7

BILLY McNEILL

Billy McNeill came into his inheritance when it was more of a burden than a bequest. He had two spells as Celtic manager, but new financial problems had started to emerge and the club was often at a loss as to how to deal with them. Even so, nothing could have stopped him from taking the job, particularly on the first time of asking. In view of his intelligence, commanding manner and captaincy of the European Cup-winning side he was bound to hold the post sooner or later, and it was apt that the approach inviting him to leave Aberdeen did not come from some obscure middle man.

In 1978 Jock Stein was getting ready to part company with Celtic and join Leeds United. He first had a part to play in arranging the succession at Celtic. McNeill's work at Pittodrie had made him Scotland's manager of the year. Stein complimented him, while also mentioning that the prize ought rightly have gone to Jock Wallace, who had just completed the Treble with Rangers. McNeill had received his reminder that trophies are the sole vindication for whoever is in charge of an Old Firm side.

There can have been little about Celtic that needed to be explained to him. McNeill was so well integrated that he had been seen as a natural emissary from an early stage. On the eve of the away leg of Celtic's European Cup tie with Nantes in November 1966 there was a dinner for the visitors, and McNeill was present to give a speech of thanks in French. Regardless of any basic knowledge of foreign languages, the tall, striking player was always well suited to representing the club, but he did much more in leading Celtic.

In the summer of 1978 he was rejoining a club that had just come an unconscionable fifth in the League under Stein. Worse still, the slump was easy to explain and tough to address. The European Cup-winning players had all gone, even if McNeill would bring back his former teammate, the then thirty-five-year-old Bobby Lennox, from Houston Hurricanes in the US. In addition, Kenny Dalglish, Lou Macari and David Hay had left for English clubs.

The new manager had been a Celtic player until his retirement in 1975 and understood that little attempt had been made to keep outstanding footballers for even a little longer. Lavish TV contracts and the formation of the lucrative Premier League in England were almost a generation away, yet Celtic still lacked even the modest commercial acumen to pay the sort of wages that might have retained a star for a while.

'I always felt the board didn't appreciate what they had there at that time,' says McNeill. 'They took the easiest way out. David Hay, Kenny Dalglish, Lou Macari – they were the Quality Street kids coming through, but they disappeared into the sunshine down south. It was a money thing. With us the board had capitalised on the fact that we were a group who wanted to play for the club. The younger ones were more sensible than us.

'Players at clubs like St Mirren were getting paid the same kind of money. That was during the 1960s and into the 1970s. The comparison with English teams was frightening. Everybody told each other [in Scotland squads] what they were earning. They weren't bigger clubs [in England]; they were clubs prepared to pay players decent money. There aren't many clubs anywhere bigger than Celtic, and its problem is that it plays in a smaller league. That wasn't so obvious then.'

While McNeill could be relieved to have Danny McGrain on

the staff, the player had been affected by diabetes, a fractured skull and an obstinate ankle problem. The latter injury, in effect, kept him out of action for sixteen months, from September 1977 until January 1979, but at his peak McGrain had been a credible rival to West Germany's Paul Breitner as the best full back in the world. While the problems took their toll, his know-how was precious to McNeill when he did re-emerge.

In the meantime, the new manager had made a start on restocking the team. McNeill's main advantage was that there were footballers on the domestic scene with the necessary attributes who were affordable. The winger Davie Provan and the midfielder Murdo MacLeod, signed from Kilmarnock and Dumbarton respectively, were of great service to Celtic for many seasons, yet their combined cost was less than £250,000. While the sum looked substantial in the context of the time, the investment was followed by a large return.

McNeill had always been sharp in identifying undervalued assets. His first post was with Clyde, but he had only been with them for a couple of months before he went to Aberdeen. In January 1978 he spent £20,000 to buy a twenty-one-year-old from the Glasgow club called Steve Archibald, who had attracted little interest. The forward would be sold to Tottenham Hotspur for £800,000 and eventually joined Barcelona, spending four seasons there.

The bringing of MacLeod and Provan to Celtic had been a coup in its own way, but cash of any sort was not readily available to McNeill. Until the advent of computerised turnstiles, fans of virtually all teams were convinced that gate receipts were not declared fully. Whatever went on at Celtic Park, it was normal practice at one medium-sized Scottish Premier League club during the 1980s for the door of the secretary's office to be closed firmly at half-time while the official attendance figure was established or, more likely, concocted.

All the same, football was relatively cheap then and Celtic, in common with other clubs, issued just a small number of season tickets. Most people regarded them as precious heirlooms that would remain in the hands of a relatively small number of families. It was the preference of the board to settle for whatever cash happened to be proffered at the turnstiles on any particular Saturday. Going to a game was still a casual matter on an ordinary weekend, and this was highly affordable entertainment, even if the cheapness was reflected in the squalid conditions on the terracing.

The directors, with few exceptions, were slow to appreciate that football matches might be promoted in the same way as any other type of entertainment. Clubs seemed to operate on the assumption that it was in the nature of things for their income, at best, to be stuck at a particular level. The chairman during McNeill's first spell as Celtic manager was Desmond White. He would question expenses containing the sort of petrol costs that resulted when he used the car for scouting trips to England. 'What do you want me to do,' McNeill cried, 'put coal in it?'

People tended not to feel much of an affinity with White, and the manager's exasperation stretched back for decades. McNeill was so irritated by him that, as captain, he even exploited the clinching of the 1973 League title to relieve his annoyance. After the win over Hibernian, the captain got on the team bus and asked for one of the expensive cigars that White carried for personal use. On such an occasion the chairman was in no position to refuse. McNeill then took a couple of puffs before chucking it out of the window.

The two men could never have been complementary. It rankled with McNeill that when White phoned and his wife answered, he would immediately ask to speak to the manager rather than exchange pleasantries with Liz. McNeill himself is a popular person who chats easily with the hordes of people who approach him to this day and he disliked the chairman's curtness. White had trouble putting himself or others at ease and, while that is a common enough limitation, it was a notable shortcoming for a person in his post.

McNeill could scarcely help but make comparisons with Aberdeen, although he was not aware then of just how unusual the board there had been: 'I remember talking to Dick Donald [the then chairman] at Aberdeen and he said, "You'll nae enjoy working for that lot as much as you've enjoyed working for us." I didn't know what he was talking about.' There may have been a hint for McNeill in the presence of Charlie Forbes, a board member known as the social convener because he was in charge of pouring the drinks.

That easy-going ambience, however, did not mean that there was anything slipshod in the way Aberdeen went about their business. There had been a course of instruction for McNeill in how to manoeuvre a board into authorising a signing. The Aberdeen director Chris Anderson advised that a manager could not ask the chairman baldly for funds to buy a player. 'He would help you roll it around until the money was there for you,' McNeill says of Anderson. 'I am quite sure Dick enjoyed all that.'

Aberdeen would have appreciated the manager's wisdom in purchasing Archibald. McNeill might not have been quite so inspired at Celtic, but he did buy very well. Shrewdness was essential in that first season as manager of his old club. John Greig was also new to the post at Rangers, but he inherited the team he had captained the season before and looked on course to retain the domestic treble. The side had even knocked out Juventus in the European Cup that season. However, the work-load was enough to make Rangers creak.

The weather meddled with the schedule and the second leg of the European Cup quarter-final had to be put back twenty-four hours. Rangers were pedestrian in the goalless match with Cologne at Ibrox and a 1–0 aggregate defeat eliminated them. They had not capitulated, however, and a victory at home to Celtic was reassuring. Their ambitions were the greatest burden and they would eventually secure the Scottish Cup by defeating Hibernian in the second replay of the final. Prior to that they had to squeeze in the away match with McNeill's side on 21 May 1979.

A persevering Celtic would be League champions so long as they beat Rangers. It might have taken McNeill aback to have such an opportunity. In the first half of the League campaign, his team had taken a mere seven wins from eighteen fixtures. Anyone of good sense would have deduced then that the manager would need a lot more time to get within reach of Rangers. Celtic, however, picked up momentum after a mid-season break in Portugal that did appear to bring more vigour and self-belief.

Implausibly, the decisive game with Rangers was ideal for one twenty-year-old, but this was an unusual youth. Roy Aitken's debut had come three seasons earlier. He could play in central defence, but it was more apt for him to be a midfielder since it did not suit him to be as watchful as a centre half must be. He craved instead to be in the middle of the action, at the core of the mayhem. The timing of his emergence, roughly coinciding with Stein's departure from the club, denied him the nurturing that had been vital to Celtic players who were just a few years older.

There were still medals to come, as well as fifty-seven caps for Scotland and the captaincy of the club in the centenary season, but expectations were such that it did seem he had suffered in the anti-climax once Stein was gone. For all that, there was nothing subdued about the 1979 clash with Rangers. Aitken occasionally had trouble detaching himself from the frenzy of a game, but there was no cause for anyone to stand apart that evening.

Celtic looked outmatched as they fell behind to an Alex MacDonald goal in the ninth minute. That opportunity had been set up by Davie Cooper, who effortlessly beat two opponents before sending in an accurate cross. It could have been taken as corroboration of the theory that Rangers, with their experience, were better placed for such a match. Celtic's disadvantage deepened when their winger John Doyle was sent off ten minutes into the second half for kicking the scorer, but there was an equaliser from Aitken, who was especially suited to a night of such fervour and force. Never bashful, Aitken was stimulated by the challenge of being in an outnumbered line-up.

Although Celtic took the lead through a hooked shot by George McCluskey, Rangers levelled, and the passion of it all made for intoxicating mayhem. McNeill's side went ahead in the 85th minute after the visitors' goalkeeper Peter McCloy pushed a driven cross by McCluskey against his centre half Colin Jackson for an own goal. Celtic made it 4–2 at the very end, MacLeod lashing the ball home from long range when he would have been almost as happy to see it vanish into the crowd as time ran out.

In Greig's first season as manager Rangers did win the League Cup and the Scottish Cup, while also making their mark in the European Cup. In the four years that followed there were just two trophies for him, and neither of them was the League championship. The ascent of Dundee United and Alex Ferguson's Aberdeen restricted Greig, but the setback against Celtic was also noteworthy since it stopped him from making the kind of spectacular start that would have given him immediate status as a Rangers manager. After resigning in the autumn of 1983 he gave up his aspirations in that line of work and afterwards was variously a pundit, a member of Rangers' public-relations staff and then a director of the club.

While there is no tragedy in any of that, it was not a course he would have foreseen when all possibilities looked open to him prior to the 1979 match with Celtic. McNeill did better, but exhilaration still has to serve as compensation for an Old Firm manager who is bound to live in the greater Glasgow area and endure the footballing animosities that can spring up in the street as well as in the stadiums. McNeill's wife had never wished to leave the picturesque town of Stonehaven, where she and the children were based while he held the Aberdeen job fifteen miles up the coast. Apart from the appeal of the harbour setting, she would have been relishing the north-east, among other things, for the escape from the west of Scotland sectarianism that is unavoidable for a player at an Old Firm club and his family.

There were to be a further four years for her in the Glasgow area during her husband's first spell as Celtic manager. In his second season the side took just the Scottish Cup, when Danny McGrain, whose shooting was usually a failing, hit a drive that was deflected into the net by his teammate George McCluskey for the only goal of the final with Rangers.

McNeill would win the League three times in the five years of that stint at the club before he took up the manager's job at Manchester City. There had been silverware and an excitement that was often generated by the imaginative, skilful attacker Charlie Nicholas, until he moved to Arsenal for a reported £400,000 in the summer of 1983. McNeill, with no prior consultation, was told flatly by White that a price, which the chairman declined to reveal, had been agreed. The manager's suggestion that more money could have been obtained if other clubs had been lured into an auction was rejected. White replied that he preferred to do business with Denis Hill-Wood because the Arsenal chairman was 'an honourable man', although it looked as if he thereby failed to get the best price for Nicholas.

Apart from being separated from a footballer of huge potential, Celtic lost someone whose effervescent originality and skill were not to have quite such impact in London. McNeill was once unsettled to hear of misconduct by the player, but was mollified to learn that the issue concerned daftness rather than destructiveness. It turned out that Nicholas and Danny Crainie, another youngster at the club, had been kicking a tennis ball around to the inconvenience of buses and cars in the Lanarkshire town of Kilsyth. Regardless of the juvenile behaviour, there were grown-up issues to be faced. The sale of Nicholas was an inevitability and it happened before he was ready to enjoy the pleasures of London without hampering his career at Arsenal. A transfer out of Scotland looked like normal practice, but there was no true parallel with, for instance, the sale of Kenny Dalglish.

Nicholas, at twenty-one, was five years younger than his predecessor had been when he set off for Anfield. For all that the forward had achieved even at that age, Celtic were learning what it felt like to be parted from a player whose career they would once have expected to control. Others had gone in the past, but Nicholas's move gave the most vivid insight into the future. Although nobody would have conceded the point thirteen years before, when Celtic were European Cup finalists, the transfer of Nicholas opened a window onto the sometimes sombre future of club football in Scotland.

Rangers alone would go on to buck the daunting trend in the latter part of that decade. They spent lavishly to recruit players during the five-year period in which English clubs were banned from European competition after the attack on Juventus supporters by Liverpool fans had contributed to the disaster at the 1985 European Cup final in Brussels' dilapidated Heysel Stadium. Someone as eminent as the England centre half Terry Butcher was ready in 1986 not just to leave relegated Ipswich Town and play for the newly appointed manager Graeme Souness, but also to spend four seasons in Glasgow. Celtic, in 1983, could not have anticipated the transformation of Rangers, and when it started to take place some at the club liked to suppose that the alterations at Ibrox were purely cosmetic.

In Celtic's experience the movement of talent across the border had almost always been in the opposite direction. Nicholas had company when leaving the premises in 1983. McNeill, too, was on the move. The decline in Celtic's European performances was under way. His side might have taxed Real Madrid in 1980 by beating them 2–0 in Glasgow before going down 3–0 at the Bernabéu in the return leg of the European Cup quarter-final, but by 1982 McNeill got no further than the second round before the team went out to Real Sociedad in the autumn. Comparisons were starting to do damage and Aberdeen would, for instance, win the Cup Winners' Cup by overcoming Real Madrid themselves the following year.

If the Celtic manager was being measured against that standard, it was, in retrospect, a severe judgement since Alex Ferguson was already on his long ascent towards the pinnacle of football history. For all that McNeill is imposing, engaging and articulate, he is also emotional about football. En route to a Cup Winners' Cup match with the Hungarian club Diósgyör Miskolc in 1980 he had punched the journalist Gerry McNee, with whom a prolonged antagonism had developed. The potential for conflict, of a non-violent sort, with Desmond White was realised once Nicholas was gone.

From McNeill's perspective the chairman appeared to niggle and quibble. In 1983 White wanted the assistant manager, John Clark, to be replaced by Frank Connor, a coach who had played in goal for Celtic in a couple of matches at the start of the 1960s. McNeill was able to safeguard his friend then, but there was no true security. In any case, he had an incentive to break free of the club in 1983 once he had heard that there were five other managers in Scotland who were better paid. This was not solely a question of pride. His business interests, in a company called Milnrow Developments, had collapsed, forcing him to sell the family home and move to a smaller property.

A request for a salary review was rejected by the Celtic board. He had, by his own admission, been hot-headed when clashing with White over particular issues, but his four seasons in England, with Manchester City and Aston Villa, were at least informative. McNeill was responsible both for achieving promotion with the former and for taking the latter to relegation. Villa sacked him in 1987. He was thus denied the fulfilment of an ambition that underlined just how unhappy McNeill had been with the Midlands club and, specifically, a certain Doug Ellis. 'My great ambition', he says, 'was to keep the club in the First Division and then hand the chairman my resignation.'

While McNeill was absent from Celtic Park, his former teammate David Hay was in charge, and he squeezed in some remarkable moments. After the two sets of fans had barracked the visiting prime minister Margaret Thatcher at the 100th Scottish Cup final in 1985, Provan's goal from a free kick was the winner that completed a late recovery from 1–0 down against Dundee United. It was notable that this was Celtic's first trophy since 1982, but a year later the League title was taken on goal difference. On the last day of the season Celtic won 5–0 at St Mirren, while the leaders Hearts, for whom a draw would have sufficed to make them champions, were beaten at Dundee.

Hay would be tantalised and aggrieved in European competition, especially by the notorious Cup Winners' Cup tie with Rapid Vienna late in 1984. Celtic had been beaten 3–1 in Austria, but appeared to have gone through to the quarter-finals after a 3–0 victory in Glasgow. The visitors appealed that their defender Rudolf Weinhofer had been struck by an object hurled from the crowd. His head was indeed bandaged in a fashion that suggested brain surgery had been carried out, but the footage shows that a bottle had landed yards away from him, and it was alleged that any cut was made by a member of Rapid's backroom staff.

UEFA initially planned to fine both clubs, but then persuaded themselves that Weinhofer had been hit by a coin. With the result in Glasgow annulled, a third match went ahead at Old Trafford to settle the tie. Celtic were not entitled to be sanctimonious in view of the fact that bottles had been thrown in Glasgow, and a vile evening saw Hay's side become overwrought and lose 1–0. During the game a fan burst onto the field from the Stretford End to attack the goalkeeper Herbert Feurer. At full-time another Celtic supporter kicked the scorer Peter Pacult in the testicles before he could get to the sanctuary of the tunnel.

At least UEFA had misgivings about the whole affair and went no further than ordering that Celtic's next home match in European competition be played behind closed doors. The other, informal punishment was the sight of Rapid going far in the Cup Winners' Cup before there was the relief of a defeat to Everton in the final.

In retrospect, the development with the most severe consequences for Celtic in that period was the appointment at Ibrox in 1986 of Graeme Souness, a manager with the funds and the prestige to set Rangers apart in Scotland and at least raise hopes of high standing in Europe. His impact was immediate, with the League title arriving at Ibrox the following year, despite the fact that Hay's side had held a nine-point lead at one stage. There were troubles at Celtic then that were far more profound than a bout of unhappy form. In the course of the season Hay wanted new players, particularly defenders, in the hope of checking Rangers. He was not only rebuffed but almost mocked by a new Celtic chairman so lacking in good sense that he publicly rebuked his manager. 'If Davie Hay wants to bring those players to Celtic, then he will have to pay for them himself,' said Jack McGinn.

Celtic were lacking in defence and it was tormenting for Hay to conclude that he might be able to deny Souness an immediate League title if only he was allowed a meaningful signing. Circumstances seemed almost designed to exasperate him. When he eventually got the forceful centre half he wanted in Manchester City's Mick McCarthy, the deal went through on 20 May 1987, eleven days after the close of Celtic's season. The manager was sacked on 28 May by a board with more on its mind than usual.

The 1987/8 season was about to take them to their centenary, and pride demanded that it be marked by something more than further scars inflicted by Rangers. At least one footballer craved prominence then because his family history cried out for it. Paul McStay was a footballer with an excellent sense of positioning who still put himself in the wrong place at the wrong time. He did nothing to resolve that in the obvious way. Rather than move during a stretch of bad years for the club when he was at his peak, the great-nephew of Willie and Jimmy McStay seemed bound to Celtic by history if not genetics. He had thought of detaching himself and threw his jersey to the crowd at the close of the 1991/2 season, when, at twenty-seven, McStay ought to have been in the middle of his best years.

A few months later, though, he was still captain of the club where he would spend his whole career. If that made him a throwback, then so, too, did the composed passing and the classic, straight-backed manner in which he studied the scene. Given the family tree, he was sure of attention, but he would have received it early in any case as captain of the Scotland side that took the Under-18 European Championship in 1982. Fulfilment for him and so many others in the Celtic team and on the terracing would come in the centenary year.

There had to be an influx of more than just emotion since Celtic could not hold on tight to Maurice Johnston, Murdo MacLeod and Brian McClair, who all moved to other clubs in that summer of 1987. McNeill, crucially, came back for another period as manager. Appointing so prominent a person might have looked like a decision that could be taken virtually by reflex, but Celtic were already on edge after their first experience of a revitalised Rangers. When McNeill attended a dinner to mark the twentieth anniversary of the European Cup win, the chairman McGinn was also there and saw proof in the ovation from the audience that the fans still rallied around him automatically.

McNeill had been expecting to take up a post in Saudi Arabia, but four days later he was Celtic manager once more in place of the sacked Hay. In the circumstances, negotiations had inevitably been furtive, with a key meeting held in a car park, but the outcome cannot really have been in doubt. It seemed only right, after all, that he should be the leader once more as the club saw its 100th anniversary coming into view. He was to be aided by an uncommon practicality, for that year Celtic did more than merely pine for the footballers it had lost. Rather than buy makeweights, they paid West Ham £750,000 for Frank McAvennie.

The forward had swagger, hunger and a reliable finish. Nowadays the price for such an attacker would be well beyond Celtic's means, and even the signing of him in October 1987 was exceptional. 'It only lasted one year to galvanise the team,' says McNeill of the investment in the squad as a whole. 'We were very lucky with McAvennie. He was totally disgruntled because he got hit by the property crash in London.' It is conceivable that the signing-on fee made the return to Scotland particularly appealing. 'I lost a lot of money on houses,' McAvennie said. 'I had two at a time in London.'

He was back with West Ham by March of 1989, and would have returned to London even sooner if McNeill had not succeeded in fending off a series of transfer requests. In some ways, Celtic in the centenary year could be depicted as con men who had concocted the appearance of splendour. All the borrowed props would have to be returned when the scam was over. Even so, it was a joyous illusion for as long as it lasted. The crowd sang 'Happy Birthday' to the club in many games, and did so with more and more hope that there would be a genuine cause of celebration.

As in the earlier phase, McNeill made smart use of his budget. He sought stability in buying known quantities. Having signed Mick McCarthy as his centre half at Manchester City, McNeill then worked with him again in Glasgow. Billy Stark, a thirty-year-old midfielder with know-how and a noteworthy ratio of goals to games, came from Aberdeen for £100,000. McAvennie was not to be the sole recognised scorer in attack either since McNeill had again exhibited astuteness in the transfer market when spending £600,000 on Motherwell's Andy Walker.

By its own standards, the Celtic board had adopted extreme measures to try to mark the 100th anniversary. The recruits were still arriving as late as November 1987, when the winger Joe Miller joined from Aberdeen. It was as if the club were running up bills on the credit card and accepting that there would be thrift to follow at a later date. There was no obvious means under the regime of the time for Celtic to compete regularly with Rangers over an extended period, but if the centenary season was an anomaly it was also a beautiful blip.

Glasgow being as it is, there had to be ugliness as well, and an Old Firm match at Ibrox in October 1987 raised questions over the part the law should play in sport. During the 2–2 draw at Ibrox, a fortnight after he had been bought by Celtic, McAvennie was involved in a confrontation with Chris Woods that soon drew in the Rangers defenders Terry Butcher and Graham Roberts. The goalkeeper Woods and McAvennie were sent off. Butcher would follow them to the stands later, and Roberts, deputising between the posts for Woods, had a bit of spare time that he used to conduct the home crowd in a sectarian singalong.

In such a moment it is hard to tell whether the Old Firm antagonism is more absurd than it is malevolent. The Scottish legal system took a straightforward stance, charging all four players with behaviour likely to cause a breach of the peace. It was a course of action that was unsettling to more than just the accused. People were left to wonder, for instance, how large the crowd at a game had to be before the prosecution was justified for misbehaviour on the pitch.

McAvennie was found not guilty and Roberts received the distinctively Scottish verdict of 'not proven'. Woods and Butcher were convicted and fined. The match itself had another casualty. It had been Jim Duncan's first Old Firm game as a referee and, in the aftermath, he had to spend a week in court. Disenchantment on his part was understandable and he stopped officiating at the top level four years later. He has not stepped inside any of the Scottish Premier Division stadiums since then. Duncan was instead at ease as a committee member of Arniston Rangers, a Junior club.

In 1987 Celtic and Rangers probably drew only practical conclusions from the result at Ibrox. The home side had avoided defeat despite being outnumbered for a while. For his part, McNeill had watched a line-up with new players avoid a disheartening result. While Celtic achieved cohesion, there was disruption for Rangers. Butcher broke his leg in a defeat at

Aberdeen in November, and his team came third in the League. A win there for Celtic the previous month triggered an insistence in a team that lost only once in thirty-four League and Scottish Cup matches, with the Double completed when Dundee United were beaten 2–1 by a pair of McAvennie goals in the final of the latter tournament.

McStay made history and swathed himself in it that season. As captain, he lived up to all the expectations that had surrounded him so claustrophobically since youth, and secured, at twenty-three, the position in Celtic lore that had also been his destiny. He won both of the individual honours as player of the year as seen in the eyes of his fellow professionals and journalists. McStay's background guaranteed that he not only saw the possibility of making history but also had the craving to seize it. His passes were honed and disruptive, particularly since there were forwards such as McAvennie ready to make such use of them. It was the incisiveness that confirmed a vision and hunger that made him so much more than a technician.

Celtic had to keep those images fresh because there was just a single episode of defiance to follow, when they retained the Scottish Cup in 1989 by beating Rangers in the final with a Miller goal. Supporters had little else to encourage them for much of the trophy-less time that followed, until reconstruction of the club began with the takeover by Fergus McCann in 1994. If achievements were absent in a blank interim, the void was filled instead with dissent. Managers became inadvertent casualties since they did not have the calibre of players to wrest attention back to the pitch itself.

The true contrast with Rangers in a period begun by Souness and extended by Walter Smith lay in the fact that Celtic's manager, whoever the unfortunate happened to be, normally lacked such breadth of means. His club felt the pain keenly whenever it stretched to afford a key player who was supposed to galvanise the team. Rangers, with their means and modern stadium, were not at such a pitch of constant anxiety. One episode epitomised the helplessness of Celtic then and entrenched the fear that Rangers could impose their will on any set of circumstances.

Maurice Johnston was the means by which they demonstrated the fact. The forward, brought from Watford to Celtic for £400,000 in November 1984, had been a well-judged acquisition by Hay. He was adroit and sharp, with the spring to get in front of a defender or even above him when there was a prospect of scoring. In the 1985 Scottish Cup final he had been part of the Celtic line-up that came from behind to beat Dundee United. Johnston was at the heart, too, of that even more memorable afternoon the following year, scoring a couple of goals in the victory away to St Mirren that made Celtic champions.

There were no trophies in the season that followed, and a £400,000 transfer took Johnston to Nantes in the summer of 1987. It seemed that he had simply been a brief if eye-catching entry in the club chronicles. In fact, he had paved the way for a more melodramatic and inflammatory episode. He returned to Celtic at a cost of £1.2 million in May 1989 – or so it seemed. Johnston was certainly at the ground, where he held up a scarf and announced that 'There is no other British club I could play for.' In fact, it turned out to be possible for him to join another team in the same city. Despite having signed an agreement with Celtic, he joined Rangers in July.

Disbelief flooded McNeill as much as anger. His captain Roy Aitken had come back from an international match to let him know that his fellow Scotland international Johnston wanted to rejoin his previous club. A sceptical manager said that the forward should phone him. Johnston did so. McNeill then discussed the matter with the Celtic board before agreeing that the proposed transfer could go ahead. The merit of the deal looked the sole topic and it was beyond anyone's conception then that Celtic's opinion would not be the key factor.

This was more than just a matter of a rival bidder coming up with a better offer, although Souness could count on the means being available. While Johnston was hardly the first Catholic to play for Rangers, his fame was great enough to constitute evidence that there would be no element of sectarianism in football affairs to impede Souness as he went on modernising the club. The then manager had the double joy of landing a terrible blow on his rivals while completing a transfer that looked high-minded in its contempt for religious divisions in the west of Scotland. Celtic, on the other hand, were startled and befuddled.

Their pre-contract agreement with Johnston was deemed legally binding by FIFA, and the club could have frozen him out of football until an acceptable settlement had been reached. An old-fashioned Celtic board, however, was content to be vindicated by the authorities and took no further action. They lapsed into a peculiar piece of chivalry as they gave up all rights to Johnston. It satisfied them that the world had been shown that they had acted properly. The stance appalled McNeill because of its weakness. Buying Johnston would have established that Celtic would at least attempt to meet Rangers on equal terms.

Allowing him to go was nothing more than capitulation in McNeill's eyes. The manager had been preparing for a struggle: 'I said to [the agent] Bill McMurdo and Maurice Johnston, "I am not going to say aye to this." I said to Johnston, "You might no play for a year or two if I get my way."' That stance was not echoed by his employers, even if it took a phone call from the journalist Alex Cameron to let him know, while he was in Florida, that the club planned to waive its rights to Johnston.

'I went mental,' McNeill remembers. The news was bad enough in itself, but it was made worse by the fact that Celtic had chosen not to involve him in the issue. McNeill was reduced to seeking Cameron's help. 'The whole situation was desperate. I was on holiday when I found out. I said to Alex, "Could you do me a favour and get [the chairman] Jack McGinn to call me?"' He was to realise that his directors still had the quaint outlook that had already left them so vulnerable.

The board washed its hands of the Johnston issue, and McNeill recalls the directors saying, 'We feel he has insulted Celtic.' It was as if distaste led them to give up the fight. 'Rangers saw an opportunity to put one over on their biggest rivals,' McNeill says. 'You can't argue with that. They knew they had an adversary who wasn't going to be as positive as they were. Celtic backed out of it. Can you imagine what would happen nowadays?'

Some Ibrox fans had also been incensed upon learning that Johnston would be joining their club. They spoke of returning their season tickets, and scarves were set alight, but the move was still a coup. Apart from proving conclusively that there was no longer a sectarian employment policy at Rangers, Souness had also exposed confusion and lack of leadership at Celtic. The aim in the East End of the city was not to come out on top in the struggle but to seize the moral high ground.

Celtic's position in law had been strong, yet no use was made of it and Johnston was free to do them harm. His impact was not particularly great for his new club over the span of Old Firm games, but in November of 1989 he scored the only goal in a defeat of Celtic at Ibrox. While a perceived mercenary did not usually draw all that much affection from the stands there, his effect was profound. 'I felt the manner of the move would damage [Celtic] for a number of years,' Souness said when he eventually looked back on that period. He would also point out that it made sense to buy a striker of such quality. Once Johnston had won the League title in consecutive seasons at Rangers he moved on to Everton.

Individuals might come and go, but the underlying factors did not alter. McNeill asked his board for a transfer fund of £5 million and was told they could run to no more than £1 million. The centenary season might as well have been a hallucination when hard facts showed the club's position to be hopeless. A manager is bound to aim for the best, and McNeill wanted to buy Stuart Pearce. The England left back was said to be available that year, but only to a club of means. Celtic did not have the sums to test the feasibility of such reports, and he remained at Nottingham Forest.

McNeill was an employee of a club who understood that a larger budget was essential, yet wanted, in essence, to keep power solely in the hands of the Kelly and White families. Innovations were attempted, but they could not go far enough. Terry Cassidy was appointed as chief executive. McNeill, generally good-natured, would sum him up as 'a thoroughly unpleasant, untrustworthy, overbearing, offensive individual'.

Results against Rangers deteriorated and a win in, say, a Scottish Cup tie fooled no one into supposing the balance of power had budged. It was the struggle within Celtic that was sustained. There was a cynicism to that clash, and a leaked memo, written by Cassidy, appeared on the front page of the Scottish edition of the *Sun*. It concerned the means by which a change of manager could be made smoothly. Without new revenue, Celtic could only contemplate alterations of a relatively low cost. The identity of the manager was no longer the principal factor, but it was an area where the club could seem bold.

McNeill was sacked in 1991, and Celtic's logic was illustrated as it enjoyed maximum effect when making the next appointment. Liam Brady was one of the most cultivated midfielders of his time, particularly with Arsenal and Juventus. He therefore brought with him to Glasgow a distinction that endeared him to supporters who were also receptive to a former Republic of Ireland international. Brady would be in the Celtic post for two years, in which no trophies were gathered. He could be scoffed at as an idealist, but Brady was among a generation of managers who had acquired personal wealth and did not have to scramble desperately for a salary.

Regardless of his own means, though, funds were tight and there was little margin of error. That was confirmed in a disturbing 5–1 away defeat to Neuchâtel Xamax in the second round of the UEFA Cup in 1991. Brady may have established a grim trend there since later managers such as Gordon Strachan and Neil Lennon would also have mortifying results while attempting to settle down in European competition.

There were specific flaws in Brady's scheme that contributed to the capitulation in Switzerland. Neuchâtel, who would come fifth out of twelve clubs in their domestic league that season, were assisted by the Celtic team selection and tactics. Injuries did compel some adjustments, but Brady's approach to the whole affair was a risky experiment. He had Dariusz Wdowczyk, a left back, as a sweeper and there were three attackers. Reports at the time claimed that the Swiss club was distracted and vulnerable. In the event Neuchâtel trounced the visitors and negotiated the return leg with no difficulty at all.

Such results drain people of patience and confidence in their manager. Brady would therefore be chastised all the more for having spent £1.1 million on a former Ireland teammate, Tony Cascarino, in July 1991. The forward scored four goals for Celtic before being bundled off to Chelsea seven months later. That deal saw Celtic receive Tom Boyd in exchange, but the worth of a sound defender was not fully appreciated in Brady's short tenure.

The signing of Stuart Slater during the summer of 1992 was indicative of the manager's quandary. He cost £1.5 million from West Ham and had an adhesive first touch that confirmed his technical excellence. Slater represented the ideals that the manager thought he could implant in the Celtic squad. Brady, who had been his teammate at West Ham, called him 'the type of player to put bums on seats, then get them off seats'. Fans would indeed leap to their feet at the sight of the winger, but did so mostly to howl their criticism. A hardier temperament was called for from any newcomer when Rangers were in the ascendancy. The manager himself had shown his mettle on the pitch with clubs of high standing, but getting the most out of players capable of far less than him was a different objective.

It was understandable that he would move for a veteran who had prospered with Celtic before, but the physical decline of a thirty-three-year-old McAvennie at Aston Villa, where he had not scored in his few appearances, meant that there was little remaining worth in him. There were some goals for Celtic, but too few to counter the argument that his reappearance embodied everything that had gone wrong at the club. It misses the point, all the same, simply to grumble that Brady had miscalculated, even if he frankly admits that too few of his additions to the squad were effective.

At Ibrox, Walter Smith, the successor to Souness, also made errors, but if someone such as the accomplished yet listless Alexei Mikhailichenko was an underachiever, the overall strength of the side compensated for it and, in any case, Brian Laudrup could be bought to take over the Ukrainian's duties. Smith was always in a position to tolerate the foibles of Mikhailichenko in any case and made a joke of the player's lethargy by applauding his 'great economy of movement'.

At Celtic, the margin of error was much too tight for someone like Slater to be excused, particularly for a manager attempting to learn how to do the job while carrying it out. Brady resigned following a defeat at St Johnstone in October 1993 that had left his club ninth in the table. Lou Macari filled the vacancy, and could initially tap into the residual fondness supporters felt for him, but the identity of the manager was not the key issue any more.

Macari's tenure lasted eight months. The better players looked disillusioned and there was talk of scorn towards him from the team, although that sort of gossip has the convenient side effect of deflecting attention from the squad itself. Wayne Biggins was a thirty-two-year-old forward whom Macari bought in November 1993, and he swiftly demonstrated why he was so little known. He did not score at all in his few months with Celtic and his name has become a byword for haplessness among fans.

It would still be naive to hold Macari wholly accountable for any fiasco. Biggins, for instance, was only on the books because the manager had needed a new forward of some sort once Andy Paton, a Brady signing who had served the manager well, insisted on going back to England. Macari was in charge for the first time when Paton made his last appearance for Celtic in a 2–1 win at Ibrox on 30 October 1993. While there would have been personal factors, it was still damning that he preferred to sign for Barnsley, who that season came eighteenth in the English second tier, then known as the Football League First Division.

The larger context lay in the state of a club so reduced in finance and expectation that its manager and board told themselves that even a player of Biggins's humdrum capabilities ought to be taken onto the payroll. Macari did flounder, but it would have taken an exceptional manager to make his voice heard above the roar of anger and protest. Supporters recognised that the entire basis on which the club then operated dictated the shabby look of the team sheet. The fear and insecurity at Celtic Park persisted no matter who sat watching from the dugout.

Long after Rangers had sold Maurice Johnston, Celtic were still trapped in an angry yet fatalistic frame of mind. Souness himself exchanged Ibrox for Anfield by becoming manager of Liverpool in 1991, but his purchase of Johnston went on working exactly as intended.

8

FERGUS McCANN

It is meant to be a good day when a club buys a player. The chairman can bask in the occasion after appeasing, if never completely pleasing, sceptical supporters, but Fergus McCann was permanently different. In December 1997 Celtic announced the signing of the Norwegian striker Harald Brattbakk for £2 million. 'Boring, isn't it?' McCann said to me as he walked from the television cameras to his meeting with my fellow members of the written press. He could be idiosyncratic when subjected to media rituals he found tedious. A journalist asked the bespectacled Brattbakk what his day job had been when he was a part-time footballer in Trondheim. 'He was a loan shark,' McCann barked, startling a player with a blameless past in financial services.

Snappy, impatient and incapable of soft-soaping his way through life, McCann was the extraordinary owner of Celtic from 1994 to 1999. He always seemed to be at war, but with the passage of time the smoke of those battles drifts away and he can be seen clearly as one of the greatest figures in the club's history. Belatedly, McCann has started to become popular with those who once accused him of a miserly attitude, and nowadays there is a supporters club named after him in Rio de Janeiro and another called the Wee Bunnet, in honour of the headgear he favoured, in Camberley, Surrey. He did transform the club, ripping it from the hands of the Kellys and the Whites, who viewed

CELTIC

their families' historic 'stewardship' as justification for never-ending control, even when the business of football was evolving in ways beyond the scope of many in the boardroom.

The stubborn McCann was the right answer to Celtic's problems, but it was an exhausting one. He and his critics reached common ground in agreeing that the five years of his torrid tenure were more than enough. If anything, he had an aversion to courting popularity. On 1 August 1998 he came out before the stands of the rebuilt 60,000-seat Celtic Park he had envisaged and prepared to unfurl the League flag marking the return of the championship to the club after ten years. A substantial part of the crowd reacted by booing him with every cubic centimetre of lung capacity it possessed. The fans were riled both by the departure of Wim Jansen, the manager who had won the title, and by the lack of new arrivals to improve the squad.

'My wife, who only went to two games in five years, felt it,' says McCann. 'She was really quite upset by that. It didn't bother me as much as you would think. I was not there to get thousands of people cheering or to get rounds of applause every time I showed up. The plan was to make this thing work.' It is an irony that the conversion of Celtic into a supposedly soulless plc has been accompanied by the ascent to the chairmanship of people like him and his successors Brian Quinn and John Reid, who were rank-and-file supporters from boyhood.

There has been an almost perverse reluctance from McCann to trade on that background, even though it might have helped mollify fans craving a squad to overturn the domination of Rangers entirely. Extreme circumstances were needed to force him into summoning up his past.

As another miserable campaign was confirmed in the spring of 1997, he wrote to supporters urging them to renew their season tickets. His mind turned in that letter to the debut of Jimmy Johnstone, which he had witnessed at Kilmarnock in 1963, but McCann's purpose was to recall, as well, a 6–0 defeat for the side on that occasion. 'Being a Celtic supporter is not always easy, but it is always worthwhile,' he argued. This aphorism would be a good motto for the five years in which he ran the club. McCann himself sometimes found it agonising before he got his remarkable reward by selling the shares that had cost him £9.5 million for £40 million. As he was preparing to leave, he promised to put £1.5 million into Celtic's youth policy if a certain percentage of his holding was taken up by fans.

The sale fell short of that benchmark and McCann hung onto the money, indifferent to suggestions that he would be hailed for his magnanimity if he handed over the sum. He had still kept to his original stance by making his offer to supporters. There had been reports in 1998 of a takeover attempt by a group including Kenny Dalglish and Jim Kerr, the Simple Minds singer and song-writer, even if a formal bid was never received. 'I have not given years of my life to Celtic, along with my fellow directors, to take it from bankruptcy to a point of strength and then recommend a proposal which fails to reflect Celtic's values and aspirations,' McCann said then. 'Aside from being below market value, the consortium's proposals take no account of the value to Celtic shareholders of having a significant say in the future of their club – something that, until flotation, Celtic supporters were denied for over 100 years.'

McCann was never apologetic and, after getting that £40 million in 1999, said that every shareholder had enjoyed a better deal than him. The reason? The worth of their stake had grown at precisely the same rate as his, but they had not needed to work for the club every day. That obstinate pithiness was typical of this surprising person. He was a fifty-three-year-old bachelor when he bought a majority stake in Celtic. By the time he left in April 1999 he had a wife, Elspeth, a corporate lawyer he met while she was involved in the takeover, and three children, the youngest of whom was the twelve-day-old Malcolm when the family flew out of Scotland. The timing, with the season still in progress, was reportedly connected with tax planning. There was also relief at escaping a harassed life in Glasgow. He and

Elspeth, for instance, would be doorstepped by reporters pursuing unfounded rumours that the marriage had broken down. McCann must have wondered if these tales were being peddled by one of his enemies.

When I visited him on a summer's morning, he had just driven the kids to their holiday pastimes, with the two daughters going horse-riding. We met in a downbeat office near his home, to the west of Boston, Massachusetts. Despite having four season tickets for Celtic Park, he never plays the part of the diehard transatlantic fan. His connection to the club has none the less been a major factor throughout his life and he continues to be better informed about the minutiae of players and results than the critics who branded him a mercenary would suppose.

His father, a headmaster, first took him to watch a Celtic match early in the 1950s, although the main image he retains is of a bald East Fife defender, most likely Sammy Stewart, thumping the ball away. The family were then living in the town of Kilsyth, a historic bastion of Protestantism that, in the west of Scotland's antithetical landscape, is close to the ultra-Catholic village of Croy. McCann would go on, as a young man, to become social convener of the Croy Celtic Supporters Club.

He soon grasped that such organisations are as tortuous as a Trotskyite cell. 'No meeting was less than four hours long,' he remembers. 'That was just brutal – the price of the bus, who's not been paid, who's going to be banned and all that stuff.' Uproar arose when, because of limited interest, there was a need to travel jointly with the 'rebel' St James CSC of Coatbridge, which was not a member of the Celtic Supporters Association, on the then arduous journey to Inverness. Compensations did exist, however. 'They subsidised the trip by buying beer at a great discount,' McCann explains. 'So they had sixty dozen bottles of beer in the trunk of the bus. And they would serve shots of whisky. The economics were very unstable. Having left at midnight we got there about six o'clock in the morning. There was a bar on the bus and it was open all night.'

McCann had a desire to follow Celtic abroad, and just before he emigrated to Canada he pulled off the then uncommon feat of watching the side in an away match in Europe. This was financed by persuading two Scottish newspapers that they should let him cover the Cup Winners' Cup game with Basle in September 1963. The embryonic, demanding McCann is there in his quibbles about a 5–1 win. 'The side', he grumbled in the match report, 'has weaknesses at wing-half which would undoubtedly have been exploited by a faster team.'

He may have been writing with a trembling hand because no press seat had been arranged. McCann only got in at all because a ticket for a place behind the goals was rustled up by a Celtic director called Desmond White. By 1972 McCann was staging a delayed, 'as live' broadcast of Celtic's European Cup semi-final with Internazionale at the Maple Leaf Gardens in Toronto. The offer that the club made him was his single piece of luck. 'I bought the rights from Desmond White for £300,' says McCann. 'He gave me a pretty good deal on that.'

In theory there was poignancy in the fact that White's son Chris should be forced out of Celtic by the putsch in the spring of 1994, although McCann could never be hampered by sentimentality. He was undoubtedly a fan, but that attachment also made him acutely conscious of the club's potential in commercial terms. After turning his back on a career as a chartered accountant, his first substantial venture was the showing of that semi-final in Toronto.

This was a crash course in misfortune. Costs were far greater than he had bargained for and the Italian community in Toronto he had been counting on did not show up in the numbers anticipated because they believed, wrongly, that Inter would be knocked out after being held to a goalless draw in the first leg. McCann had been hoping for 12,000 customers, but had to make do with 7,000. Extra time and a defeat for Celtic in a penalty shoot-out also meant that he had to stump up for 152 minutes of satellite time.

The event obliterated him financially. 'I didn't buy any clothes for two years,' explains McCann, who thinks it might have been as much as ten years before he cleared the last of the debts. The man from whom he had bought the advertising for the event was retired and living in Vancouver when the account was settled. 'He was astounded,' says McCann, 'when he got a cheque in the mail for the amount plus interest.'

That hapless piece of entrepreneurship might have deterred Celtic's future owner since, as he recalls, 'all my money was gone, and I hadn't had that much to start with'. That misadventure, though, convinced him of his own durability. 'The thing I learned', McCann remembers, 'was that the school of hard knocks gives you the best MBA you can get. You understand that you're dealing with rascals at times and that you have to be quick on your feet. You have to be able to take the knocks. Not many people can handle that, and I found that I could. The short, sharp lesson lasting three weeks in 1972 I value now very highly. At the time, misery.'

The following year he had started a golf-holiday business that sent its first party of Americans to the 1973 Open Championship at Troon. 'I would charter planes, 707s, to cross the Atlantic,' he says. 'That's risk. And I've got ads in *Golf Digest* and I've got seats to fill. I realised that to make money in the travel business you have to be the principal, not the agent. You have to be the person that carries the risk.' McCann was aggressive in developing this venture and the story goes that, once it had started to flourish, he relayed the good news to a British Airways executive who had previously spurned an invitation to become involved. The phone call, according to a newspaper report, wakened the man at his home in the middle of the night.

After selling up in 1986 McCann had the basis of the fortune that made him a realistic bidder for Celtic. Other interested parties included Gerald Weisfeld, who had built up the What Every Woman Wants chain with his wife Vera. What made McCann different was the belief he had in the potential of the club. It was a peculiarity that a person living in Montreal should have a much better grasp of this than those for whom Celtic was the focal point of their everyday lives in Glasgow.

Those of us in the press, with our own limited perception, could barely decide which was the crazier of his claims. Was it the assertion that the club would prove 'a good investment'? Or might it have been his argument that a 60,000-capacity ground was appropriate, just when attendances for a failing Celtic could dip below 15,000? McCann had foreseen the gentrification and expansion of the football audience, partly because he was conscious of that long-established trend in North American sport. Others with a desire to win control of the club envisaged bolting seats into the concrete terracing of the existing ground to comply with the Taylor Report. Had this gone ahead the sole advantage would have lain in meeting the 1994 deadline without needing temporarily to become tenants at Hampden Park, but the club would have been lumbered with an unsatisfactory stadium in which Celtic's prospects would have been as diminished as the crowd capacity.

McCann understood that there was a market for modern amenities in the old game. 'It's not all people', as he puts it, 'who are drinking beer and fighting.' With his own money at stake, he examined the matter at length. 'When I did a survey, it turned out that 69 per cent of Celtic supporters owned their own home. If I'd asked you in 1994 how many you thought it would be, you'd have said 25 per cent or something like that. The media underestimated the financial strength of the support.'

McCann had long wished to become involved with Celtic, seeing a commercial opportunity at a club of which he was also a supporter. His first approach to the board came in the late 1980s, when McCann suggested to the then chairman Jack McGinn that the marketing skills honed in the golf-holiday business could be employed to sell far more Celtic season tickets. That sort of aim ran contrary to the instincts of the people then in charge at the club.

'They had about 7,000 season tickets, which were very expensive,' says McCann. 'They wouldn't issue any more and they always said it was too complex to do so. The real reason was that if "these people" got season tickets, they would want everything: away tickets for Aberdeen and Rangers, Cup final tickets. To hell with them, that was the attitude. The supporters are the enemy.

'I could see that capital was missing and that an understanding of marketing was totally missing. Management of the operation was missing and also, eventually, the integrity was missing. That was the key thing. They would say one thing and mean another. All they cared about was their own position. Fear of losing that was all that really mattered. It was all they had. These were people who would otherwise not have anything. They were directors of Celtic and that's what they did have. That was something they would not give up. Also, as they saw it, they had a huge moral obligation not to risk ownership of this institution going to someone who they would later be blamed for [allowing to take over]. That meant anyone. There was no list of people who were OK. No one was OK.'

Celtic were trapped in a syndrome that frequently affects family concerns. It has been observed that such businesses are often established by one generation, developed by the next and ruined by the third. That pattern was taking shape in Glasgow. The resurgence of Rangers was met first with complacency at Celtic and then by panic when excellent players such as Terry Butcher took the Ibrox team to a far higher plane. A dynamic Rangers made the most of perfect circumstances. In that period, when television revenue was a minor factor, Rangers could afford to employ footballers like Butcher and, much later, Paul Gascoigne.

One complacent Celtic director had so misunderstood the enterprise that he maintained for a while that their rivals were simply spending in an effort to make up lost ground. Talent was too thinly spread in his own boardroom to cover the many issues that needed to be addressed. By contrast, Rangers, in the aftermath of the Ibrox disaster that killed sixty-six people in 1971, had rebuilt their ground as an exemplary all-seater stadium. Celtic could not grasp that a trend had been set. Developments at Celtic Park, while welcome, rested on the assumption that the vast majority of the crowd would go on watching the games from the terracing. After one haphazardly conducted survey Celtic felt confident enough to announce that their supporters preferred to stand.

That policy contained the implicit conviction that football is primarily for men, since women are not generally tall enough to get an unobstructed view from packed terracing. McCann, interestingly enough, had shown his usual blend of pragmatism and idealism over the expansion of the football audience when arguing in his Croy days that women should be allowed to become full members of the supporters club. Nowadays it would not be feasible for the club to sell 56,000 season tickets, as it did for several years, without the appeal to both sexes.

It took McCann a while to appreciate that change was dreaded by a sclerotic Celtic board that presided over an anachronistic, elderly ground and could not bear to break away from the vacuous parts of its tradition. Prior to the publication of the Taylor Report in 1990, with its recommendation that Britain's top-flight stadiums should be all-seated, he had suggested lending the club £6 million so that two stands containing 12,000 people apiece could be built. The redevelopment would have allowed for terracing at each end with room for a total of 48,000 fans, so giving the ground an overall capacity of 72,000.

McCann states that he was ready to lend the money at half the bank rate as part of an arrangement that would have seen him take a commission on the season-ticket sales, which he would promote. Celtic turned him down, and it is claimed that they did so because they did not believe in his financial projections. McCann's acumen could have been trusted in view of the favourable terms on which he was offering his cash. He took the rejection by the board as proof that there would be no part-nership with the directors. 'That was treated with total terror,' he says of their reaction to the scheme he laid out. 'The better that offer sounded, the more terrified they became. That was the interesting thing. What was there to lose? This guy's crazy. You get money at half-rate, he's going to be at risk, he gets no shares, he gets no vote. He's in for £6 million, we run the show and he gets commission. What was there to go wrong? You grab it with both hands. I realised at that point that there was no way to work with these people unless you got some control.'

One capable person did, none the less, take a seat on the board. Michael Kelly was of imperial blood, since his grand-father James Kelly had been the leading player when a Celtic team first took the field in 1888. He had much more than that to commend him. Michael Kelly, who had been the youngest Lord Provost of Glasgow since 1782, was not blind to the flaws of the others on the club's board and, in passing, often portrays them as hapless in a memoir that refers, for instance, to another director, Tom Grant, acting independently and binding the club to a stupid deal for £120,000 worth of office equipment. None the less, Kelly absurdly depicts the takeover by McCann as the destruction of a great tradition, of the 'real Celtic'.

Kelly was fully conscious of the lack of ability in the board-room. This was addressed with a directorship for David Smith, a Celtic fan who had been behind the £2.3-billion takeover of the Gateway supermarket group. Although that acquisi-tion soon ran into difficulties, Smith could reasonably be por-trayed as the kind of substantial and cosmopolitan financier never before appointed to the board. He and Kelly, however, were thwarted by a fanciful ambition. It was Kelly's aim to find someone who would inject capital while also recognising 'fam-ily tradition'.

Overtures, indeed, had once been made to McCann when he might have been regarded as the saviour of the old regime rather than its nemesis. 'Michael Kelly came to Montreal with David Smith,' McCann remembers. 'He came with some city of Glasgow souvenirs, brass cufflinks. He had no real interest in doing any business at all, but they were desperate. He was intelligent enough to know that they had to get capital from somewhere. But the only terms would have been, "Write me a cheque and I'll let you know how I get on."'

Kelly's view is that McCann did not intend even to enter a proper discussion that day, but no one else was swayed either by the sort of proposals being put to them. The club, in consequence, could not change hands in an amicable manner. There were protest movements involving supporters groups such as Celts for Change and, all the while, the satire and detailed analysis of fanzines such as *Not the View* rallied dissenters. Public meetings stoked the desire to remake the club. They were often addressed by Brian Dempsey. He had established his own house-building company and also had the fluent oratory that perhaps reflected the fact that he was the son of an MP. Where McCann had an aversion to speechifying, Dempsey's knack of engaging with an audience and strengthening its commitment was priceless in that period. 'You are the salt of the earth,' he would tell them earnestly.

Dempsey had already been a member of the Celtic board, taken onto it at the same time as Michael Kelly in 1990. The latter, however, joined with others to prevent the appointment of Dempsey being ratified at the next AGM. Whatever the motives in that specific case, the directors were in a hopeless situation. By and large, they lacked talent and, even with the advent of David Smith, looked like anachronisms on a football scene that was getting ever more complex and dangerous.

The board were made to feel embattled. McCann's campaign was plotted by David Low, a financial analyst whose manoeuvres kept the board under strain. There are colourful tales about his jaunts around the border areas of Northern Ireland to buy up shares in Celtic. On one occasion, Low, wearing a costly tailor-made suit, found himself sitting on a milk urn in a cow shed in South Fermanagh. The farmer began by swearing that he could never sell a holding that been in the hands of his family for generations. He had a change of heart once the offer was raised by £1,000. Celtic, as a private limited company, could routinely block their transfer into hostile hands. Low countered that veto by having the owners assign the voting rights to him immediately while entering into a contract to transfer the shares themselves whenever that became possible.

This, in a way, was nothing more than showmanship. The board, to the end, had sufficient votes to defeat any hostile proposal that was tabled, but they could no longer function since their every step met with scepticism, if not ridicule. The misery of their situation must also have taken its toll. With three minutes gone of the home game against Rangers on New Year's Day 1994, Celtic were 2–0 down and the crowd was in revolt. One man tied his scarf in a noose and swung it from side to side in front of the directors' box. The Rangers manager Walter Smith could not help but glance at the scene. 'What are you looking at?' screamed a fan. 'It's got fuck all to do with you.' For the first time some figures at Rangers reckoned they were no longer hated above all others by these supporters. They had been displaced by the Celtic board.

The following month David Smith was to the fore as he startled the press with an announcement that the club had cornerstone finance of £20 million that would let it embark on the building of a new stadium in Cambuslang, to the east of Glasgow. This funding was supposed to be coming from a merchant bank called Gefinor, but its representatives were soon denying that any such agreement existed. The impression of chaos was so great that it made the continuation of the existing regime at Celtic an impossibility.

The Celts for Change group called for a boycott of the home match with Kilmarnock four days later. They then kept their own tally and claimed that there had been 8,225 people present, rather than the officially declared attendance of a still paltry 10,882. Those who did attend saw a fox race onto the pitch, and added to the animal's fear with their roars as they took it as a symbol of a different sort of hunt that was in progress. Key people had come to consider the Celtic board as quarry. The Bank of Scotland no longer needed to dread the bad publicity that would come from throwing the club into crisis. That, indeed, was what most fans had yearned for.

Five Celtic directors had previously struck a binding agreement that none of them could sell his shares unless they all did. They had been united in opposition the previous year when McCann and others offered to invest £13.8 million into the club, but when the Bank of Scotland asked for personal guarantees from the board members and threatened to put Celtic into receivership it became inevitable that there would be a revolution.

The businessman Gerald Weisfeld was close to completing a takeover, and thought on at least one occasion that he had done so. He was thwarted because the pact designed to bind five of the club's directors left them at the mercy of one another. Two of them rebuffed Weisfeld, just when McCann had all but despaired. He had feared that Kevin Kelly, Michael Kelly's cousin, and Tom Grant 'would never get off the bloody fence'. At the last moment, they split with the other three pact members, Smith, Michael Kelly and Chris White. Kevin Kelly and Grant had the support of fellow directors Jack McGinn and Jimmy Farrell, and the quartet comprised a majority of the board. Rapid steps then had to be taken lest the club really was forced into receivership. Eight minutes before the Bank of Scotland deadline of noon on Friday 4 March 1994 documents were signed and £1 million of McCann's money was lodged to stabilise the club's financial position.

McCann had won but it galled him that he would have to buy the shares of Michael Kelly and others that same day, so rewarding people he had accused of ruining Celtic. 'Not one thin dime,' he snapped, before being talked round by his advisers. Sums of up to £300 a share were agreed. 'I regretted bitterly paying them,' McCann admits. 'When Kevin Kelly [eventually] sold his shares he didn't get the same because the price had come down to a realistic level.'

Once the takeover was concluded, McCann had no taste for courtesy. 'We're all glad you're going,' he said to Michael Kelly. 'You've been a disaster for Celtic.' Kelly regarded that as loutish behaviour. For McCann, it was overdue frankness. Late that Friday evening Dempsey stood on the steps of the main entrance to the stadium and addressed the fans who had gathered in the car park, which by then had become a habitual scene of protest. In a remark that is now part of the lore of the club, he said, 'The battle is over, the rebels have won.'

Little more was heard from him in that period. Dempsey did not invest in the ensuing share issue and he would occasionally be caustic about the way McCann ran the club, accusing him of protecting the value of his shares in the short term with a conservative attitude that stopped Celtic's potential from being tapped to the full. It was Dempsey's belief that the club should build a new ground to the north of the city in Robroyston, an area in which he had plans of his own for housing development. McCann chose instead to rebuild Celtic Park.

The idea had been that Dempsey would be one of four people putting in £1 million apiece to a new share issue, while McCann invested the £8.25 million – by his calculations, two-thirds of his fortune – that ensured his personal control of Celtic. In the event, Dempsey bought none of the shares and McCann stumped up a further £1 million to make up the shortfall.

In retrospect, Dempsey does look an implausible member of any supporting cast. McCann's mind goes back to a meeting with the accountants advising him in the fight for Celtic. 'I remember we were at Pannell Kerr Forster,' he says, 'and we were trying to get this thing done. Is he [Dempsey] going to put in his money or not? And he said, "I want to be chairman of

Celtic, don't you understand?" When he lost his rag it finally came out.'

McCann, taking such a gamble with his wealth, could never have shared power, particularly not with someone putting a far smaller sum at risk. The withdrawal of Dempsey was damaging. Perhaps he and McCann could never have operated in tandem, but Dempsey's charm and presentational skills might have eased Celtic away from some shuddering conflicts. It became normal instead for McCann to resign himself to disputes. Many wondered if he could have been more selective about the fights he took on.

The judicious Brian Quinn was Acting Deputy Governor of the Bank of England before resigning in 1996 to join the board of Celtic. Four years later he became chairman of the club. 'I've had a lot of experience speaking to businessmen, bankers and the like, but he was unique,' Quinn says of McCann. 'He had tremendous focus; he was not deflected by anything. He wasn't a warm man. He wasn't a nasty man either, very far from it. He wasn't vindictive. He was there to do a professional job, not to make friends and influence people.

'He is a disputatious person. He was almost always right, although we have all learned in life that that doesn't necessarily suffice. He knew when something had been done that wasn't right. Fergus was argumentative; he was litigious, too. Whenever there was something done that he thought was against the interests of Celtic or improper in some sense, he would not hesitate. He would consult the lawyers and send a writ off to the company or to the individual or to the newspaper or to whoever it was.

'My attitude to this was that I thought it was excessive. I think we spent too much time doing things that had no reasonable prospect of success and could be counterproductive when you take the longer-term considerations into account. It's not even a question of not making friends. You don't create the right impression; in commercial business you don't have the right kind of relationships with people if you're known to be a person that always sues. Fergus sued often enough to take me to the view that we were too much involved in litigation.'

McCann caused a certain sadness with his sacking of Lou Macari, who still benefited from the popularity he had enjoyed as a Celtic player when he came back to manage the club in the autumn of 1993. A manager who is a remnant of the previous regime is always in danger, and he was dismissed by McCann in June of the following year. Macari had laboured with a poor squad, and his team was an ugly one. It would have been a surprise if he had been retained, but another proprietor would have come up with a compensation package. Not McCann.

Macari had kept his family home, which was near Stoke-on-Trent, after being told that he must base himself primarily in Scotland. To McCann's mind this merited dismissal. Macari accounted for his movements by saying that he had been scouting players south of the border. He also sued in the Court of Session. The judge, Lady Cosgrove, called McCann 'a rather devious individual', but found in Celtic's favour. An imprudent Macari then took his case to the Court of Appeal in 1999 and lost again, adding to the terrible costs he had already incurred. Lord Rodger of Earlsferry commented: 'Perhaps predictably, Mr McCann's approach was wholly different from the one followed by the previous board of directors. In particular the old board had adopted a somewhat laissez-faire attitude to management, exemplified by their perception that the manager must be allowed a free hand and left on his own to get on with his job.'

With his personal fortune staked on Celtic's results, McCann had no reason to be so detached, but it would have been feasible to reach a compromise with Macari that did not hurt the club discernibly. The confrontations seemed never to be ducked and the relentlessness could feel debilitating. 'We were in dispute with Lou Macari, we were in dispute with David Hay [a later departee who had come back to the club as chief scout in 1994],' says Quinn. 'We were in dispute with certain newspapers, and my view was that we had much, much more important things to do than expend our energies on all the [law] suits. There are occasions when it can be justified to settle with someone, where the PR damage or the energy loss is too great.'

Quinn had it firmly in mind 'to avoid excessive litigation' once he was chairman. 'In terms of turnover,' he said, 'we are not all that big a company. You can't afford to be involved in that too much.' Even so, Quinn appreciates the conditions under which McCann operated. In the summer of 1994, for instance, Celtic grudgingly contemplated a year as tenants at Hampden, where they were often at odds with their landlords. The club had hoped to remain at Celtic Park even while major parts of the rebuilding were in progress, but the Scottish Football Association would not allow that and £600,000 had to be spent on renting the national stadium. They had also failed to qualify for European competition. McCann knew by then that he could not count on the fans to stand unflinchingly behind him. For his first home game as owner, the attendance was 36,199. For the last of that season, six weeks later, the crowd was down to 16,827.

Steps were taken to revive the morale of supporters, and there could not have been a more popular replacement for Macari than Tommy Burns. No player's life has ever been so indistinguishable from that of the club. Burns, born close to the ground, was educated for a time in the school beside St Mary's, the church where Celtic had been formed. As manager and, later, coach he would attend Mass there at lunchtime. Players used to remark on the fact that a fiercely driven figure on the training ground in the morning would be at peace in the afternoon. His funeral, too, was held at St Mary's after he died from a recurrence of malignant melanoma, at the age of fifty-one, in May 2008. As the journalist Glenn Gibbons put it, Burns had the background of someone who would have been among the club's founders had he been born in the nineteenth century.

There were practical reasons for Celtic to covet him in the summer of 1994 since he had done good work as manager by keeping Kilmarnock in the Scottish Premier League. McCann, intolerant of the protocols, went so far as to approach Burns without first getting the approval of his club. After Kilmarnock protested, Celtic were fined £100,000 and eventually ordered to pay £200,000 in compensation. This deepened the resentment of McCann towards the SFA, but in the end he would have his triumph by demonstrating that the ruling body had discriminated against Celtic in another matter.

In the Burns affair, he contrasted the punishment with the footling £5,000 fine imposed on Rangers for 'tapping up' the Dundee United striker Duncan Ferguson the year before. Indignation, though, did not climb so high in the latter dispute since United received the solace of a £4-million fee for their player. Celtic could hardly be convinced that they had been dealt with impartially over Burns, but there was no prospect of a relaxed view being taken of any topic at a club in steep decline. It had not won a trophy in five years and had come no higher than third in the League since taking the title in 1988. No one, least of all McCann, was capable of being laconic, while Burns, admirable in many respects, was an emotional character who could not help but increase the volatility at the club.

In September 1994 he approached Motherwell and agreed to buy the midfielder Phil O'Donnell for £1.75 million, which was perhaps double the realistic valuation. The deal had not been sanctioned by McCann and the sum was so large that, at the time of writing, it continues to be the record amount ever received for a player by the Lanarkshire club. Burns once said that Celtic's then owner dealt with profit and loss, while he dealt with dreams and ambition.

'I've got some dreams and ambitions as well,' McCann replied in comments made before the death of Burns. 'Maybe I've got a different view of it. If he tells the guy at Motherwell that £1.75 million will be fine for Phil O'Donnell, what am I going to do? I tried to speak to the owner at Motherwell [John Chapman] and he said, "I just leave that to the manager." Quite right, too, because he had already got the deal done at twice the price.' O'Donnell's worth was to be a moot point since he was often injured. He died of a heart attack in 2007, while playing once more for his first club, Motherwell.

Burns did make Celtic more attractive, and his fourth competitive match in charge was an enlivening 2–0 win over Rangers at Ibrox. The gulf had not really been closed and Celtic would fail as usual to put up any fight for the title. Early efforts to rebuild the squad were dubious. Charlie Nicholas, for instance, had little left to offer when Billy McNeill brought back from Aberdeen for a second spell with the club. Macari released him, but Burns then re-signed the striker. Impatience would have been a key factor in the ill-starred move for O'Donnell that provoked McCann without improving the side.

Celtic could not even bumble along unobtrusively. They got to the League Cup final and lost it to Raith Rovers, opponents from a lower division. Burns's side were 2–1 ahead but conceded a late equaliser. Raith won the Cup in a shoot-out, with the Celtic captain Paul McStay in tears after missing the key penalty. It would have been a devastating loss for the club at any point in their history, but the misery had come just as Celtic, following the initial investment by McCann and his associates, was preparing to offer new shares to its supporters and other parties.

Raith Rovers beat Celtic on 27 November 1994. The closing date for the share issue was eight weeks away and there was a prospect that emotionally spent supporters would be too impoverished by Christmas shopping to commit themselves to investing a minimum of £620, even when low-interest loans were on offer. Many believed it inconceivable that Celtic would stick to their proposed schedule, but McCann discerned that people would dig deep precisely because the club was in such a plight. He decided against postponing the whole exercise.

'The thing that sticks in my mind most from all the time I was there', says McCann, 'was that night when the deadline was the next day. I was sitting inside Celtic Park at 7 p.m. when there was pouring rain outside. In the first couple of weeks, typically, there hadn't been much response to the share issue, and then the money started coming in. By that night there were long queues outside waiting to get in the door and up the stairs to the Jock Stein lounge so they could put their money down. I said to myself, "I cannot let these people down." Really, it was the most daunting time I had there. I thought, "I cannot piss their money away."

'You had to think of the dangers of going out to buy a star player and getting it wrong because you wanted to be make yourself a hero, which is the [then Rangers chairman] David Murray approach. You'd be doing it with someone else's money, not just your own. I really felt a great, heavy burden. People had put their cash down. I learned at that moment that I was right and that the supporters were going to be there. My plan was going to work.'

McCann was correct about his strategy, but the process was excruciating. Burns did win the 1995 Scottish Cup final, and a trophy that Celtic would later see as being of secondary interest looked like a gleaming promise of better days to come. Celtic had tormented themselves in beating Airdrie that afternoon and one of the main images associated with the match is of a tackle in the penalty area made by Peter Grant, who took part despite being barely fit after injury, to guard the 1–0 lead. The goal had come from Pierre van Hooijdonk. The Dutchman had been signed from NAC Breda in January and to Burns, in the wake of the final, he represented all that could be achieved if McCann were not, as he saw it, so parsimonious.

Immediately after the game the manager tried to use his new status by making comments intended to put pressure on McCann to allow him a greater budget and the freedom to use it entirely as he saw fit. It was a foolish ploy to adopt against an owner who was sure that Celtic could only advance step by prudent step. Burns, always prey to his own emotions, could not work in harmony with McCann. The manager went through the subsequent two seasons without winning a trophy and his contract was not renewed when it ended in 1997.

Burns did return to the club eventually and, at the time of his death, was first-team coach under Gordon Strachan. It was the type of post, tied to the training ground and far removed from the boardroom, that fitted him well. Aiden McGeady, an emerging star who sometimes looked wrapped up in his own virtuosity, recorded how Strachan's criticism of his performance would sometimes see Burns springing to his defence. McGeady may also have been young enough not to realise when a good cop–bad cop strategy is in progress.

The role of Celtic manager had not been so easy for Burns to fill, but there may have been no one else available who would have coped with the circumstances. He did buy exciting if unreliable footballers. The striker Jorge Cadete was to damage far more than defences. Celtic had such difficulty in registering him after concluding a deal with Sporting Lisbon that he was not eligible for a 1996 Scottish Cup semi-final with Rangers in which Celtic were beaten 2–1. Cadete was the focus of great hopes, and on his debut in the Scottish Premier League six days earlier the roar when he scored against Aberdeen was so loud that it blew the microphones and put BBC Radio 5 Live off air for a few moments.

A more lasting uproar would be caused by the SFA's refusal to register Cadete sooner. Internal investigations insisted that the chief executive Jim Farry had acted properly, but McCann could not be fobbed off. No one supposed he was bluffing when he threatened to take the matter to court, even if clubs are supposedly prohibited from suing the ruling body. The SFA ultimately agreed to an independent inquiry that took place nearly three years after the signing of Cadete. It was a debacle for them. Farry fared so badly under questioning by Celtic's legal team that the SFA abandoned the case. They sacked Farry for 'gross misconduct', made a written apology to the club and paid compensation to Celtic. 'He had an attitude that went beyond practicality,' McCann recalls. 'What his logic was in not registering Cadete was beyond me.'

The SFA reached a financial settlement with Farry, which probably explains why he never commented in detail on the affair. He died of a heart attack in 2010 at the age of fifty-six. It is hard to come up with another example anywhere of it being proven that a football association has acted improperly towards a member club. The SFA had been humiliated by this demonstration that it could be not be trusted. Officials from that time will suggest that Farry had kept them in the dark over certain matters, but that simply underlined the fact that no one could have faith in them to investigate vigorously. Celtic, for their part, had a ready answer whenever anyone in the future came up with old accusation that the club was paranoid.

All the same, I have never believed that Farry was consciously pursuing a vendetta. I liked him and felt that the bureaucratic circumlocutions in which he spoke were usually made with tongue in cheek. He could be stubborn, and I was among those who admired his desire to go ahead as planned with Scotland's match against Belarus on Saturday 6 September 1997, even though Princess Diana was to be buried that morning. He felt it apt and sufficient that a lone piper should play a lament before kick-off, but Farry was criticised by the then prime minister Tony Blair and the Secretary of State for Scotland. Three Rangers players said they would withdraw from the squad, and the SFA eventually put the fixture back a day.

Farry was not so much unfeeling over Diana's death as repelled by the vacuous sentimentality underlying the grief that had seized the country. He might have wondered what had happened to Britain since 30 January 1965, when Winston Churchill, war leader and conqueror of fascism, had been buried on a Saturday morning before a full programme of football was played throughout the UK that afternoon. I chatted about all this with Farry, who mused whether those who were so overwhelmed by the death of Diana could be counted on to check on an elderly neighbour whom they had not seen for a few days.

In practice, though, his judgement of the realities bearing down on the Belarus match was flawed. His course of action regarding Celtic was misconstrued as well. It was uppermost in his mind that the SFA must maintain its independence in the face of powerful bodies such as Celtic and Rangers. Furthermore, there had been friction with McCann, who resented the treatment his club allegedly received as tenant of the national stadium in 1994/5 and derides the partly rebuilt Hampden, completed in 1999 at a cost of £59 million. 'It is basically a white elephant,' he says. 'The guy in the back row at each end is a hundred yards from the goal-line. When we finished Celtic Park, the guy at the back was fifty yards from the goal-line, looking down.' No one can show what effect all the contention had, but the SFA belatedly took the view that Farry had been wholly wrong to delay the completion of Cadete's move to Celtic.

The ramifications can still be felt. Celtic, who often thrive on the notion of themselves as outsiders, had been at odds with the governing body for generations. The club now fights its corner harder than ever. When a supposed touchline incident brought a four-match ban for the manager Gordon Strachan, Celtic were still not placated when the sentence was halved on appeal. The issue was taken to an independent committee chaired by Lord MacLean, which cleared the manager entirely in November 2007. Afterwards the referee, who must have fared poorly under questioning by Celtic's solicitor, struck a note of self-pity. 'When you start having lawyers and lords against a humble referee, we can't compete,' said Stuart Dougal.

Celtic were well aware before that incident of frostiness from the ruling body that did not stem purely from the disgrace of their exposure in the Farry affair. 'Among the Establishment, including the SFA, there is still a feeling that Celtic are too big for their boots,' says the former chairman Quinn. 'My view is that the SFA think Celtic have been captured by the money men and that all that matters to Celtic are commercial considerations and that we have no interest in the community side of football or the grass roots. So there is a predisposition against Celtic among the SFA. We've got to work that bit harder if we're going to be accepted.'

He was not implying that the club should accept a perceived wrong with stoicism. There is merit, as the Farry confrontation showed, in ensuring that the SFA are held to a high standard. In 2011 Celtic, admittedly to their own benefit, had turned to the QC Paul McBride, who exploited flaws in the rules to ensure that a pair of four-match touchline bans for the manager Neil Lennon were served concurrently since the flawed regulations did not state that the sentences in such a case should run consecutively.

In his own way, McBride was following in the footsteps of McCann. That, admittedly, will not lead to the former owner being seen as a benefactor to Scottish football. Even so, it would be grotesque to deny the good that he did, which was not to be found solely on the balance sheet of his club. Specifically, McCann did not attempt to curry favour with platitudinous tributes to fans, and he was under no illusions as to the unsavoury attitudes among an element of the Celtic support that held fast to its sectarian views.

Only McCann would have decided that there should be a minute's silence before the Old Firm match at Celtic Park in January 1996 to mark the 25th anniversary of the Ibrox disaster, in which sixty-six Rangers fans had died. Rangers were fearful that this proposed commemoration would turn into a debacle, but McCann, as was normal with him, could not be talked out of it. The minute's silence was observed imperfectly, but the noise seemed to come in part from fans arriving late at the turnstiles, unaware of what was taking place inside Celtic Park. A relieved member of the Rangers staff struck the correct note when he said, 'We just about got away with it.' McCann recalls the night in similar terms. 'It could have gone wrong,' he agreed. 'I just said, "It's the right thing to do, it's the logical thing to do." We had to make some sort of gesture.'

The owner did not stop at that. Later in 1996 Celtic launched the Bhoys Against Bigotry campaign. There had been hopes for a co-ordinated venture with Rangers, but the Ibrox club did not believe then that this directly confrontational stance would be productive. It took seven years for a reappraisal of this approach, with Rangers announcing the Pride Over Prejudice initiative in 2003. Elements of the Celtic support have an exaggerated view of their own virtue, but there had been plenty of scope for improvement. McCann's stance was one element in securing it. UEFA and FIFA would both make awards to the Celtic fans for their conduct while in Seville for the 2003 UEFA Cup final. Rangers' slowness in facing up to their problems may, conversely, have contributed to the sort of scenes that had UEFA fining the club £8,800 after accusations of sectarian chanting at both legs of a UEFA Cup tie with Villarreal in 2007.

None of that should be a basis for smugness among Celtic's support. There were despicable episodes when Rangers clinched the League title in front of them with a 3–0 victory on 2 May 1999, and Celtic would ultimately be fined £45,000. The referee, Hugh Dallas, eleven years before his controversial departure from the SFA, was struck by a coin thrown from the crowd. Two of the three players sent off were Celtic's. Some of the club's fans came onto the pitch when the visitors were awarded a disputed penalty and, in a lighter moment on an anarchic night, another supporter tumbled from the top tier of the north stand, thankfully without coming to harm. The full-time whistle was followed by the Rangers players forming a huddle in mockery of Celtic's pre-match practice. If Dallas was relieved to exchange it all for the sanctuary of home, he was unwise. A neighbour who had been at the game smashed two of his windows with a bottle.

McCann had left Scotland by then and cannot have regretted missing the Scottish Cup final with which Rangers completed the Treble by beating Celtic once more. Progress on the field had been agonisingly slow and the 1990s turned out to be as poor a decade, in terms of winning trophies, as the club had ever known. It was McCann's right to insist that it had been his mission to reshape Celtic so that there would be achievement in the longer term. Burns did bring dashing football, but there was instability at the core of it. While the manager recruited well to reintroduce flair, Van Hooijdonk, Paolo di Canio and Cadete also caused mayhem before leaving. A sardonic McCann called them 'the three amigos'. Di Canio and Van Hooijdonk both made financial demands that were spurned, with the latter announcing that the £7,000 a week reputedly on offer in 1997 might be 'good enough for the homeless' but not for him. Cadete seemed to suffer from depression and, after going back to Portugal, faded out of top-flight football. Di Canio and Van Hooijdonk moved on to other clubs and into further squabbles.

Celtic were sturdier without them on the pitch and had a trace of stability. Burns had been replaced by the Dutchman Wim Jansen, an outstanding midfielder in the Feyenoord side that beat Celtic in the 1970 European Cup final. The new manager had an obstinacy often associated with figures in Dutch football, and that led to a clash with McCann. Before that happened, the team was steadied by the purchase of players such as Marc Rieper, Craig Burley and Paul Lambert. The uncanny coup was the acquisition of Henrik Larsson. The Swede was out of favour at Feyenoord, where he was being downgraded to the status of utility player and substitute, but Jansen knew that a clause in his contract meant he could leave for £650,000. Larsson himself believes that his seeming troubles in Holland had been of benefit. 'It didn't go well where I played – right, left, centre, everywhere,' he says. 'Now, when I look back to that I see it was a great school. I learned how to be a professional football player. I saw what it takes, what is expected of you and how to live, how to prepare, how to learn a language. To learn all those things was part of the reason that I succeeded with Celtic.'

Larsson's first notable deed for his new club, all the same, was to pass carelessly to Chic Charnley, who then scored the winner for Hibernian on the opening weekend of the season. A struggling side often gets engulfed in garish disputes, and a training-ground confrontation in November ended with the left back Tosh McKinlay head-butting Larsson. The team was at least dogged, and Rangers, obsessed with breaking Celtic's record of nine consecutive Scottish League titles, had become prone to short-term thinking.

Life was still muddled and overwrought at Celtic, who were debating in mid-season whether they ought to sack Jansen. It was then the club's policy that no player should be signed unless he had been watched, in person, by the manager. Jansen was indifferent to the edict and refused to watch Rosenborg's Harald Brattbakk, arguing that the opinion of the chief scout David Hay was good enough for him. Celtic's offer to lay on a private jet so that he could fly to Norway and be back for training the following day cut no ice. McCann and others toyed with dismissing the Dutchman because they suspected him of ducking responsibility.

Jansen was retained because in mid-season all that mattered was sustaining a challenge in the League. In January 1998 Celtic started to gain credibility six days after a loss to St Johnstone by beating Rangers at home, with goals from Burley and Lambert. The Ibrox club, understandably fixated with winning a tenth League title in a row, had lost any long-term perspective in team-building. With Celtic's resources just as uneven, the struggle was both ham-fisted and fascinating. Even the subplots caused recriminations. It emerged that Jansen would leave in the summer no matter what, having decided that he could no longer work with the general manager Jock Brown. The latter, brother of the then Scotland manager Craig Brown and himself a well-known football commentator on television, became in those histrionic days a hate figure to some Celtic fans, who blamed him when the club looked inert in the transfer market or insisted on believing that he was a Rangers fan. Brown lasted less than a year and a half in the job, until even McCann, usually so defiant of public opinion, decided that to keep on employing him was unworkable.

In 1998, however, Rangers were also overwrought, and by then the manager Walter Smith had already confirmed that he would be leaving in the summer. His side had been eliminated in quick succession from the Champions League, in the qualifiers, and the UEFA Cup. But two weak clubs can still have a struggle of overpowering emotion. On the penultimate weekend of the League season Rangers were beaten at home by Kilmarnock, and Celtic needed simply to win at Dunfermline the following day. They could do no such thing and, after going ahead, were limited to a 1–1 draw. Jansen's side therefore had to beat St Johnstone at home in their last League match to take the title. That fixture was to be as close to unendurable as any game Celtic have ever played, since Rangers, winning at Dundee United, were maintaining the terrible pressure.

Larsson himself was shaken. It was as if he had unwittingly become part of a duel, even though he had not been fully aware of the cause to which he was giving himself when he left Rotterdam for Glasgow. 'If I had known everything I would not have gone there,' he told me with feeling more than twelve years later. 'There was a mountain to climb if we were going to stop Rangers because the team they had was very good. We had about seven or eight new players.'

Larsson did open the scoring that afternoon, but the side slowly succumbed to the paralysis of fear, and George O'Boyle might have levelled for St Johnstone. In the heart of all that suffocating dread, Celtic lifted themselves to produce a moment of cogency that reflected a mettle lacking in previous line-ups over the course of the Rangers ascendancy. Fleetingly, a series of players surpassed themselves. Tom Boyd had enough poise to hold the ball until the overlapping Jackie McNamara was in position. The right back's low cross was uncommonly well judged and Brattbakk, whose irregular scoring showed how inhibited he was by expectations at Celtic, had the sangfroid to wrong-foot the goalkeeper by tucking the ball into the small space at the near post.

The dry facts speak of a commonplace match, but the result was a liberation. Here was a demonstration that the rebuilding of the club could be achieved and would not prove illusory. For any owner other than McCann it would have been a moment to caper and wallow in appreciation. True to idiosyncratic type, he felt no temptation to bask in the glory and, after going down to the tunnel area, had left the ground before the celebrations were in full swing. 'I had to be back because of the babysitter,' he now explains with utter seriousness. 'The other thing was that I didn't want to get involved in the on-field celebrations. The players would have been chasing me and so forth. It was something for the players and fans, and it's not really my thing. I should just stand back. I always felt that football is about players. That is still the truth. That is why in a public argument in the media between a shirt [jersey] and a suit the shirt will always win.'

Hardly any followers of the club were as circumspect as McCann. One pub in the East End was so jammed with revelling supporters for hour upon hour that the staff could only create space to collect empty glasses by bawling 'Huddle!' The fans would then spill out into the Gallowgate, stopping the traffic while wrapping their arms around one another's shoulders in the manner of their team before kick-off. It would have been silly to snub the bacchanalia or make it an early night because occasions of this sort had been few, with no certainty that they would come round again soon.

Celtic had already won the League Cup that season, but there were to be a paltry three trophies in McCann's time. His last season was barren. With Jansen gone, the distinguished Slovak Josef Vengl8 was in the dugout. The then sixty-two-year-old was a knowledgeable man, but he did not exude dynamism, and his patchy English was a further limitation. He was culti- vated in a way that cast him as an outsider. One slow day the UEFA Cup draw was made and Kilmarnock were pitted against

Sigma Olomouc. A journalist realised that Vengloš might high-light, say, a blistering winger or wily poacher at the Czech club. 'What do you know about Olomouc?' he was asked. 'Olomouc', said Vengloš reflectively, 'is the coronation city of the kings of Moravia.' Not a pen moved among the press pack.

While Vengloš was no longer cut out for the front line of management, his acumen was appreciated, never more so than in the purchase of the veteran Slovak L'ubomír Moravčík, whose virtuosity delighted fans. He also encouraged the club to persist in the tangled negotiations to take Mark Viduka from Croatia Zagreb (as Dinamo Zagreb were briefly called). In that period Celtic could not simply bring in a strong, skilled, imaginative striker for £3 million and proceed to prosper. Viduka had no sooner reached Glasgow in November than he walked out on the club. The factors involved never became public knowledge, although the working hypothesis for any enigmatic affair in contemporary football involves money. His debut did not come for another three months.

With or without Viduka, there were appealing displays under Vengloš, which included a 5–1 defeat of Rangers in 1998, but no trophies came to Celtic. McCann will be remembered for one key League title and also for a vast and enduring achievement. He created favourable conditions by rebuilding the stadium and, with it, the club's finances. The confrontations were essential yet debilitating, and the tricky objective for McCann's successors was to bring joy to those crowds and so continue filling Celtic Park.

9

MARTIN O'NEILL

Whenever a club is feeling the heat, there is a temptation to step into the shade of its own history. After Josef Venglos had left in 1999, Celtic turned to Kenny Dalglish. It was a resonant appointment and few guessed that his stay would be brief, with Martin O'Neill soon to make an impact instead. While a transfer to Liverpool in 1977 had confirmed that a player of Dalglish's talent must find Scottish football too small a stage, his return, in a wholly different capacity, implied that a revived Celtic were intent on proving that they could transcend their parochial surroundings. If Dalglish was prepared to come back to the west of Scotland, then others, in theory, would accept that a serious enterprise was being undertaken there. This was a shortcut to credibility.

Dalglish has one of the most noteworthy managerial histories of modern times in Britain. He won three League titles during his first period in charge of Liverpool and, more remarkably still, another with Blackburn Rovers. At Ewood Park, he had initially to ensure promotion to the old First Division in 1992. The wealth of the owner Jack Walker was available to him, yet few have ever spent so shrewdly. The signings were bold yet practical, and this was one of the rare exceptions in football where an apparent splurge could accurately be termed an investment. Of the side that won the League in 1995, recruits such as Alan Shearer, Chris Sutton and Graeme Le Saux would ultimately be sold for profits, respectively, of £11.7 million, £5 million and £4.3 million.

There was a deep seam of practicality that, for a time, made Dalglish a fine manager. He had first taken on those duties for Liverpool on the day after the Heysel Stadium disaster in 1985. As player-manager, Dalglish would be highly successful, but the toll that the post took on him became extraordinarily severe four years later when there was further carnage. At a 1989 FA Cup semi-final, ninety-six Liverpool fans died as a result of a crush while they were attempting to get into Hillsborough, the Sheffield Wednesday ground.

Subsequently, Dalglish attended many funerals and made himself available to the bereaved. The stress he was experiencing increased over a period of almost two years prior to his resignation in February 1991. His return to management halted once Blackburn took the 1995 League title and he then became the club's director of football. He re-entered the dugout with Newcastle United, but was sacked twenty-two months later, in 1998. At that juncture Dalglish harboured reservations about placing himself in the front line of a club, and the deal that took him back to Celtic the following year smacked of compromise.

With Jozef Vengloš gone, a board meeting was held in Dublin to discuss his replacement. Fergus McCann, preparing to sell up, did not insist on dictating the outcome since it was his successors who would have to deal with the consequences. Brian Quinn, the director who would become chairman in 2000, remembers ambivalence towards the principal candidate. 'There was quite a lively debate about Dalglish coming to the club. There were those who were more in favour rather than less and those who were less in favour rather than more. Nobody said outright, "This is wrong." And nobody said outright, "This is just the answer to a maiden's prayer."

'What did happen was that the board couldn't come to a decision, so they said to me, "Why don't you meet with Kenny Dalglish, because you're a Glasgow person and Kenny's a

Glasgow person. Spend as long with him as you need to make up your mind." I went out to dinner with Kenny in London and spent the evening with him. I came back and was asked by the board what I thought. I said to them, "I have to tell you that after four hours I don't know any more about Kenny Dalglish than I did before." I still had reservations, but it was decided that we would go ahead notwithstanding.'

In hindsight, Dalglish's reluctance to take up the post of manager ought to have disqualified him entirely. Celtic were already in a difficult situation, and the merest suggestion of equivocation by him compounded the problem. Dalglish, none the less, was to be director of football, with his former Liverpool teammate John Barnes installed as head coach. The latter had no substantial coaching experience, and following his short spell at Celtic he had to endure a life of punditry until, in 2008, he became manager of Jamaica, the country of his birth. There were then a few months with Tranmere Rovers before he was removed.

Quinn is frank about the botched thinking that took Barnes to Celtic in 1999. 'It was a bad judgement, a really bad judgement to do that. We'd already had one misfire with Liam Brady, whose first managerial job was with Celtic. I don't think there is sufficient recognition of the big step that it requires when moving from the playing side on to the management side. Especially in those days when the manager wasn't dealing just with the football.

'Nice fellow that he is, Barnes just wasn't up to it. And so he made lots of mistakes, in the players he signed and the way he handled the players.' Conversations with him were reassuring purely at a superficial level. 'His tactical plans made a lot of sense,' says Quinn. 'But it was one of those cases where he knew the words but didn't know the music. When we went out on the field we were all over the place. Dalglish did not provide the guidance that we thought he would. Kenny did not deliver.'

Barnes had an obstinate idealism that ignored the limitations of a squad whose members, by and large, did not meet the standards he himself had reached as a player. The novice had a misguided self-confidence and pursued a refined vision. In the course of that season there was a bid to repair relationships with a sceptical press over dinner. At one stage, I asked Barnes why he sometimes used a 4–2–2–2 formation. He replied that it was how France, then the reigning World Cup holders, and Brazil, the beaten finalists, played. That system calls for formidable full backs and, indeed, was probably born out of the fact that those countries possessed them. France had Lilian Thuram and Bixente Lizarazu, while Brazil called upon Cafu and Roberto Carlos. These were some of the greatest players of the age in any position. Celtic's full backs, Vidar Riseth and Stéphane Mahé, were not even noteworthy at their own club. Barnes was pursuing an ideal without the means to realise it.

At that same dinner, the then Celtic chief executive Allan MacDonald left the room to take a call. He returned to tell us with satisfaction that a deal had been struck to buy Rafael Scheidt. The congratulations were tentative because we had no clear idea who this player was. Scheidt went on to great and unfortunate fame. Barnes, having studied him purely on video, had a false impression of a Brazilian footballer who now takes his place on lists of the worst signings ever made anywhere. Scheidt was then a defender with Gremio, in Porto Alegre. Despite costing close to £5 million, he would only start two competitive matches for Celtic and make three appearances as a substitute before the club at last got him off the premises with a loan to Corinthians of São Paulo late in 2000.

All that lingered of him in Glasgow were the recriminations and the debate over whether Celtic were the victims of their own incompetence or, as conspiracy theorists would have it, a scam. Quinn admits that the recruitment process had been less than rigorous, with Celtic's contracts manager the single member of staff who might have seen the defender in the flesh. 'Jim Hone went out, only to discover that it was the interval between the two halves of the Brazilian season,' said Quinn. 'He didn't see

Rafael play, so Rafael was brought to Celtic Park and he played in practice matches with the rest of the team. A number of things were wrong with that. I was never happy with that at the time, and certainly not afterwards.'

Hone would have been blameless even if he had watched Scheidt in action since he was not a scout. The impression was of a floundering club. Barnes disproved the adage that results are all that matter by winning eight of his first nine League matches, without convincing anyone that he had a line-up of real substance. He was handicapped, too, by the freakish accident in a UEFA Cup tie with Lyon when a seemingly mild challenge left Henrik Larsson with a broken leg. The Swede had by then begun to thrive with Celtic and he could single-handedly have bought Barnes time. As it happened, the coach was long gone before Larsson made a comeback in the last game of the season.

Barnes departed following a defeat to lower-division Inverness Caledonian Thistle in the Scottish Cup. Celtic, at home, were 2–1 behind at the interval, but a troublesome situation was inflated into a full-blown crisis. There were recriminations involving players and coaching staff in the dressing room. In the circumstances, that cannot have been unexpected, but Mark Viduka chose not to appear for the second half. 'We had a bit of a problem,' Barnes conceded. The thirty-six-year-old Ian Wright came on, but it was Caley Thistle who took over as they scored a third goal. As Barnes has subsequently recognised, his lack of experience meant that he did not have enough authority among a squad who felt entitled to doubt him.

'I had scored thirteen goals before I broke my leg,' says Larsson. 'We had a decent team but the time wasn't right for John Barnes to have the Celtic job. He had trouble as an Englishman coming in. He wasn't very experienced. He was unlucky that I got injured.' The coach could not draw either on the reserves of credibility that Dalglish possessed thanks to past achievements. The Scot appeared detached and was scouting at a mini-tournament in La Manga involving Nordic clubs when

Celtic lost that match. Dalglish was believed to have been reluc-
tant to return immediately from Spain after the Scottish Cup
loss and was flippant with the photographers waiting for him at
Glasgow airport. 'Do you like my tan?' he enquired, before stepping into a post that has left many people pale.

With Barnes sacked, Dalglish became interim manager two
days after that defeat to Caley Thistle. He rashly attempted to
be a populist and, for instance, held a press conference in Bairds
Bar, a pub that is a Celtic supporters stronghold. The journalists
would have been uneasy at going about their work while fans
criticised the supposed bias that lay behind the questions, but
there was a phoniness to the whole exercise. Dalglish is much
too watchful and wary to come across as a man of the people
in any role except that of star footballer, from which age had
disqualified him. It was simple to appreciate why he wanted no
more to do with management in that period, even if he would
take up such a post in January 2011 when Liverpool shifted him
into it on a caretaker basis and then saw him prosper to such a
degree that the appointment was made permanent.

Celtic won the League Cup in March 2000 by beating
Aberdeen, but an entire project had collapsed. Dalglish left in
the summer and his friend Allan MacDonald, a former managing director of British Aerospace for Asia and Africa, resigned
in September. The chief executive had a compulsive boldness,
arguing that the club had to go into considerable debt if it was
to have a squad to compete with Rangers. His forthrightness
was less tenable when he revealed that he had commissioned
a behavioural psychologist called Chris Lewis to report on the
way in which the referee Hugh Dallas had conducted himself
after being hit by a coin during Rangers' 3–0 victory in the 1999
match. Pundits naturally preferred to conjecture about the mental state of MacDonald and Celtic.

The club, in any case, gathered its thoughts in 2000 as, for
the fourth summer in succession, it went looking for a manager.
This time the emphasis was on candidates built to last. Guus

Hiddink was close to being appointed, but Dermot Desmond, a billionaire whose stake of just under 30 per cent gives him the largest holding of Celtic shares, flew out to Spain, where the Dutch coach was then employed by Valencia. He sensed at a meeting that this candidate did not have an all-consuming desire to be Celtic manager. 'I looked into his eyes and didn't see it,' Desmond has said, 'didn't see an understanding of the whole history.'

The search then had him seeking the advice of Sir Alex Ferguson. The Manchester United manager came up with his personal shortlist: Alan Curbishley, David O'Leary and Martin O'Neill. It was the last of them that appealed to Desmond. O'Neill was a striking character with a virtually flawless record who had even brought trophies, in the form of two League Cup successes, to his then club Leicester City. According to Desmond, Ferguson agreed to sound out Desmond's preferred appointee. An answer was soon relayed. 'What took you so long?' said O'Neill.

The Northern Irishman is a compelling presence. Having identified him as the right choice, Desmond, using the suite he had at the Dorchester in London, introduced him unannounced to the other directors, with only Quinn tipped off about the identity of the surprise guest. 'Martin wasn't appointed unanimously by the board,' says Quinn. 'He was appointed by acclaim. Martin was absolutely brilliant. He spoke as only Martin can for the best part of an hour. We asked him to leave then. I was chairman in Frank O'Callaghan's absence, so I said, "I'm going to go round the room because we've made mistakes before and I want to be clear what your views are." It all came back very, very strongly in favour of Martin.'

O'Neill is conventionally described as charismatic, but his personality is more complex than that term would imply. While he does have a galvanising impact, he is also a careful man. Having got the job, for instance, he addressed the hundreds of fans standing outside the main entrance to Celtic Park. 'It's an absolute honour for me to be the manager here,' he said, 'and I will do everything I possibly can to bring some success here to the football club.' The response from those supporters was as loud as it was ecstatic, but O'Neill had avoided giving hostages to fortune. There was no promise of anything at all. It was the force of his character that registered with an audience determined to believe in him.

Much as he inspires footballers and supporters, the innate realism of O'Neill had been entrenched from the start by a need to cope with strict limitations. As a player, his international career had been with a disadvantaged Northern Ireland that he none the less captained to a victory over the hosts Spain at the 1982 World Cup finals. In management, he had already been in charge of Shepshed Charterhouse, Grantham and Wycombe before he got as far as Leicester. Selecting him amounted to an act of atonement by Celtic following their gamble on the gauche John Barnes.

It was part of O'Neill's seriousness to negotiate a budget that would ensure he had a squad that meant business. He bought Chris Sutton from Chelsea for a club-record sum of £6 million, rejecting the concerns of Dermot Desmond about such an outlay on a player then viewed in England as a misfit. Barnes had spent nearly as much on Eyal Berkovic, but O'Neill was in a position to embark on a more intense programme and there was, for example, £3.75 million available to bring in the Belgian centre half Joos Valgaeren. A little later that season, in December 2000, he paid nearly £6 million to take Neil Lennon from his former club Leicester. I once put it to Lennon that he must be close to the manager. He was incredulous over the implication that O'Neill would make a pal of a player. The manager's record of inspiring footballers at all levels is a long one, but he has that knack of keeping a healthy distance while still forming a connection to his squad members.

There is a structure that O'Neill installs at each place of work. He attends training a little more often than is supposed, but Steve

Walford, who had the uncompromising habit of wearing shorts on the most unrelenting winter day in Scotland, is in charge of it. O'Neill will go over and speak quietly to Walford if he has a point to make. His other assistant, John Robertson, can be seen as an intermediary with the squad. However, O'Neill also values his judgement of players, whether they are on the books already or prospective signings. The methods of this manager and his staff virtually come under warranty. That did not stop Celtic from experiencing moments of desolation, but his overall effect was to regenerate confidence at the club. Fans would simply chant the name Martin O'Neill with euphoric relentlessness. What else, they seemed to imply, was there to say?

The man himself must have enjoyed the devotion, but the intensity of the club still took him aback. 'One night John Robertson and I went to a little Celtic supporters club in Perth, just to present some prizes,' says O'Neill. 'There must have been 250 people there, and 150 of them would have been season-ticket holders. That was an eye-opener to me. This was their life. If you woke up in the morning and realised what that club you were managing meant to everybody, you'd pull the covers back over you again and decide not to go to work that day. Sometimes you think, "I could do with a break from this," but the minute you get the break you start to wish you were back in it again. They were five of the most rewarding years I have spent on this earth. The great thing is that I believe my wife and my daughters shared in unique experiences.'

Their home was in the West End of the city, part of a cosmopolitan area around Glasgow University. The family lived near to an award-winning restaurant, One Devonshire Gardens. The neighbourhood was not the sort of tedious executive housing development where ennui is the price of security. Shortly after Celtic had lost a midweek League Cup semi-final to their great rivals, some Rangers fans stuck a Union Jack in O'Neill's garden. This was harmless enough, but the manager had not got home by the time that happened. It was at least unsettling that he should not be with his wife Geraldine while intruders were prowling around on his property. However, O'Neill determinedly made light of it, joking that the Rangers manager Alex McLeish must have made good time from Hampden to plant the flag.

As the first Catholic to captain Northern Ireland, O'Neill was sure-footed as he picked his way around the fault lines of Glasgow life. 'If my wife and I wanted to eat out, particularly during the week,' he says, 'then we would nip down to a restaurant at about six o'clock and be out by 6.45. It never presented any real problems. I could have taken a lot more abuse than I did. I wouldn't say Rangers fans came up to me with open arms, but they allowed me to pass.' However, the divisions that persist in the west of Scotland, regardless of its relative affluence and middle-class lifestyle, would not always be ignored.

In November 2004 O'Neill, after a 2–0 loss at Ibrox, put his arm round Neil Lennon, marched him towards the Celtic supporters and waved a clenched fist. The manager explained later that he was championing a midfielder who had been 'verbally abused in a racial and sectarian manner'. For some Rangers fans, the events were histrionics that diverted attention from Celtic's defeat. The risk that Lennon runs, though, has proved to be real.

Glasgow may have felt congenial to O'Neill when circumstances there favoured his career, even if he did take a serious interest in becoming Leeds United manager as his first contract with Celtic was nearing its end in 2003. The Irishman was fortunate in the timing of his arrival in Glasgow. Henrik Larsson constituted what may be the most freakish piece of good fortune Celtic have ever known. His career had been at a low ebb and he exercised a release clause in his contract with Feyenoord because he knew he was about to be treated as a deputy for any forward or wide midfielder who happened to be missing. Larsson's life as a footballer had gone drastically off-course since the summer of 1994, when, at twenty-two, he had been part of the Sweden squad that finished third at the World Cup. Three years later, he understood that it was essential to leave Feyenoord, but he might simply have gone back to play in his own country.

Pride was the factor that directed him to Scotland instead. 'I was talking to Helsingborg,' he says, 'and I told them that if a club from any other country came in, I would rather stay outside Sweden because I didn't want to come home with my tail between my legs because I could never have gone abroad again.' The trip to Glasgow, however, was a voyage of transformation.

Larsson is an unflinchingly matter-of-fact person. I was once trying in a no doubt elaborate manner to get him to explain what set him apart. 'I have a good jump,' Larsson replied, realising that something had to be said if the formalities of a press conference were to be observed, so the emotional fashion in which he reportedly discussed the journey to Glasgow is rare for him, perhaps unique. 'When I flew into Scotland for the first time,' he once said, 'I was too excited to eat, too excited to read. I knew this was my chance, and below me there was this pretty landscape with small lakes scattered around and a hilly landscape glowing in the sun.'

That regeneration stayed with him throughout his seven years with Celtic. The broken leg in his second season did not snap his momentum, even if it devastated John Barnes's prospects of being a successful coach at the club. Supporters, with some justice, took it for granted that when a match was going wrong, Larsson would put it back on a favourable course. There was synergy because Celtic were also the making of him. With his days in Glasgow behind him, Larsson went on to entrench his fame globally. Arsenal were winning 1–0 in the 2006 Champions League final despite having their goalkeeper Jens Lehmann sent off, only for the substitute Larsson to set up two goals in his last match for Barcelona. The following month, England were 2–1 in front against Sweden at the World Cup finals, but all leads are provisional while he is on the pitch and Larsson secured a draw.

He was thirty-four by then, having reached his peak in his years with Celtic. In modern times there can scarcely have been a great footballer who has chosen to devote himself, when his powers were at their greatest, to a team in a footballing back-water. 'When you're an absolute hero at a club it's sometimes difficult to give it up,' says O'Neill. 'And it would also have been difficult to lose confidence at Celtic Park because even when Henrik made a bad pass, it was someone else's fault. I'd have loved to have had that in my own playing career.'

It was with Celtic that Larsson turned into one of the princi-pal players of his time. Tommy Burns believed that the Swede had been the best to appear for the club in the previous forty years, a period that encompassed Jimmy Johnstone and the other European Cup winners. In 2000/01, the season after breaking his leg, he heaped up fifty-three goals for Celtic, thirty-five of them in the League, to take Europe's Golden Boot award. The immediate achievement of supreme form after terrible injury typ-ified his single-mindedness. Larsson was good in the air, sharp-witted, skilful and competitive, but beyond all that there was a rare capacity to gather himself in major matches and complete a task in which others would have fallen short. In O'Neill's first Old Firm game, he put Celtic 4–1 in front by anticipating a lay-off from Sutton, seeing that he could go clear because there was space to slip the ball through the legs of the advancing centre half Bert Konterman, and then realising that the best way to fin-ish was with a chip over the advancing Stefan Klos. Larsson was the embodiment of an incontestable superiority over Rangers that Celtic had not enjoyed since the early 1980s.

The ramifications of that 6–2 spree were great. In a statement made in the spring of 2000 that slowly became infamous, the then owner of the Ibrox club David Murray said: 'For every fiver Celtic spend, we'll spend a tenner.' It was a clumsy assertion that spoke of alarm. That commitment took on a farcical truth when he paid £12 million for the highly unsuccessful forward Tore André Flo. The Norwegian had cost roughly double the price of O'Neill's record signing, Sutton. Rangers lost their poise. At far steeper expense they became at times the counterparts to the cack-handed Celtic of the 1990s. O'Neill, who lost his second

Old Firm match 5–1, had days of anguish when Rangers, in 2003 and 2005, snatched the title on the final day. No matter how deep the pain, however, the ramifications were not extensive. In the summer of 2008 Celtic reached the end of a period that saw them become champions in six out of eight seasons.

That success, all the same, arose during years in which they and Rangers increasingly struggled to define a place for themselves in a football environment dominated by clubs from England and Spain, whose means were of an utterly different magnitude because of the scale of their domestic markets. It was a great achievement for Rangers to overcome the odds and get to a UEFA Cup final of their own in 2008. At the start O'Neill could afford Sutton and Lennon. Prior to his second season, the manager brought in John Hartson, another striker who cost £6 million. Thereafter, the general unfeasibility of such deals for Celtic was underlined as they instead made the sort of signings that were designed primarily to patch up the team. In the 2004/05 season, O'Neill's last with the club, the struggle to establish an advantage in a contest for the title that eventually ended in triumph for Rangers was manifested in a deal that took Craig Bellamy on loan from Newcastle United for the closing five months.

Celtic had been scrambling to find a way of pursuing their ambitions while preserving financial stability. Following the 3–2 defeat by Porto after extra time in the 2003 UEFA Cup final there was a meal that Quinn remembers as 'the most sepulchral occasion I had ever been at', but the gloom spread to a dinner with O'Neill, his wife and daughters in Glasgow the following evening. 'We had to explain to them then that we had lost £7 million or thereabouts that season,' Quinn says. 'He was flabbergasted. He said, "You mean we've been to the UEFA Cup final and we're still losing money?" I said to Martin, "All you need to do is look at the wage bill. I am not holding you personally responsible. We agreed to it. But the fact of the matter is that we are spending in excess of our income, and that can't go on. We have to do something about it." First of all, he couldn't believe what had happened. And he couldn't believe the timing. I think in retrospect it was a bit brutal.'

The 2002/3 campaign had been a high-water mark, even if there were no honours for Celtic. Early in the season the team was knocked out of the Champions League by Basle in the third qualifying round. The side would have advanced had a curling finish from Sutton gone into the net instead of hitting a bump and running wide. As the shot was struck, O'Neill walked from the dugout as if drawn forward by the roll of the ball. As it missed the target the manager was stepping unwittingly onto the pitch, where he sank to the turf. Those steps, though, were part of a long, memorable journey, as Celtic went on to thrive in the UEFA Cup.

In the quarter-final, for instance, Liverpool had taken a 1–1 draw in Glasgow, but Celtic reacted with a 2–0 win in the return match, with Alan Thompson scoring from a free kick before Hartson cut across Dietmar Hamann to crunch a twenty-five-yarder into the net. 'He still thinks it was the highlight of his career,' O'Neill remarked after the striker had retired. The press area is near the directors' box at Anfield, and as he walked past at full-time Quinn leaned over and said to me, 'It's the best night since Lisbon.' He was speaking as any Celtic supporter might have that night. The O'Neill era was successful in practical terms, but thrilling, too, in its hints of what the club might achieve.

'I still get goosebumps when I think about it,' says Larsson of the Anfield victory. 'We had been close, trying to make our mark in Europe. That year we really did it because we beat a lot of good teams.'

Celtic had already eliminated Blackburn in the second round of the UEFA Cup. The visitors, under the command of the former Rangers manager Graeme Souness, had not deserved their 1–0 loss in Glasgow, and he presumably meant to hearten his players by telling them that the game, despite the result, had been 'men against boys'.

Once the remark became public, O'Neill used it to goad his men into excellence. The return at Ewood Park was won 2–0, with Celtic in complete control. More than the results themselves it was O'Neill, then, who inspired a faith that the club had the potential to take its place among the upper echelon. He is highly demonstrative on occasion and also had the persuasiveness to talk directors into spending sums on players that would have been unfeasible if balancing the books had been a priority. There was a delirium about Celtic in the months that led them to the final in Seville. Virtually everyone present was breaking new ground, and that showed in unconfined excitability. 'One memory I have is of Martin,' says Quinn. 'I have never seen a more agitated man in my life. On the way to the stadium the team bus took a wrong turning and he was jumping up and down with anxiety.'

The thrill of the adventure swept everyone along, but the wider truth was that the club, while living beyond its means, still could not afford enough players of the highest calibre. Larsson seemed to take on José Mourinho's Porto single-handed in the 2003 final. He looked capable of having the better of that struggle when he equalised twice, but Celtic could not hide the uneven quality in the team and were beaten 3–2 after extra time. Porto had nine players in their starting line-up who would be Champions League winners the following year, with a 3–0 trouncing of Monaco that completed Mourinho's renown.

The Portuguese, who seems to take pride in gamesmanship, had a side adept at breaking up the momentum of a match whenever it suited them. 'We lost the game after Porto had spent most of the time cheating on us,' says O'Neill. Larsson, too, continues to feel wronged by the defeat even now. 'We were the better team, but we lost that one and it is still sore. Our first goal especially was a great one. It would have meant so much to pick up the trophy because it would have been excellent to have that in my collection.'

His sense that Celtic had not deserved to lose is open to

serious dispute all the same since the side had flaws. Bobo Balde, a Goliath of a centre half who was nimble enough to cope with mobile strikers, had an intermittent rashness in him and was sent off in Seville after a second booking in extra time when he attempted a tackle in an area of the field where it had been unnecessary. Derlei's winner resulted from a mistake by the goalkeeper Rab Douglas. Larsson continues to feel frustrated by that evening and is tantalised by the conviction that Celtic were not far from being able to engage as equals with mighty clubs. 'After the run to the UEFA Cup final, if the club had put in a few more quid we would have been even better,' he says. 'Unfortunately the funds weren't there to do that. If you look at it, Porto went on to win the Champions League the year after.'

While Larsson would eventually win that trophy with Barcelona in 2006, leaving Celtic had not been a matter of urgency. 'There is not a better place,' he says of Celtic Park. 'The sound level is completely different. Camp Nou was a great experience, but if it comes to El Clásico versus the Old Firm game, the Old Firm game wins every day of the week. It's a battle and there is so much at stake. For the week before the game everyone is talking about it. It was just fantastic to play in so many of them and be on the winning side more times than not.'

Scotland is a small place and much of its drama is crammed into the Glasgow area. It is a piece of territory drenched in football, and there is an intensity at odds with the fact that the prizes at stake are minor in the eyes of the world at large. It is not uncommon for footballers to undergo a self-imposed house arrest at times. Larsson found a more relaxed tone in places with a higher profile than Glasgow on the football scene. 'There is always somebody watching you, and if you do something that is not good, somebody is going to react to it,' Larsson says. 'That's part of the reason why I thought, "I can't be bothered," and stayed home instead. It was easier in Manchester [where he played for United early in 2007]. No one cared. Even in Barcelona it was easy. I can remember walking from my hotel to the training ground in my first few days with Barcelona. In Manchester you could walk about in the city. People recognised you but it was OK. I loved living in Scotland and Glasgow. I had seven great years there, but it's a small city and those two teams are so important to the people.'

Larsson did not know of Barcelona's interest when he stuck to his plan and chose to leave at the end of his contract, in 2004, but he had not lacked for suitors. 'There were chances all the time really,' he says. 'I didn't want to go and I don't regret it now. As a Celtic player you have everything to lose whenever you go onto the pitch because you are expected to win. More often than not we managed to do that under O'Neill. That's a quality to have as well. If it's that easy why can't everybody do it? A lot of Scottish people will always belittle themselves.

'That's the way it is, and that's how it's always going to be. The standard is not always the greatest, but in my days there was a very good standard at the Old Firm, and Hibs and Hearts would always be there or thereabouts. Some people will have said I could only do it in Scotland, but then again there were two World Cups, European Cups and European Championships where I also managed to score. That discussion more or less finished between 2002 and 2004. Those were my peak years.'

Celtic were excellent in some areas, and Larsson still relishes the thought of his partnership with the perfectly complementary Sutton, but the standard of the squad was uneven. While the club had gone to its limits in terms of expenditure, there were still members of the team who had to be regarded as stopgaps. None the less, there was a hard-nosed tone about the side under O'Neill. He did supervise marvels, but he was no dreamer. O'Neill accentuated power and endurance by, for instance, ruling that the muscular Johan Mjallby, who had been bought as a midfielder by Jozef Vengloš in 1998, would henceforth be at centre half, where his gift for leadership was great.

When reflecting on his early days in Glasgow, O'Neill once commented that he had inherited players who were capable in possession but did not cope so well when the opposition had the ball. The manager fixed that, and it is startling to remember that Celtic, in March 2004, could protect a 1–0 lead from the home leg to see out a goalless draw in the Camp Nou and so eliminate Barcelona from the UEFA Cup. Over longer periods, however, the strain on uneven resources was apparent. Following defeat in Seville, Celtic had to complete their League season with an away match at Kilmarnock. Despite winning 4–0 there, they ended as runners-up, with Rangers, smartly managed by Alex McLeish, taking the title on goal difference after beating Dunfermline 6–1 at home.

O'Neill had given Celtic a season that was both unforgettable yet, in practical terms, unsuccessful. He has a knack of rousing players, and they became all the more determined because of that lack of trophies. The campaign that followed was an act of vengeance on the fates and, of course, the other Scottish clubs. After a draw at Dunfermline, Celtic won twenty-five League matches in a row, and the title had been regained by April 2004. So far as the settling of local scores was concerned, the side won all five Old Firm games, including a Scottish Cup semi-final. Celtic went on to take the trophy in what was Larsson's last competitive appearance for them. His contribution that day was a golden stereotype of what he had come to mean to the club. After Dunfermline had scored in the final, two goals from him righted the afternoon and led to a 3–1 win.

It was correct, all the same, that he should leave. It needed those two years with Barcelona to silence anyone who still thought that his exploits should have an asterisk beside them because they had come in a backwater. By the time he had his two-month loan spell, during Sweden's close season, with Manchester United at the start of 2007 he was cherished. Any withholding of appreciation during those seven years with Celtic reflected the fact that Scotland, like the great majority of nations in Europe, had been marginalised because its television market was feeble by comparison with those of England, Spain, Italy and Germany.

Celtic had become a club uncertain of its strategy that scrabbled to plug gaps in a team that was breaking up. By August 2003 the strains were already unmistakable. While with the squad for a Champions League qualifier in Hungary, O'Neill put the emphasis on his desire to sign new players, but back in Britain on the same day the chairman was confirming that there was no money to spend. Quinn, years later, explains the contradiction: 'Martin is very persuasive and he knows what he wants. He was doing what he had been trying to do all along, which was to try and force the issue.' That is normal practice for managers, and O'Neill was speaking, too, in the same terms as many fans. 'We were', Quinn recalls, 'under tremendous pressure from the supporters who came to the AGM and said, "You are far too conservative and you should build on the success of Seville."

'We went on for another year without really having a radical change in the way the finances of the company were being run. We had a rights issue which we used to pay off the debt, which was accumulating. The hope still was that we would be able to do well in Europe and do well domestically. It was a difficult year but we kept on going. Then we went to Shakhtar Donetsk in October 2004 and lost 3–0. All my doubts were resolved, in the sense that I knew exactly what had to be done. I sat with Peter Lawwell [the chief executive] and with Dermot Desmond in the hotel after the game and said, "We have to have a radical change, not just tinkering. We cannot keep going back to shareholders to cover current expenses. When you raise money from shareholders, it should be for capital expenditure, such as building a training ground and improving the scouting structure."

'I said, "We have to run our affairs so that we break even at least, year by year." Dermot, of course, was absolutely on board. We sat down that night and had a look at the team. We had a look at who were the big earners. We told Martin immediately that we couldn't go on like this. We needed to change things. We told him that we were far from being in trouble but that we would be if were to go on like this for a few more years, and that can't be. Martin said he accepted it, but his wife was already quite ill [with lymphoma]. By the spring [of 2005] he said to me, "I can't do it. There's just too much effort and time required whenever I need to be with Geraldine. I can't bring about the changes which you are asking for because it is a big transform-ation." He told us around March that he was almost certainly going to go.'

Around that time, Quinn dialled the wrong number when try-ing to reach PR man Alex Barr and left a message on the answer-ing machine of a Walsall teenager called Kayley Elkington. In a comment that was soon passed to the press, the chairman was adamant that Celtic's wage bill then was exceeded by just five clubs in England, despite the manager's scepticism over that issue. 'I am not going to be made a liar by Martin O'Neill,' said Quinn on the recording. This episode showed the strain on the club more than any sort of sustained feud between the two men.

Regardless of the payroll, which would eventually be brought under control, Celtic could not balance the books while buy-ing costly players. Since O'Neill's departure, the biggest piece of expenditure in the transfer market has been the signing of Scott Brown from Hibernian for around £4 million in 2007. That trend was unavoidable, galling as it was to realise that the reso-nance Celtic had would not be reflected in the means actually at their disposal. 'Even with the financial restraints they have at the moment, I would say Celtic are one of the top ten clubs in the world. They could easily be in the top three,' O'Neill continues to insist.

'It's just that Celtic is a monolith stuck in a place that, at this moment, cannot sustain it. I would never take Celtic out of Glasgow because it's part of the city. With Rangers, you have two fantastic football clubs, but in this day and age where money counts for so much I would be all for a change of rules that allowed them into the English Premiership. Celtic already attract 60,000 people for their games, and if they were in the

Premiership they would immediately go to 80,000 when they expanded the ground. It would be sensational.'

That vision was rejected once again by the leading English clubs in November 2009, and the prospect of it coming to pass already felt remote when O'Neill's tenure approached its end. The club pondered its future then and was counting on a team that was stagnating. Celtic struggled on and would have been champions in 2005 if their result at Motherwell was no worse than Rangers' against Hibernian at Easter Road. At Fir Park, the opposition, managed by the great former Rangers centre half Terry Butcher, had to send out a side containing a smattering of youngsters. None the less, Celtic's situation gave the fixture an urgency that stimulated Motherwell.

By then O'Neill's team was malfunctioning. There was no longer the freshness to impose their will. Celtic did take the lead, through Chris Sutton, but hardly anyone acted as if they were convinced they could determine their own fate. The kit man John Clark had his eye on a TV monitor and eventually had to pass on the news that Rangers, too, were winning. Celtic did not have Larsson any more to trump the opposition at a moment of danger. The team struggled towards full-time and could not keep their lead intact. Two minutes from the end Scott McDonald, who would be bought by Celtic in 2007, scored with a hook shot in the goalmouth as a defence on the retreat was flooded with confusion. That sufficed to make Rangers champions, although the Australian struck again for a Motherwell win.

The reaction to McDonald's opener had been revealing. Players were shouting at the bench, asking for the score at Easter Road. Celtic, in 2005, had lost the belief that they could shape their own fate. They yearned to be helped out of their troubles by a third party. It was one of the unhappiest afternoons in Celtic's history. 'I don't think I'll ever get over it,' O'Neill said years later.

A week after the debacle, the manager did take the Scottish Cup in his final competitive game in charge. The most any fan would have said of the win over Dundee United was that at least the season had not got any worse. None the less, O'Neill's period with Celtic had lasting consequences.

For much of his five years in Glasgow, they were a side with the attitude and ability to dominate Scottish football. When it went wretchedly wrong, the sense still was that Celtic had merely themselves to blame. At their best, O'Neill's team were redoubtable. In the schismatic environment of Scottish football, the first decade of the twenty-first century would therefore develop into one of the more trying periods in Rangers' history. O'Neill's drive, intelligence and capacity to inspire players had brought about a turning point in the history of each club. It was a vivid period when Celtic's fans felt the urgency of the team's enterprise, and even the miseries made those years among the most gripping in the club's history.

'I should judge it by the amount of exhilaration and pride at managing the club or being a custodian of it,' O'Neill says of his period in command. 'Sometimes the pressure might have to be endured at the time and then enjoyed later. That's the nature of football. My wife's experience of Seville would have been a white-knuckle experience. I have nothing but fantastic memories of the football club itself because I loved being there. The heartache of losing in Seville was only surpassed by losing against Motherwell. Nothing will ever come close in football terms to that particular day, more so even than Seville.'

An expensive effort had been made to lift the side to a new level, yet wealth had still not inundated the club. Previously, other endeavours to put Celtic in a different, more lucrative context had come to nothing. In 2001 common cause had been made with prominent clubs abroad whose restricted means were stopping them from living up to reputations forged in previous generations. The concept was termed an Atlantic League.

Under this proposal the best sides from Scotland, Holland, Belgium, Portugal, Sweden and Denmark would all leave their domestic scenes behind. Encouragement was received unofficially from the governing body of European football. The then president of UEFA Lennart Johansson had a soft spot for Celtic while his fellow Swedes Larsson and Mjallby were in the side. That factor might have been marginal, but it was still heartening. Celtic, Rangers and others were encouraged to think that they would be allowed to escape from their domestic situations, with compensation paid to the clubs left behind. There was also an unwritten understanding that the football associations of Scotland, Holland, Portugal and the others would retain their status within UEFA.

Matters went quite far. A meeting, for instance, was held at the Perthshire home of the then Rangers chairman David Murray, with people like the PSV Eindhoven chairman Harry van Raaij present. Some were always anxious that UEFA's seeming sympathy was a sham since the body could be sure that FIFA, the ultimate authority in world football, would block the whole project by threatening to ban the clubs. Aside from that, there was also a lack of impetus about an initiative involving a range of individuals from a variety of cultures. The clubs, too, could be consumed by their immediate aims, so the level of commitment fluctuated. The Portuguese were said to have been the first to drift away from the initiative. Momentum had never been developed.

There were also distractions, since the involvement of so many parties stopped confidentiality from being achieved. The need to form relationships was also in conflict with the wish for discretion. That gathering in Perthshire, for example, could not go entirely unnoticed. In addition, there was hostility from the ruling bodies in each country. The Scottish Football Association appreciated that its continuing existence would be of no comfort if the domestic scene, with Celtic and Rangers gone, became a backwater comparable to, say, the League of Ireland.

The scheming did not stop there. In 2002 the Old Firm explored another approach once the then chairman of the Football League Keith Harris had called for Celtic and Rangers to be allowed into its lowest level, known nowadays as League Two. The argument went that they would use their superior means to ascend the pyramid until they got to the top of the present-day Championship. At that juncture, according to the strategists, the members of the Premier League would let the Old Firm in because they would bring wealth with them. This approach was quickly dismissed, and among the opponents was Adam Crozier, the then chief executive of the FA, despite the fact that he is a Scot and a Celtic supporter. Any blurring of the distinction between Scottish and English football would have revived the argument that each is simply a regional body within the UK. The logic gallops on to the conclusion that there should be just one seat at FIFA for a British FA.

Resistance to Celtic and Rangers leaving their domestic setting was implacable. With higher revenues beyond their grasp, Celtic could not go on as they had been doing and, in a sense, there was no intention of doing so. O'Neill's successor would have to conduct his affairs in a different manner. 'Over the period from about 2000 to 2005 we had lost 50 million quid,' says Lawwell. 'The job was to put in place a sustainable business model while continuing to be successful on the pitch. I remember saying to Brian [Quinn] a few months into the job, "If I can get the club to make a bit of cash, would the board invest it in the team?" Brian said to me, "I love an optimist."' The club had to commit itself to tight budgeting if the losses were to be halted. That process was not an easy one. The desire, after all, still existed to sell some 55,000 season tickets, yet there had to be a spectacle to entice so many fans.

There is great sneering when supporters are referred to as customers. It is true that they are not mere shoppers and, often, a devotion to a club has become instilled over generations. None the less, it is the case that attendances will ultimately collapse if a team's failure seems entrenched. Whoever succeeded O'Neill had to deliver honours, yet do so with a more frugal approach.

Gordon Strachan was an unexpected choice. While O'Neill

embodied an Irish affinity with the club, Strachan had no such connection. Indeed, as an outstanding midfielder he had been one of Celtic's chief tormentors in the great Aberdeen team that Alex Ferguson would manage to victory over Real Madrid in the 1983 Cup Winners' Cup final. Strachan had even been attacked by a supporter on the pitch at Celtic Park in 1980.

There could be no crude populism from Strachan twenty-five years later. He dislikes playing to the gallery and is liable to head off in a contrary direction if a journalist's line of enquiry tries to lead him on too obvious a course. Celtic were still wise to pursue him. He had been a badly underestimated manager who was available simply because he had chosen to stand down from the Southampton post.

A qualifier for the Champions League in July 2005, his first competitive match with Celtic, ended in a 5–0 trouncing by Artmedia Bratislava. 'It was terrible for the man,' says Quinn. 'He was very, very upset. I remember speaking to Dermot [Desmond] about it and, without breaking stride, we agreed that it was just a one-off mishap. So we stood behind him.' Celtic fell short in the return match, where they won 4–0, and their interest in European competition was at an end by 2 August. Between the games with Artmedia the side had drawn 4–4 with Motherwell in a chaotic contest at Fir Park. Strachan looked as if he might be no more than a human buffer zone before a new period for the club began under someone else.

There is, however, a persistence and perceptiveness to him. In his periods on the sidelines of the sport his work as a match analyst on television regularly identifies aspects of the game that never seem to occur to anyone else. Strachan's effect was particularly potent at Southampton and, having taken them to the 2003 FA Cup final, where they were defeated 1–0 by Arsenal, he had the team as high as fourth in the Premier League in late December of that year. His intention to give up the job became public knowledge and he therefore left in February 2004, when the club was safe in mid-table in the Premier League. By the summer of 2011 there had been eight 'permanent' successors and Southampton were relieved to get out of League One, England's third tier.

Strachan's move to Glasgow still might not have been anticipated. Leaving Aberdeen for Manchester United, he had gone to England in 1984 and stayed there ever since. Despite that, the attraction of Celtic was simple and vigorous. From the start, as player-coach at Coventry, he had spent far too much time at clubs that can readily be earmarked for demotion. 'The "next level" is mythical,' Strachan says. 'Your job with these clubs is not to get relegated. It was the same with Southampton. The formula seemed to be the same for staying up: the training, the motivation. I didn't know if I could do it three times on the trot. I seemed to be getting jobs that were too similar, and I wanted something different.'

Glasgow was alien to a man accustomed to the east coast of Scotland, where he had been born in Edinburgh before going on to play for Dundee and Aberdeen. 'I had never had anything to do with the west coast,' he says. 'Once you go past Harthill Services [twenty miles from Glasgow] it's a different world.' He knew the sectarianism there as well as the way it can be woven into football. 'It's not a goldfish bowl,' he says, 'it's a piranha bowl.' There was a disquiet, too, about taking his wife Lesley into that environment. 'She found it extremely hard,' he says. 'So did my mother. I don't think anyone minds when people criticise you for your decisions, but they get personal in Scotland and that's what hurts your family.'

Any joy in the new job was accompanied by the knowledge that money could not be spent freely. By 2005 Celtic were more committed than ever to living within their means. Peter Lawwell had understood the economic pressures from the time he was given the job, towards the end of 2003. His immediate task then was to cut non-football expenditure by 20 per cent.

No one could mistake him for a bloodless bookkeeper. He is a big man with a vivid personality and a passion for Celtic.

Fans who railed against his economising still could not reject him with any plausibility as an outsider. In September 2008 Lawwell would decide against leaving to become chief executive of Arsenal. 'I was flattered and honoured to be offered the job,' he says. 'They are a great club and Arsène Wenger is an incredible man, but in the end I wasn't 100 per cent on it. This is where my passion is. Arsenal, for all its attractions, would have been more of a job. Here, it's not. You need that at times. It's 24/7. You need that passion. Unquestionably I have that for Celtic. I want to see it through.'

Strachan came to Glasgow knowing that it was one of his principal duties to control costs. By combining that with some strong campaigns in Europe, he helped the club accumulate an operating profit of £36 million over the course of his last three seasons, to the summer of 2009. The most expensive of Strachan's recruits was Scott Brown. This former Hibernian midfielder has extraordinary energy levels that can seem to swamp his judgement, as he gives possession away cheaply. It still cost £4 million to land a footballer who had to be viewed as a work in progress. The accelerating growth of salaries in England also leaves Celtic gasping. 'The ridiculous £30,000 and £40,000 a week wages in England are now £70,000 and £80,000,' says Lawwell of the severe inflationary pressures in the sport that have gone on to take payments higher still.

He is not prone to laments, and the club has sought to flourish by other means. The scouting network is far more extensive, experts in sports science map out programmes for the players, and Lawwell himself has been able to negotiate better commercial deals. With the world economy shrivelling, Celtic were still capable of extending a contract with Nike worth £5 million a year until 2015. Even so, the Deloitte Football Money League showed that Celtic's turnover put them outside the world's top twenty in 2010, since the tenth-highest match-day income did not make up for small television revenue.

That sort of outcome had been foreseeable for several years, but restrictions do not always lead to paralysis and Strachan had rapidly overhauled his squad. Of the starting line-up for the drubbing by Artmedia in July 2005, just half a dozen would begin the 1–0 victory over Hearts with which Celtic regained the League title nine months later. The manager went on recruiting extensively, and those who wish to reproach him can find examples of acquisitions who have flopped. This ignores the fact that Strachan had to deal in areas of the market where there can be no complete confidence in the goods acquired.

A few successes vindicate a manager in those circumstances. Two such cases had a vast impact on Celtic's fortunes. In November 2006 the club advanced from the group phase of the Champions League by beating Manchester United 1–0. The goal itself was delivered with a free kick from thirty yards struck by the slightly built Shunsuke Nakamura. It spun and dipped with such virtuosity into the top corner of the net that the goalkeeper Edwin van der Sar might have been leaping merely for appearance's sake. With a minute remaining, United could have equalised, but the Celtic goalkeeper Artur Boruc hurtled to his right and saved Louis Saha's penalty. 'Rod Stewart was there and he was crying after the game,' says Strachan. 'It was so much for people to take in.'

The key contributors were both men whom wealthier clubs might have declined to buy. Nakamura has great stamina, technique and vision, yet he is slight and one-paced. The defects rule him out for those with the budgets to be extravagantly fastidious, but he and Celtic were of benefit to one another in ways vaguely reminiscent of Larsson's impact. Nakamura's standing in Japan was validated globally when he could be seen getting the better of United. In the process, the midfielder turned out to be a boon to his new club commercially, even if, despite larger prices quoted in the press, he had cost a slender £1 million from the Italian club Reggina.

Boruc's case history is very different. It had also taken a paltry sum (£600,000) to buy him, but the signing from Legia Warsaw has not always had the streamlined appearance of a dedicated professional. Boruc would be suspended by his country in 2008 because of a broken curfew following Poland's friendly in Ukraine. The following year his teammate Aiden McGeady received a black eye after an altercation with the goalkeeper at the Celtic training ground. Strachan was keenly aware of the contrasts between Nakamura and Boruc, the men who had done most to bring about the defeat of Manchester United. 'One was the perfect example of how to run your life,' says the then manager, 'and the other was the perfect example of how not to run your life.'

Strachan regards the latter as the best goalkeeper he ever worked with, and the Pole's talent could potentially have made him a success with even the most exalted clubs. Boruc, in practice, would be sold to Fiorentina in 2010, and Nakamura, with his contract at an end, had gone to Espanyol the year before. The line-up assembled by Strachan was beginning to be dismantled. He had gathered half a dozen trophies in four years, with at least one in each campaign. None the less, he had stayed longer than intended, having originally planned to stand down in the summer of 2008. The moment would have been right in some respects because Celtic, having been seven points behind with a game more played, still managed to overhaul a Rangers side that was tiring as it encountered fixture congestion on its way to the UEFA Cup final, which would be lost to Zenit St Petersburg.

There were two Old Firm matches at Celtic Park in April of that year, because one of the games had been postponed from January. Celtic defeated Rangers narrowly on each occasion, with the winner in the first match coming three minutes into stoppage time from Jan Vennegoor of Hesselink. Strachan's side retained the championship in 2008 after winning at Dundee United, although Rangers' loss at Aberdeen on the same evening would have confirmed the title in any case. There was a profound poignancy rather than exhilaration because Tommy Burns had died a week earlier, with the funeral taking place two days before the game. After the title had been won, the Celtic squad re-emerged in T-shirts bearing his image.

Strachan had a cuppa. 'I am a tea addict,' he says. 'I'll only drink on special occasions. After that I thought, "Right. It's been a real hard year." I wanted to make sure that my family were all right because they were at the game. The woman who is always there offered me a cup of tea. Tommy had died. I had to celebrate but I didn't feel like celebrating. For the staff, it was too much for us.'

Strachan would also say that 'being Tommy's mate was the best part of joining Celtic'. He is a reflective person and when people think he is being awkward on purpose, it is usually because of his aversion to platitudes. His remark about Burns would not have been made simply to serve up a sound bite. Strachan is an original thinker about the game and he is candid about himself. After leaving Celtic in 2009 he had a dreadful spell with Middlesbrough, where he lasted a year before a parting of the ways in which he waived his right to compensation. 'It was the wrong club for me and I made the wrong moves,' Strachan now says. 'The pre-season was wrong, a couple of the signings were wrong. So I obviously hadn't put enough thought into it. I can usually sniff when it's time to go.'

Strachan seems detached but his refusal to play to the gallery is at heart respectful to supporters. He recognises that his life is more privileged than theirs. 'You hear managers saying they can relate to the fans,' he says. 'It's bollocks. I don't know what it's like to work all week in the pissing rain or down a mine or in a factory that's crap. When they spend money to watch a bad team, well, I'm sorry, I don't know what that's like. I wouldn't start the nonsense about "I've always loved this team" because I didnae.

'I supported Hibs up until about I was fourteen, and that's it. I couldn't tell you what Hibs had done from when I was fifteen. I didn't have a clue. As a professional I wanted to get on with my job and make everyone happy. But I couldn't be turning round and kissing badges because it just wasn't me. I see players kissing badges and saying, "I love you." And then I see them hiding as they go out the door instead of signing three autographs for people who have been standing outside for an hour.'

It was typical of Strachan's independent streak that he had it in mind to step down from Celtic after three seasons, but he became uneasy about that. At Coventry City he had been player-coach and then manager for six years, and after the board had talked him out of leaving his tenure came to an ugly conclusion following the club's relegation in 2001. He regretted not having resigned when he wished to do so. At Southampton and Celtic he took charge of the timing. Even so, Strachan would have left Glasgow sooner had it not been for Burns's death. 'When Tommy died, I felt it maybe wasn't right to go,' he said.

Until then Strachan had lived in Bothwell, to the south-east of Glasgow, but the arrangement had only been for the three years he proposed to spend with Celtic. He then relocated to the West End of the city. 'When I had my day off on a Wednesday I used to go to the Oran Mor [a cultural centre] at lunchtime for "A Play, a Pie and a Pint". Some of the plays were fantastic, with really top actors. The Comedy Club was just down the road and I used to go there with my hood pulled up. It was a wee enclave of sanity, the West End. When you went to the cinema in Ashton Lane, no one bothered you.'

The satisfactions were more elusive in his last season with Celtic. The League Cup was won against Rangers, but those opponents overhauled Strachan's side to take the League in 2009. It is a teasing thought that Celtic might have had a fourth consecutive title under his management. Had they won their last two matches, instead of recording goalless draws, it might have been feasible for them to have edged out Rangers on goal difference. However, that lack of effectiveness in the penalty area was a blight that worried Strachan and he had wanted to remedy it in the January transfer window.

His aim was to buy a Hibernian forward. 'We tried to get

Steven Fletcher,' Strachan remembers, 'but Peter [Lawwell] said it was too expensive [Hibernian sold him to Burnley for £3 million in the summer of 2009, but he was reportedly priced at £4 million in January of that year]. When Peter said that, it was fine. There was never a grumble. Fine. So I got on with it and we went seven points clear at the end of the year and won the League Cup. I did think, "We can do this." But then the goals dried up.'

It was an episode that epitomised Celtic's commitment to living within their budget. Some would term it a false economy since they had denied themselves the scorer who could have made all the difference. However, Fletcher scored a modest eleven goals for Hibernian that season, and no one can be sure that he would have enlivened Strachan's attack sufficiently. In any case, there may have been a more unsettling matter than that for Celtic.

The manager informed the board in mid-season that he would be leaving in the summer. His decision soon became public knowledge, and it might have been a factor in the side's lack of consistency. Strachan, all the same, believed it would have been wrong to conceal his intentions. 'It was always on my mind to do that,' he explains. 'I said to Peter [Lawwell], "Four years is enough for me." That might have affected how we played over the closing months of the season, but if someone had said to me, "What are we going to do about next season and signing people?" it would have been very unfair to Peter if I had said, "We should get this one and that one," and then I go. That's not fair to anyone. It's not fair on the player who has been signed. It's not fair on the club. It's not fair on the next manager.'

Strachan, on the whole, was poorly treated by the Celtic supporters. It is implausible that their attitude was still dictated by an antagonism towards him that had been felt a quarter of a century before, when he was with Aberdeen. He did not have an inclination to play to the gallery and some felt that the style of football was drab, although anyone with a real taste for the more refined aspects of the game would have still been enraptured by

Nakamura's mastery. The set-piece against Manchester United had sent the club to the knockout stages of the Champions League in 2006/7, where they went out to Milan at the San Siro in extra time as Kaká scored the only goal of the tie. Strachan's side also got to the last sixteen the following year before being beaten by Barcelona. The Artmedia experience had been as misleading as it was devastating since many of Strachan's best days came in the Champions League.

Nights in that tournament sometimes liberate Celtic from the claustrophobia of the domestic competition. 'It's the best feeling in the world,' says Strachan, thinking of the 2007/8 season. 'That can be a big problem for people who leave Celtic. To get there you have to play Spartak Moscow in the knockout round, then you have to beat Milan, Benfica and Shakhtar at home. That's four teams to get to the last sixteen.'

Strachan is right to be proud, considering how many of his predecessors had fared. The stress of even attempting to live up to the standards of days gone by is readily gauged. In the 103 years from the first match up to 1991 there had been six managers (with Billy McNeill having two stints). By the summer of 2010 that total had risen by eleven, if Kenny Dalglish's name is included for his few months in the post. That acceleration, with all its risk of a crash, shows Celtic straining to stay the pace in contemporary football, yet there can be no scope for excuses and complaints. This is no sudden change. Despite the enterprise of the founders, it has been natural for the club to recognise that there will always be rivals of greater means in larger countries.

It is futile to mope or brood over the wealth of clubs in England or Spain. Celtic have to make ingenious use of their budget, but important if intangible assets are also present. There is a benefit to existence in the Scottish Premier League since it can offer an access to the Champions League that is far harder to attain in the larger countries. None the less, piecing together a team that can cope there is a steep challenge.

Strachan's successor failed the test. Tony Mowbray, a former

Celtic centre half, was known for his idealism, but his side was neither effective nor all that attractive and he was sacked in March 2010. Neil Lennon followed him, initially in a caretaker role, and then embarked on shaping what was largely a new side. In effect, he pieced it together with the proceeds of Aiden McGeady's sale to Spartak Moscow for £9.5 million. Some of the recruits, such as the Honduras left back Emilio Izaguirre, were bafflingly good at a cost of just £600,000, but Celtic, in the throes of team reconstruction, were drummed out of both the Champions League and Europa League qualifiers by 26 August 2010.

While the team went on to play some expansive football, the remodelled line-up was not quite dependable enough to win the League title, which went to Rangers for a third season in a row, and Lennon had to make do with the 2011 Scottish Cup as Celtic's reward for the season. There is, even so, a greater challenge for Lennon and his successors than regaining an edge over Rangers. It is, indeed, a danger that the Old Firm rivalry may become the sole context in which each club exists.

Given time, people may yet come to see Strachan, who handled the Champions League challenge well, as the embodiment of the sort of manager equipped to offset the intrinsic disadvantages of life in a small marketplace. Lennon, though, has not quite given up hope of ever bringing in an elite footballer. 'We are still looking at top players at the moment, but whether we get over the line with them is another thing,' he says. 'Scotland is becoming a harder sell.'

Roy Keane did leave Manchester United to spend the closing six months of his playing career with Celtic in 2006, collecting a League winners medal, but he was thirty-four by then. Much as he is a hard-bitten individual, there was a dewy-eyed tone to that period. It was still appreciated as a break from normal practice. A club with a relatively humble income when compared with the grandees of La Liga or the Premier League has to be sharp-witted and seize its opportunity to buy players who are, for the moment, beneath the notice of richer rivals. Above all, there is a need to be more efficient in the honing of youngsters, who nowadays can quite often come from outside Scotland.

Celtic explore the overseas market with a particular intensity. Izaguirre had counterparts in the Israeli Beram Kayal and Ki Sung-Yueng, a South Korean midfielder. The search is on for the undervalued asset. If a club such as Celtic has any advantage over wealthier clubs, it lies in the fact that its commitment to nurturing footballers with potential is wholehearted. Those players, in turn, can think themselves lucky to be playing before large crowds, while recognising that there is an opportunity to move on to one of the more affluent leagues.

Research is critical. If Lennon is complimented on his recruits, he automatically gives the credit to John Park, the head of the recruiting office set up in recent years, for landing someone like Izaguirre. Ipswich Town's interest in the Honduran had come to nothing a couple of seasons before, but his transfer value to Celtic was being put at £10 million in 2011.

'We did a 2010 World Cup project,' says the manager, 'and the guys upstairs looked at players for certain positions, and we did have a number of options. But Emilio kept coming to the fore. We watched him against Spain, when he was up against Jesús Navas, who is a top right-winger, and he played him very well. We felt that for the money it was a gamble, but not a great one. Then he comes in and – Christ – he played so well from his debut on and has never looked back. He's so confident in any area of the pitch and he sometimes gives you the heebie-jeebies. He's clean-living and very religious, deep into his [Christian] faith. Honduras is one of the unfashionable places, but having watched him and watched him we just felt we had a good player here.'

Lennon is not deluded enough to think that he has found a perfect alternative to the era when Celtic could afford to buy him as a player. 'The gamble there', he says of candidates from the more obscure markets, 'is you don't know what sort of temperament they are going to have. You can do a little bit of homework by speaking to people about them and by getting to know them, but the proof of the pudding is when they actually come into the British game. The pace is different, the physicality is different. I suppose you need a little bit of luck in that respect, but signing someone like Kayal is just perfect for the game here. He can break the play up, he has a change of pace to go past people and he also has a good passing range.'

For all the initiative that Celtic showed in securing Kayal, Lennon pauses when asked if he would sign for the club as a player now, as he did in 2000. He then replies that he probably would 'if Martin O'Neill was the manager'. This is a neat answer, although, in turn, it raises the issue of whether someone like O'Neill would take the job under the present conditions. Lennon looks to the defeat of Manchester United in the 2006 Champions League game as confirmation that the club, on a given day, can still lift itself to meet a great challenge. As he points out, that match was not so very long ago and Celtic's means are much the same now.

In the summer of 2011 there were new murmurings about a breakaway league for European clubs, but Celtic have heard all that before. The wisest course is to avoid being infatuated by such speculation. Rather than distract themselves with what are, for the moment at least, daydreams, the club needs to live at peace with realities that have applied for decades. The experiment in spending enough to buy Chris Sutton or keep Henrik Larsson failed the economic test. Success on the field still did not make Celtic rich enough to afford such men easily.

Perspective was lost. Apart from the bullishness of the club's early days, when Queen Victoria was on the throne, Celtic have known that they are at a financial disadvantage while confined to Scotland. The striving to succeed despite that fact is itself an element in the fixation with the club. Celtic are far stronger in organisation and finance than they were when Jock Stein made his return to the club in 1965, but the reserves of passion are their true wealth.

On 15 May 2011 Rangers clinched the League title at Kilmarnock as expected, but 57,837 spectators at Celtic Park made a loud and passionate pretence of indifference to that while Motherwell were being beaten 4–0. The attendance did not reflect a belief that Lennon's side would be champions that afternoon. People had gathered as an act of faith or, more precisely, to stage a colourful display of bloody-mindedness. The passion and exuberance, 123 years after Celtic's first game, were as vast as they had ever been. On such a day it was impossible to think of Celtic as peripheral. Those ambitious men at the end of the 1880s would have been proud to know that the club continues to be a gathering place for multitudes with the conviction that Celtic can still be a gleaming presence in the world.

ACKNOWLEDGEMENTS

I am particularly indebted to Pat Woods for the generosity with which he shared his knowledge of Celtic. My thanks also go to Paul Brennan (celticquicknews.co.uk), Peter Broughan, Donald Cowey, Jim Divers, Gerry Dunbar (ntvcelticfanzine.com), the late Joe Fisher, Glenn Gibbons, Kevin McKenna, Peter McLean, Andrew O'Hagan, Brendan O'Hara, Barry Quinn, Brian Quinn, Nik Quinn, Susan Shaw, Andrew Smith, Jack and Isobel Stewart, Roddy Stewart, Derek Taylor (Kollectables, Glasgow), Kevin Turner, Hamish Whyte, the Mitchell Library, the British Library and the people behind thecelticwiki.com, kerrydalestreet.co.uk, etims.net and celticgraves.com.

Thanks to Newsquest Glasgow Herald & Times for providing some of the photographs.

INDEX